VLADKA MEED

On Both Sides Of The Wall

MEMOIRS FROM THE WARSAW GHETTO

INTRODUCTION BY

ELIE WIESEL

Translated by Dr. Steven Meed

HOLOCAUST LIBRARY

**Published in conjunction with the
United States Holocaust Memorial Museum**

Published in Yiddish by the
Educational Committee of
the Workmen's Circle New York, 1948

Published in Spanish by
Sociedad Pro Cultura y Ayuda de Mexico
as "Desde Ambos Lados del Muro," Mexico City, 1959

Published in Hebrew by
Beit Lohamei Hagetaot, Israel, 1968

Published in English
by Beit Lohamei Hagetaot,
Ghetto Fighters' House, Israel
and Hakibbutz Hameuchad Publishing House, Israel, 1972

Library of Congress Catalog Card No. 78-71300-W
ISBN 0-89604-013-5

Printed in U.S.A.

A Memorial Candle for my Unforgettable Parents
Hanna and Shlomo,
to my Sister Henia
and Brother Chaim
who shared the fate of the millions of Jews, Hitler's Victims,
and perished in the gas chambers
of the Treblinka death camp.

I wish to express my gratitude and appreciation to my husband, Benjamin. Together we went through the Holocaust. Without his comfort and support, I might never have survived those horrible years. Without his assistance, I would never have brought myself to write down my experiences. Finally, without his help and guidance, neither the Yiddish original nor this English edition would have become a reality.

Vladka Meed

TABLE OF CONTENTS

INTRODUCTION

by Elie Wiesel

Nothing. Nothing was left me of my past, of my life in the ghetto—not even the grave of my father . . .

With these words Vladka ends her recollections—and, perhaps ours too. For in the ruin of her childhood lies the memory of humanity, and possibly also its salvation.

You read what this Jewish girl from Warsaw says about Warsaw, about Warsaw's Jewish children and their murderers, about the starving ghetto-beggars, about the young ghetto fighters who, like avenging angels, poured the flames of vengeance on their enemies—and you do not know whom to pity first or most.

You may at times, be seized by rage. We had so many enemies! This cry is almost a leitmotiv in Vladka's book, the isolation of the Jews. Not only within the ghetto walls, but even more on the outside, the Jews were ostracized, isolated, hated aliens. The Germans murdered, the Ukrainians killed, the police tormented and the Poles betrayed them. True, here and there a "good citizen" was found whose cooperation could be bought with Jewish money. But how many good-hearted, upright Poles were to be found at the time in Poland? Very few. And where were the idealists, the universalists, the humanists when the ghetto needed them? Like all of Warsaw they were silent as the ghetto burned. Worse still: Warsaw's persecution and murder of Jews increased once there no longer was a ghetto. Many ghetto fighters died long after the uprising, because they could find no hiding place in Warsaw.

Who most earns our outraged anger—the murderers, their accomplices, the *szmalcownicy*—the blackmailers—or the common citizenry pleased in their hearts that Poland will be rid of her Jews, or perhaps the so-called democracies whose unconcern in those crucial years seemed almost to tell the executioners: "Do what you will with Europe's Jews."

If your shock is great, Vladka's must have been infinitely greater, not only because she herself saw everything, experienced everything, but because she had so deeply believed in humanity, and had expected understanding, help, succor from her fellow men.

Of Feigele's emotional stress and trauma, Vladka writes sparingly. Indeed, little about Feigele. Perhaps she is right. Perhaps the world did not merit her own youthful hopes; certainly it was not ready to embrace the ideals of her friends—Zygmunt, Mikolai, Abrasha Blum, Berek, Yurek and the others.

As one of the handful of survivors who not only shared the Jewish agony, but participated in the Jewish armed struggle, Vladka brings us an eye-witness account, the more hair-raising and heart-rending because it is so straightforwardly factual.

Incredibly—but true—on the first of May, 1944, a group of her friends celebrated, in various Warsaw *melinas*—hiding places—International Workers' Day! Do you hear? In Warsaw! After the destruction of the ghetto, after the extermination of Polish, Lithuanian, Ukrainian, and Czechoslovak Jewry! When every wall had ears, when death lurked in every doorway, the handful of persecuted, starving, desperate Socialists of the "Bund" found the strength, the courage to

> "*send greetings—in unadorned language—to all those in the world who struggle for freedom, primarily to our brothers in the concentration camps, the forests, and the bunkers. These greetings are filled with the faith and hope that we, the remnant, will in the end live to see the defeat of our bestial foe. Will avenge the crimes that have been committed against us, and we will continue steadfastly to participate in the struggle for a righteous and just world . . .*
> *In an inspired solemn mood, we all dispersed.*"

The whole world had betrayed them; yet they fought on for its own sake.

One reads these memoirs, and, mingled with the grief and rage, experiences a strange feeling of wonder: So many victims, so many heroes! One might think—and the assassins were convinced—that the harsh German decrees would turn the Jews into animals. After all, there are limits to human endurance—of waiting in terror between one "selection" and the next, of running from bunker to bunker, crawling from rooftop to rooftop, looking death daily in the face. . . . One must break at last.

But the hangman was mistaken. Throughout the ghetto years, the Jews refused. Oh, there were exceptions—police who beat their victims, then extorted money from their relatives, opportunists who sought wealth or power; collaborators who deluded themselves that they would survive the oppressor's need of them.

But these were a small minority. The ghetto, half-a-million souls, for the most part did not become a jungle. Quite the contrary, people tried to help each other. Vladka gives examples: Schools, kitchens and nurseries were organized. Friends looked out for one another, made sacrifices for one another. The concept of friendship was never so sanctified as here. One wonders at the heroism of the fidelity of friends, just as one wonders at the heroism of the insurgents.

Where did Abrasha Blum find the strength to think first about his friends and only then about himself? And Mordecai Anilewicz: where did he draw the strength, the knowledge, to go out in battle against the most awesome army in Europe? And Vladka herself, where did she muster the courage, once on the "Aryan side," to search for *melinas* for children, to purchase arms for the ghetto fighters, to work as a courier among the Jews in the forest near Czestochowa and the Jews of the concentration camps in Radom?

Is it not harrowing to reflect that the only assistance, the only consolation, that came to the few surviving Jews hidden in caves and cellars was brought, not by emissaries of great governments, or rich Jewish communities, but by a band of frightened, dauntless Jewish girls from Warsaw itself, like Vladka and her handful of friends.

I know that many will say: "It was impossible to send anything from the outside . . ."

Impossible? No one even tried! Had there been a hundred attempts, one might have succeeded. Can it be argued that it was less dangerous for the ghetto-couriers to travel from one ghetto to another (to warn, to organize resistance, to bring assistance) than it would have been to travel to Budapest from Istanbul, and from there to Warsaw? One must marvel even more at the fighters and couriers. Instead of falling into despair, they found reasons and strength to help others. These are some of the thoughts and emotions that Vladka's book has evoked in me. The book first appeared in Yiddish in 1948. Its publication was an event of significance for it was the first authentic document to reach the free world about the uprising and destruction of the Warsaw ghetto, or about the Holocaust in general. The English translation, completed in 1971, is even more important, precisely because it has appeared so late. True, in the meantime, many books have been written on the same subject. It would seem as if no tragedy in our history has taken up as much space as the destruction of European Jewry. Hundreds, if not thousands of reports, autobiographies, monographs, documents, research, and albums have been dedicated to it. And deservedly, too. For no matter how much is written, we find that we have only scratched the surface. If one thinks that everything had been revealed, everything has been said, one is mistaken. For what is secret remains secret, still horribly hidden, like Creation and Death itself, and Time . . .

But Vladka's book is not "just another work," or merely an autobiography from the Holocaust. It is written with inspiration, with exaltation. Every sentence rings true, every scene burns itself into the reader's memory.

In the ghetto:

> "Several wagons went by, loaded with Jews, sitting and standing, hugging sacks that contained whatever pitiful belongings they had managed to gather at the last moment. Some stared straight ahead with vacant eyes, others mourned and wailed, wringing their hands. Women tore their hair or clung to their children, who sat bewildered among the scattered bundles, gazing at the adults in silent fear. Running behind the last wagon, a lone woman, arms outstretched, cried: 'My child! Give me back my child!' "

And further on:

> "At Gesia 13, from the window in the hiding place, I saw the march of the orphanage of Janusz Korczak. The children went silently, carrying blankets, walking hand-in-hand . . ."

And several pages later, she writes of Jews being driven to the Umschlagplatz:

> *"A tremendous churning, black tide . . . There were rickshas carrying invalids; men, women and children, the young and the old, trudging along. Face after face passed below us, faces apathetic, agitated, terrified, some tense, others bereft of hope. We watched intently, searching for a familiar face among the thousands shuffling past. The sight made my head reel. All the faces blended in confusion; only bowed heads and bundles and bent backs, a single wave of humanity. The marchers were silent, the atmosphere stifling, only the sound of footsteps, all sorts of footsteps—the slow and nimble, adults and children . . . its cadence pounding a final warning: 'Remember!' "*

You read the book and hear the footsteps, the heavy footsteps of the old, the tiny footsteps of the children. When you read, further on, that those that were saved, after every attempt, after every roundup, felt guilty, you yourself are overwhelmed by the same feeling of guilt. Why them and not others? Why them and not me?

I could quote more and more. But this is only an introduction, a foreword. The purpose is only to offer a taste, to sound the first notes on the strings. There are songs without number: songs of lamentation, songs of confession, words about stormy times, words about heroic figures, words about words, about their poverty and their consolation . . .

It seems as if it all happened yesterday. Some eyes haunt you with such despair, with such intensity, certain phrases pursue you with such silent pain, that you lose all sense of time and self. You stand with one foot on the threshold of the Holocaust Kingdom, see the burning clouds obliterate towns and cities, families and whole communities, like tombstones of smoke, far, far away, high above, reaching all the way to the Heavenly Seat . . .

At the same time, you get the impression that the entire period belongs somehow, not to our own history, to our own lives, but to some ancient legend that the immortal elders tell a thousand times that same night.

Something prevents belief; you are unwilling to accept that humanity once spawned so many murderers, that it remained silent at the time that, in its name, as if "for its sake," they murdered one million children. And in spite of its guilt, continued living . . .

Sometimes you want to close your eyes and say to yourself, "The whole story is nothing but a dream." Vladka herself, while on the "Aryan side," had the same thoughts. The ghetto? A dream. The Holocaust? A nightmare. Everything is as it has always been. Children are still children. Their grandfathers still sit in the prayer house and recite their prayers or study the Mishna. Soon you will awake and in place of this desolate graveyard you will find your childhood, filled with Jews smiling and dreaming, Jews healthy and sick, rich and poor . . .

But you do not, because you are afraid to close your eyes. You are afraid that you will drown in your own memories. For if you remain alone, alone with your innermost thoughts, you will lose your senses.

No . . . "Hang on, kid!" they used to say in the ghetto. And suddenly it becomes clear whom we should pity: Everyone. And even more, not for the victims (it is too late for pity) but for humanity. For with open eyes, it betrayed Feigele, and itself as well.

1. HOW IT BEGAN

WARSAW, July 22, 1942. — It is dawn. From all over the house at Leszno 72 come sounds of doors opening and closing, of hurried footsteps on the stairs. Already, in the courtyard, there is a great stir as tenants mill about anxiously asking one another, "What is the news?" The latest Nazi round-up has been on everyone's mind; the entire ghetto is apprehensive. Late into last night, nervous speculation centered on the report that the headquarters of the *Judenrat*—the German-appointed Jewish community council—was raided and sixty of its leading officials detained. There is a voice louder than the others: "We're in for real trouble now."

For more than two weeks the ghetto had lived in suspense. Terrifying rumors had circulated, most of them launched and spread by Kohn and Heller, a Jewish firm that collaborated with the Gestapo, that the Germans were going to deport all the inhabitants of the ghetto to an unspecified destination where they would be put to work. The Germans had issued no such orders and the reports had been denied by officials of the *Judenrat*.

But the more one learned about what was happening in the ghetto, the more anxious one felt. Day and night Jews were being shot in the streets and in public places, even in their own homes. Only a few days before, a number of young men had been rounded up in the street and taken away—no one knew where. There had been no further word from them. Last night's reports had been even more disturbing.

I left my apartment and went down to the courtyard. Not daring to assemble on the streets, people gathered in little groups in the doorways

9

of houses to talk. With nervous gestures and frightened eyes, their voices hushed and anxious, people spoke of the recent arrests. A strangely oppressive air hung over the courtyard. Even the children were quiet, wandering silently among the grownups. The assemblage swelled as more and more tenants emerged from their homes.

"Any news?"

"Too early for that. But we're bound to hear something today."

"Hush! All this talk will only bring us trouble."

"Whatever will be will be, no matter what we do," said an old man in a trembling voice.

"Take heart, Jews," another man called out. "You'll see, with God's help we'll overcome this new misfortune too."

In such affirmations of faith, the ghetto residents sought mutual reassurance and encouragement.

Why, indeed, I thought, should we despair? For the two years since our imprisonment in the ghetto, we had endured humiliation and hunger. Why should we now lose hope?

A sudden commotion interrupted my thoughts. Friedman, a neighbor and official in the *Judenrat*, appeared. His pale, frightened face and hasty step attracted everybody's attention. Some tried to detain him. Did he bring bad news? Since he worked for the *Judenrat*, he must surely know what was going on.

The short, stout official looked utterly worn out. Halted, he scanned the faces about him, and said: "Yes, there will be deportations in the very near future." He hesitated, then continued: "The Jews of the resettlement centers who have been living on welfare funds and the inmates of the Gesia penitentiary will be the first to go."

There were scattered sighs of relief. But others felt newly threatened.

"What about those of us who have only filed applications for support? Will we also be deported?" a woman's shrill voice broke in.

"Nonsense!" someone answered her nervously. "A few thousand more will be picked up, but then things will quiet down."

"Even *they* don't know for sure," Friedman said with a shrug. He was referring to the *Judenrat* functionaries.

"Who does know then?" several voices asked simultaneously. "A catastrophe is about to come, and there is no one to tell us what to do."

The general apprehensiveness grew. Some tenants went off to carry the latest news to friends and family; others ventured into the street in the hope of learning something more definite there. I joined a small group gathered around Friedman, plying him with more questions. He told us that the directors of the *Judenrat* were holding a secret session, but that he had no idea what might be taking place.

Out in the almost empty street, small groups of curious Jews were beginning to emerge from every doorway. Everyone looked along the ghetto wall to the corner of Leszno and Zelazna Streets, where the German patrol had recently been reinforced. The sudden appearance of this special guard had thrown the community into dismay.

A group of Jews gathered about a candy and tobacco vendor listened attentively to the story of a twelve-year-old boy, one of many children who earned their bread by slipping out through the ghetto wall to buy food from the Gentiles. Today, while checking the chinks and openings through which he could slip out to the "Aryan side," he had discovered that the entire wall was surrounded by Germans and Ukrainians. It was dangerous even to approach the wall. The youthful smuggler had almost paid with his life.

The boy broke óff in mid-sentence, as two squads of Jewish police went goose-stepping past, followed by several empty wagons.

What could it mean?

"The Jewish police has been given orders for the day," said the tobacco vendor. Several squads of ghetto police, in addition to the usual German patrols, had already passed along the street that morning. Now, as if in confirmation, the air was rent by the scream of a siren, and a car loaded with Germans sped by. Startled, the Jews fled in every direction, only to gather again as soon as the vehicle was out of sight. There was a heaviness in the air which foreboded something worse than anything the ghetto had yet experienced.

I had to see my mother. She lived at Leszno 66, just three houses down. I had moved out of the apartment I had shared with her and my brother and sister after the police had come to arrest me for my underground activity. Luckily I had been out at the time. My mother stared at me, fear in her eyes.

"Has anything happened?" she finally asked.

"Nothing—nothing at all, really," I reassured her. "Only a lot of rumors—nothing certain." I told her what I had heard.

My mother sighed resignedly, "What is the use? I no longer have the strength to cope with anything. We will go when the others go—whatever is fated for them will be our lot, too."

My mother had been suffering from a foot injury ever since the beginning of the war, but the pain was unimportant. It could be treated in another town just as well as in the ghetto. Moving somewhere else was not so terrible, as long as she could stay together with her children. My father had died of pneumonia a year earlier.

Like most of the rest of us, my mother assumed that the approaching deportations were merely transfers to some other region. After all, for months now the ghetto had been filled with trucks and horse-drawn wagons, bringing Jews from nearby towns. Now, we imagined, it would be our turn to be moved to another place. My mother, as usual, had resigned herself to the inevitable. But she was extremely worried about my fifteen-year-old brother Chaim and my sixteen-year-old sister Henia. Despite their unceasing efforts, neither of them had been able to find employment in factories working for the Germans.

The tense silence that had settled between my mother and me was broken by sounds of excited voices from the courtyard, and of doors being slammed. I hardly had time to look out the window before our own door was flung open, and our neighbor, Mrs. Zacherman, rushed in. Since the beginning of the war, when her husband had gone off to Russia, she had lived alone with her three small children.

She was distraught. "Did you hear?" she cried. "They have put up notices—posters about the deportations!"

We stood speechless. So the rumors were really true! "Tell me," said my mother, her voice trembling, "What do the posters say?"

Mrs. Zacherman seemed not to hear the question. She wrung her hands, paced to and fro, asking plaintively, "What are we going to do? What am I going to do about my children?"

I dashed outside to look at the posters. The street was already thick with people, streaming from every doorway as news spread from house to house, jostling and elbowing to get close enough to read the notices pasted on the wall. Each, it seemed, was consumed by the need to see the notices with his own eyes, to take in the announcement with his own mind, to interpret it for himself. My own heart was pounding as, having pushed my way through the crowd, I came close enough to read the printed words. The letters leaped and danced before my eyes, as if to elude comprehension, but they burned themselves into my consciousness.

> By order of the German authorities, all the Jews of Warsaw, regardless of age or sex, will be deported. Only those employed in the German workshops, the *Judenrat*, the Jewish police and the Jewish hospital will be exempt. Every deportee will be permitted to carry fifteen kilograms of luggage, including cash, valuables, and provisions for three days. Those failing to comply with this edict will be liable to the death penalty.
>
> (Signed) The *Judenrat*

The street became a human sea, as people milled about in front of the German posters, straining to read between the lines, to fathom the meaning behind the words. I found it hard to persuade myself that it had already come to this. Knots of bewildered Jews stood talking, debating and conjecturing aloud, no longer in whispers. Their one subject of conversation was the harsh fate that had been ordained for them. Scattered voices raised terrible questions that went unanswered: "Where are we going? How many will be deported?" The posters offered no clue.

"All this commotion will only last a few days, then the whole thing will blow over. They can't possibly deport an entire city," someone said reassuringly. Others, too, began to venture words of encouragement.

Some Jews turned to the *Judenrat* headquarters for advice; others stood about, consulting with family and friends, trying to decide what to do. There was no time to lose—the order was there for all to see. Already, business was almost at a standstill. Stores and stalls were being shut down; merchandise was disappearing from shop windows. Beggars scuttled away, afraid that they would be among the first to be taken. It was rumored that freight cars were being brought up and shunted onto railway sidings. Bewildered, I made my way from one group to another, the words "deportation—immediate deportation!" hammering away at my brain.

I thought back to my meeting with Leon Michelson a few days earlier. He had said, half-musingly, "Can it be that the Jews who are going to be deported will meet the same fate as the Jews of Chelmno?" I shuddered at the very thought. Several months before, three Jewish gravediggers who by some miracle had escaped from Chelmno had startled the ghetto with tales of Jews being gassed to death. Some refused to believe the story; even those who did refused to entertain the thought that we might meet the same end some day. That Warsaw, our capital, should suffer such a disaster was simply past belief.

Cries of *"Genshuvka, Genshuvka!"* roused me from my thoughts. It appeared that the Jewish prison at Gesia 24 was being emptied. If that was true then the deportations had indeed begun! Almost immediately, crowds of Jews, myself among them, began to hurry in the direction of the prison. When I finally reached the intersection of Lubecki and Gesia, the place was already swarming with hundreds of Jews. The Jewish police were guarding the prison gates. It was forbidden to use the sidewalk in front of the prison, where the empty wagons were lined up. Several vans had already been driven inside. From time to time, as I watched, the gates opened to admit another vehicle.

There were sounds of quiet weeping; men bit their lips, women clawed at their faces and wrung their hands in despair. Those most affected were no doubt relatives of the inmates—for the most part Jews who had been caught smuggling food. Every now and then some man or woman clutching a small parcel would elbow forward through the human mass, hoping to hand a piece of bread to an imprisoned relative as he was taken out. The eyes of the bystanders sorrowfully followed the prisoners, the first to suffer this new misfortune.

The throng lingered for some time. Then, suddenly there was pushing and jostling; cries of grief filled the air. Some of the bystanders had recognized their kin in a wagon coming out of the prison. Within moments, the Jewish police began to disperse the crowd. They were followed by German troopers, pouring through the prison gates. Frantically, we scattered. Above the confusion, a loud wail pierced the air, then was gradually drowned out by the rumble of the wagons and the clanging of the horses' hoofs on the cobbled street. . . That was how it all began.

2. IN FRONT OF THE WORKSHOPS

Though I read and re-read the new posters, I still could not believe that the deportation had really started. People exchanged reassuring words, perhaps seeking to delude themselves as much as to console one another. The clouds would yet disperse. At most, some sixty thousand would be deported. Certainly no more than that. This was the accepted opinion among the community leaders.

Everyone was anxious not to be one of "them." It was necessary to find work, to obtain an employment card; then, according to the German edict, one could be sure of being permitted to stay in the ghetto. The ghetto put its trust in the printed word; workers would not be deported. Life might be hard, but still bearable. However, it was as good as impossible to find a position in a German factory. Such jobs were extremely scarce. A certain amount of money had to be paid to the employer, or else you needed to have pull with the Jewish owners of a shop. Another possibility was to make friends with someone who had already been working in a German factory for some time, and could put in a good word. Barring any of these prospects, the final alternative was to own a sewing machine. If you did, you might be able to exchange it for a job.

The section around Leszno, Prosta, and Nowolipki Streets, where the German shops were concentrated, was besieged daily by Jews. Each morning after the curfew had ended, lines formed at the closed factory gates. The earlier you got there, the closer you were to the door, the better your chance of being admitted. Those not waiting in line scurried about in search of a job—any job—the key to survival. Every day new workshops were opened—sometimes without a permit.

As soon as anyone put a few sewing machines into a couple of vacant rooms and began issuing employment cards, Jews stormed the doors. We snatched at straws. Scalpers forged employment cards and sold them at exorbitant prices. A job was a precious commodity, to be sold to the highest bidder.

Every morning, my brother, Chaim, hurried to the *Arbeitsamt* (the employment office affiliated with the *Judenrat* that supplied workers for the *placowkes,* the German forced labor squads working outside the ghetto). Chaim was anxious to acquire a place in such a *placowka*, but he had no luck. Such jobs were usually obtained through bribes—which we could not afford. Henia, my sixteen-year-old sister, had decided to hold onto her position in a communal kitchen maintained by the Jewish Self-Help Organization. All such employees were secure for the time being.

The Toebbens workshop, one of the largest of the German shops, was located at Leszno 70, close to my home. Each morning I, too, joined the line, along with other Jews who were waiting outside its still-closed doors in hopes of finding a job. One morning, while waiting there, I had met Sarah Samorak, my mother's best friend, who lived at Pawia 7. She had drawn me aside and, looking furtively about her, had reached into her bosom and brought out several small shiny objects.

"My only valuables," she had said, cupping a gold chain and two rings in her palms. "If I give them these, I think they'll have jobs for my husband and me."

She had waited eagerly for me to agree. Naturally, she had a good chance of getting a job—far better than others who lacked such trinkets to offer as bribes. But she was not the only one; there was no lack of Jews bringing their last pieces of jewelry or their household treasures to the workshops. And what of those less fortunate who, like me, had no jewelry, sewing machines or useful connections? Well, they had nothing to lose, so they stood in line with the others and took their chances; perhaps they could win by showing their skill. My own hope was to be lucky enough to be given a chance to display my abilities in sewing. And if there was nothing available for me, perhaps something would turn up for my brother or my mother. All you could do was try. . . .

The summer morning had grown humid. A constant stream of people moved toward the workshop, some lugging sewing machines and folding chairs, others with children in their arms.

"We'll have to spend all day here, and there is no telling what may happen, so I felt it was a good idea to bring the children," said a young woman holding a little girl by one hand and pushing a carriage containing a younger child with the other. As the crowd increased, so did the jostling; everyone was eager to get closer to the still-locked doors. the day was sweltering; sweat formed on the haggard, weary faces. Gaunt, drylipped children prowled among the adults silently, with fearful eyes, listening gravely to what grownups were saying.

As I waited, hungry and thirsty, pressed upon from all sides by the surging crowd, I spied Anka Wolkowicz. Since Alter Bass, a co-worker from my underground youth group, had been arrested, I had been staying temporarily in Anka's apartment. For several days she had been distressed on account of her five-year-old son, Larry, who was in Medem Sanatorium, in Miedzeszyn, on the outskirts of Warsaw. She could not decide whether to leave the child there or bring him to the ghetto. In Miedzeszyn things were quiet for the time being. "What should I do?" she asked of anyone on whom she happened in the street. She noticed me in the crowd. "You haven't seen my sisters, have you?" she asked me nervously.

"No, I haven't," I answered. Anka lived with three of her sisters, who had been driven out of Wloclawek by the Germans. Only the day before, one of them had managed to get a job in a shop for the price of a sewing machine. I had heard them weeping all night long; there were four of them, and only one could be saved. Which one would it be? A single available job had thrown all four into despair. This morning, again, all four had hurried to the factory.

"So you've found nothing for yourself yet?" I asked Anka.

"No, nothing at all. I've been running around liké crazy, and worrying about Larry, too. What do you think I should do with him? Should I bring him here, after all?"

Frankly, I was not thinking about Larry, but about my own family. I was in distress myself; how could I possibly give advice or help in such a dilemma? But Anka did not wait for an answer. She was already edging her way through the crowd. Looking back, she called to me, "I can't stay here any longer. If you see my sisters, tell them I went to telephone, to find out how things are at the sanatorium." And she disappeared.

There were many others like Anka, wandering about dazed and worried about the fate of their children. Some of them could even have found work, if only there had been someone to take care of their children. I saw our neighbor, Mrs. Zacherman, making her way through the crowd. She at least had a chance of getting a job in exchange for her sewing machine. Every day she left her three children in the care of a poor neighbor. Now, agitated, she was pushing ahead to find her place in the line. Probably she had run home to look in on her youngsters, pleading with whatever neighbors she met not to forget them in the confusion.

The crush became worse, as more people joined those waiting outside. I was barely able to breathe. The crowd was getting restive. Then a shout: "They're letting people in!"

Immediately, the crowd began to surge, pushing and shoving its way towards the entrance of the employment office. I was swept off my feet, carried along in a sea of backs and elbows. Children cried; women screamed to those around them to be careful; the little ones were in danger of being trampled underfoot. But the crowd pushed on, heedlessly. I heard the sound of a door closing. The press slackened slightly, and the crowd came to a complete halt. Somehow I had been pushed out of line, far to one side of the door.

What was I to do now?

"Those who know how to use their elbows are always the first to get in!" exclaimed a familiar voice. I turned to find Mrs. Zacherman standing near me, holding onto her sewing machine and breathing heavily. "I'd had that place in line since early morning, but they locked me out just the same. It's no use waiting here any longer. They won't open those doors again today."

We looked at each other helplessly. What was there left for us to do? Waiting here could only mean the same thing all over again. What about the workshop on Prosta Street? There at least they gave out numbers at the entrance; it still might be possible to get in. We had nothing to lose. We might as well try our luck.

All around us were other Jews equally harried and exhausted. They had waited since dawn in the sweltering heat but had accomplished nothing.

Mrs. Zacherman and I, with a few others, wriggled free of the crowd and hurried toward Prosta Street. On all sides people were lugging sewing machines; some were riding on *rickshas*, others were pushing handcarts.

Everyone was in a hurry, hot and anxious. Now and then a car loaded with Germans sped through the ghetto. Squads of Jewish police marched by in formation. Conversations stopped in mid-sentence, stilled as eyes apprehensively followed the uniformed figures. Where would they stop next? Which house would they surround, to seize the inhabitants for deportation? Now and then a woman—or sometimes a man—would pass, crying, but no one paid any attention. One had to press on, attending to the most urgent matter of all, protecting oneself and one's family.

At long last, we found ourselves in front of the workshop on Prosta Street, where a jostling line, much like the one we had left on Leszno Street, had formed. Here, at least, a few Jewish policemen tried to maintain some semblance of order. We fell into line. Before long, a door opened and several Jews emerged, obviously agitated. The people waiting outside tried to stop them, to find out what was going on. But those emerging were withdrawn and uncommunicative; all they said was that they had been hired. All that these fortunates, the envy of all the rest, wanted was to hurry home.

Two more men came out, with smiles on their perspiring faces; clearly, they had been accepted. They went up to someone in the crowd and whispered to him something no one else could hear. No one wondered at the secrecy. Once you were settled, why endanger your new-found security by telling your secret to others? Those with employment cards kept to themselves, fearing perhaps that some evil eye might blight their good fortune.

Looking about for a familiar face, I spotted Sarah Samorak, who had just come out of the factory. I moved towards her quickly, hoping she could tell me something helpful. But when I stopped her she only glanced at me in a curious way. When I asked her about what had happened inside, she refused to answer my question. Uneasy, she looked this way and that; then she hurried away.

This from my mother's best friend! Just a few hours earlier, when we had been in the same boat, she had been only too eager to talk to me. Now, feeling secure, she had changed completely.

We waited in front of the factory gate for a while longer, although no one else was being admitted. Gradually the line thinned out: another day wasted. Dusk was gathering. Depressed and hungry, Mrs. Zacherman and I started home, my thoughts anxiously turning to my family. As we neared our street, we heard cries of distress. Several wagons went by, loaded with Jews, sitting and standing, hugging sacks that contained whatever pitiful belongings they had managed to gather at the last moment. Some stared straight ahead with vacant eyes, others mourned and wailed, wringing their hands. Women tore their hair or clung to their children, who sat bewildered among the scattered bundles, gazing at the adults in silent fear. Running behind the last wagon, a lone woman, arms outstretched, cried: "My child! Give me back my child!"

In reply, a small voice called from the wagon.

"Mama! Mama!"

The people in the street watched as though hypnotized. Panting now with exhaustion, the mother kept on running after the wagon. One of the guards whispered something to the driver, who urged his horses into a gallop. The cries of the pursuing mother became more desperate as the horses pulled away. The procession turned into Karmelicka Street. The cries of the deportees faded away; only the cry of the agonized mother still pierced the air.

"My child! Give me back my child!"

We stood petrified. Mrs. Zacherman, no doubt thinking of her own children, was in tears. We had come face to face with the inescapable truth. Obsessed by our frantic search for jobs, we had scarcely noticed that six or seven thousand Jews were being deported every day. But now the question we had been too preoccupied to consider could no longer be ignored. What was to be done? The deportations were expanding; any day they would engulf us, too. Where was there safety?

We were consumed now by one concern—to save ourselves. It overrode every other thought, displaced every other emotion.

3. IDENTITY CARDS

On July 23rd, the death of Adam Czerniakow, head of the *Judenrat*, became known. He had taken his own life. What had led to this desperate act? Some claimed that he had suffered a nervous breakdown; others said that he had refused to serve as a tool for the Germans. Whatever the cause, his death remained a mystery. But within a short time we had ceased to give it a second thought. We could only worry about ourselves and our families.

The roundups were now in full swing. Hour by hour, the Nazi dragnet spread out, until it had reached nearly every house in the ghetto. Gone was the illlusion that the deportations would soon end; no longer was there talk of a limit of sixty or seventy thousand Jews. At first we had counted the days, hoping forlornly that the deportations would shortly be over. But now we accepted as fact that the harsh decree would not be rescinded.

German vehicles, their sirens wailing, careened through the ghetto streets, firing into the windows of Jewish homes and sniping indiscriminately at pedestrians, who ran for cover the minute any car appeared.

Every morning at eight o'clock, the goosesteps of the Jewish police resounded through the ghetto streets, signalling the start of a new day's roundups. All other activity came to a standstill. People remained in their homes, afraid to venture out. There was no way of knowing which house or block might next be surrounded and raided by the police. Huge wagons loaded with weeping Jews passed by at intervals, headed for the deportation center, the *Umschlagplatz*, where freight cars stood waiting. Fear of what awaited us there dulled our ability to think about anything except saving ourselves; everything else, even hunger, was unimportant. More and more, we moved about in a daze, to be awakened to reality only by the occasional frantic scream of some deportee. You had to look out for yourself, if you did not want to be the next victim.

One day, while I was out, a friend left a message for me at home. I was to appear early the next morning with photographs of myself and my family at Nowolipki 25, the offices of *Zytos*, the only ghetto relief organization still in operation. I was to meet friends there, and perhaps obtain an employment card. Here was a glimmer of hope. I felt exhilarated. My friends from the underground had remembered me. I was not forsaken.

The next morning I hurried to the appointed place. Although it was still quite early, there was already a great bustle in the streets. The Jewish population did not walk, it ran—whether to work, to look for a job, or to make a necessary purchase. The street itself seemed anxious, as though infected by the hasty movements of its pedestrians. In fact, the early morning hours were the only time of relative safety; the Jewish police were still preparing themselves for another day's grisly work. You had to take whatever advantage you could of these hours. I hurried along with the rest.

At the corner of Karmelicka and Nowolipki, I came upon Cyvia Wax, a slender, beautiful girl of seventeen who had worked in *Skif (Sozialistischer Kinder Farband)*, the underground Socialist children's organization. She, too, was in a hurry, with an important mission to carry out before the roundup got underway. As we parted she whispered that she was going to distribute employment cards among her friends.

Before I had gone more than a few steps, I heard someone calling me. I recognized Jan Bilak, another youthful co-worker in *Skif*, pulling a *ricksha*. He, too, was giving out employment cards, but his were destined for those living farther away. With his *ricksha*, he could reach the more distant areas sooner. He explained that even if he were stopped by the police, he would have nothing to fear, because the Germans needed *rickshas* for transportation to the *Umschlagplatz*. I did not press Bilak to explain what all the cards meant; I was bound to find out at the *Zytos* offices.

With buoyed hopes, I arrived to find the offices crowded, the atmosphere thick with cigarette smoke. Questions were being asked; cards were being shown. Everyone was restless, unable to sit still. Whoever entered from the street was immediately besieged by questions: "What's happening outside?"

"Nothing new so far." The reply was always the same. Each time, the tenseness relaxed slightly.

Is everyone here waiting for employment cards? I wondered.

A man emerged from the offices. All eyes turned to him. "Is there any news?"

"They don't know anything in there," was the answer.

"They don't know?" someone exclaimed. "We all come here to learn something, to get a bit of advice—and they won't say anything . . ."

Scanning the scene for familiar faces, I spied Abrasha Blum and pushed my way through the crowd to him. He was talking to Abramek Bortenstein. Abrasha, an outstanding leader, the soul of the illegal Bund, was tall and dark-skinned, with a long, serious face and an ardent gaze. Even amid the general chaos, there was an air of friendly serenity about him as he spoke to Abramek, himself a leader of the illegal socialist youth organization, *Zukunft.*

The two greeted me warmly, then resumed their conversation. I listened, and by degrees began to understand what was taking place. their group had managed to obtain from the *Judenrat* a number of fictitious employment cards, which were being issued to unemployed young people. Such cards were honored by the police, and could save their holders from being deported. Efforts were also underway to organize workshops as another means of keeping young people from being deported. Such a move called for consultation with the *Judenrat.* But now the death of Czerniakow, its president, had plunged them all into confusion.

Dr. Emmanuel Ringelblum, the well-known historian, approached. Murmuring a polite apology, he drew Abrasha aside briefly. When Abrasha returned, he asked for my photographs, gave me a personal data form to fill out, and left with Ringelblum.

Abramek spoke to me of the general helplessness that had seized the community workers. They wished to help, but they were working under a severe handicap. Everywhere the Germans had appointed new people.

The Jewish officials who formerly had a measure of influence in the ghetto had been dismissed. Abramek thought that the best way to counter the roundups was to go into hiding to avoid being deported. The Germans were not to be trusted. One should do everything possible to stay in the ghetto. Here, at least, one could remain abreast of events and of what might be expected. . . . Abramek seemed tense and agitated. He had little faith in the fictitious cards which were being given out to the young people. They might be better than none at all, he said, but they did not give any real security. Each day brought news of more deportations. Everyone was helpless against the universal threat.

Despite forebodings, I heaved a sigh of relief. The dubious security which the cards provided was better than no security at all. At least I would have that much.

Kuba Zilberberg, a youth group member, came over to talk to us. He brought good news. His father, a wealthy merchant on Gesia Street, together with several other Jews, was about to open a shop within the Toebbens complex, to make German military uniforms, and hoped to hire several acquaintances without the need of bribes. They would have to be tailors, of course. Kuba had come to the *Zytos* office to obtain names of qualified applicants for the jobs. Abramek was pleased by this news. To have a job at Toebbens meant a greater measure of safety—though only for a handful of workers.

A new commotion outside sent us rushing to the windows. Police were assembling in the street below. Our bewilderment quickly gave way to near-panic. Some dashed out of the building, others ran from one room to another, or gathered in groups outside the doors of the various offices, hoping to find shelter inside. It was safer there. One might mingle with the clerical staff, and perhaps pass for an employee.

"A blockade! A raid! The house is surrounded!" someone whispered in dismay. "What are we going to do?"

I wanted to see Abrasha again. He might already have a card for me. Finally, with a few others, I succeeded in pushing my way into one of the offices. We paused just inside the door, scanning the nervous faces of the officials and staff.

"Why doesn't someone tell us what to do? We have employment cards," someone said loudly.

But no one answered him. The clerks were frightened; far too many people had crowded into their department, endangering the safety of everyone else. They tried to persuade the visitors to leave, but they refused to go. "Why should we be discriminated against?" "We don't want to be deported either." The clerks gave up trying to chase them out. In any event, nothing could be done. Each was oblivious of the other. The Jewish police might raid the office at any moment.

Drenched with perspiration, I could barely make my way to the desk of Dr. Ringelblum and Abrasha, who were still distributing cards. I managed to obtain employment cards for myself, my mother, and my brother, indicating that we were all employees of *Zytos*. At least now I had some sort of document. Any document could mean a measure of security. But I must hurry home with this safeguard before I got caught in a police raid.

Taking leave of Abrasha, Abramek and Kuba, I ran down the stairs with a few others. But it was too late; the gate had been closed. A Jewish policeman was already there, barring the exit. We pleaded with him, showed him our cards, explaining that we had important assignments to carry out—all to no avail. He insisted that he had his orders. What could we do? Go back upstairs? One of our group motioned to the policeman, took him aside, and thrust something into his hand. The policeman looked about furtively, opened the gate and told us to get out fast.

The street was deserted. Farther on, a detachment of police stood at attention, listening to an officer's orders. Another detachment was marking time at the corner of Karmelicka Street. There was the creak of empty wagons approaching. A new roundup was about to begin. We had better get out of the way. We took a shortcut to Karmelicka Street, where we were stopped by a brusque voice: "Where are you going? You're not supposed to be here!"

Once again we presented our cards, explaining and pleading. In the end we were permitted to go on. Only a few blocks more, and I was home. I heaved a sigh of relief. The fictitious cards had been of some help, at least for the moment.

4. IN THE HANDS OF THE POLICE

The Jewish police were now very important people in the Warsaw ghetto. The Nazis relied on them to carry out their roundups, to control employment cards, and to load unemployed Jews into the wagons and transport them to the waiting railway cars. Obviously, no one was very fond of the police; even in better days they had been known to badger and harass people in their daily lives by insisting on rigid adherence to the Nazi regulations. Now they had become even more hostile and aggressive. They were feared, but at the same time they were the objects of envy. For one thing, the Jewish police were secure; even the Germans thus far had left their relatives alone. They were never threatened with "resettlement."

One afternoon, during the first week of the deportations, I happened to be at home with my mother when a column of police suddenly sealed off our building. All residents were ordered to go down and assemble in the courtyard. In their alarm, people tried to snatch up a few belongings, but the raiders, some wearing white armbands reading *"Judenrat,"* told them, "You'll have time to pick up your things when the wagons get here." So, it was no longer only police, but also functionaries of the *Judenrat*, who had been delegated to assist in the task of "resettlement."

The luckless residents of the building submitted to the orders of these men. Without protest, they were herded roughly down the stairs. With the callous arrogance of the privileged, the Jewish police dragged children, the elderly and the ailing down to the courtyard. Although a number of the residents had employment cards, the faces of all were pale

26

with fear. Families clung together for whatever comfort there might be in closeness. The elderly were pushed to the rear, while the young were lined up in front. Children snuggled close to the adults. Hearts pounding, the distraught residents prepared for the inspection. Several women brushed past rudely and walked up to the police, flaunting their employment cards. "These women are going to be released immediately," one of the bystanders muttered. "Their husbands are in the police force." And, indeed, as the troopers saw these cards, their arrogance softened; they smiled and motioned to the women to return to their homes. Envious glances followed them as they hastened off.

Three men approached the police. Someone behind me whispered that they were the richest Jews of our building. It was easy to guess that their intention was bribery. The police never objected to having their palms greased. One could usually escape their clutches—for a consideration. The police could always fill their quota of deportees elsewhere; those who had neither cash nor employment cards to justify their being allowed to remain in the ghetto were the first to be rounded up. Breathlessly we watched the transaction. If the police accepted the bribe, the inspection was not likely to be stringent. Finally, broad smiles appeared on the faces of the trio. They had got the police where they wanted them.

The inspection continued as the police, without a word, examined the cards shown by the residents. Anyone who attempted to ask a question or make an excuse was ordered, "Be quiet until it's your turn!" I stood silently beside my mother and my young brother. A policeman threw a cursory glance at our cards and then moved on. What lay in store for us?

After the inspection had been completed, a few of the Jews who had neither cards nor money were ordered to step to one side. Yet other Jews in similar straits were passed over. How, I wondered, did the police decide? There were protests. In order to spare certain lives, others had to be made the victims.

Of those doomed, I knew only a few: two elderly sisters, Tzirel and Sima, who worked in a paper bag factory, and Reb Avrom, formerly a coachman, and his family. Along with the others, they were ordered to gather up their pitiful parcels and wait for the wagons. The rest of us, saved for the moment, heaved an involuntary sigh.

But the Jews who were about to be deported did not move. Ashen white with fear, they begged the police for mercy. One elderly woman, trembling like a leaf, clutched a policeman's hand and pleaded, pointing in our direction, "Please let me stay. My daughter is over there! Let me stay with her. If I'm alone, I'll die."

Fanya, the coachman's daughter, clung to her little sister, insisting through her tears, "You can see for yourself how weak and run-down we are. In another town, among strangers, we'll simply die. Have pity!"

It was no use. The men in uniform ignored their anguish. A few of the less hardened, visibly distressed by the scene, walked out of the courtyard.

We stood as though turned to stone. Near me someone muttered, "Dear God! Put an end to this misery!" Yet not one of the hundred and fifty-odd Jews who had been spared made any effort to help. They did not want to jeopardize their own good fortunes. One group gave thanks to the Lord for His mercy; the other, defeated and resigned to their fate, handed over their sacks and baskets, and climbed slowly into the waiting wagons. From there, they stared out at the remaining crowd. Some of them broke into cries of despair. What grief was reflected in their eyes! What mute reproach! We stood there, stunned, silent and conscience-stricken. As the police ordered the wagon to move, one last bundle was tossed into the wagon. Those inside gave one last glance at their more fortunate neighbors and at the big, grey building in which they had lived, now retreating from view as the wagon clattered slowly out of the courtyard. We stood rooted to the spot, hardly believing that the nightmare was over. Then, still shaken by the experience, we embraced one another, murmuring, "Well, at least we were lucky this time. . . ."

But why had no one helped the others? Why hadn't somebody—why hadn't I—pleaded for them? Flinching, I tried to silence these questions, to justify my cowardice, saying to myself, "Our own chances of being allowed to stay in the ghetto were slim enough. We could not afford to stick our necks out for others."

Shortly thereafter, the police threw up a roadblock at the corner of Zamenhof and Nowolipki Streets, where the cards of all passersby were subjected to inspection. Any Jew without the proper documents was immediately forced into a waiting wagon. I showed my card and was waved on.

A piercing voice stopped me. It came from a middle-aged woman struggling with two policemen who were dragging her towards a waiting wagon. Her cries chilled the blood. A cluster of Jews standing nearby cursed the policemen under their breath, but did not stir. Subdued, finally, and thrown by the police into the vehicle, the woman at first lay motionless, then started to cry again: "Fellow Jews, have mercy, help me! I have little children at home. Help me . . ." Her cries went unanswered, the wretched woman fell at last to quiet weeping.

A few moments later, two little girls, sisters about ten and twelve years old, weeping steadily, were hoisted into the same wagon. They made no protest, uttered no cries, but submitted passively, hand in hand, their eyes roving, perhaps seeking their mother. Seated in the wagon, they huddled close to one another, crying silently. Even the policeman on the wagon was moved. He fumbled in his pockets for something, then stroked their foreheads.

Little by little, the wagon filled up. Almost all the victims resisted; not one submitted docilely. They argued, they pleaded, and some even tried to force money into the hands of their captors. But it was all to no avail; no one was released from the wagon. The other Jews, watching the scene from afar, scanned the faces of the captives to see if any relatives or acquaintances were among them. As the wagon began to move, the screams and the cries for help grew louder, piercing everyone's heart anew. Eyes full of pity followed the departing victims, but no one dared approach them. Only after the wagon had rolled out of sight did the bystanders begin to gather up the hastily scribbled notes to relatives which the doomed prisoners had tossed out onto the street.

Many such notes eventually found their way into the hands of those to whom they were addressed. Those who received such missives had but one remaining recourse—to speak privately with a member of the Jewish police force. It was possible for a sympathetic trooper to arrange by devious means for the liberation of a condemned person before he was loaded onto a freight car for departure. True, this conspiracy had to be carried out secretly, unknown to the Germans. One had to have the right connections, influence, and above all, money.

Policemen returned home after engaging in a roundup to find themselves besieged by grieving, pleading Jews who had come to bargain for the release of their kin. Each one had brought along money or a valued piece of jewelry. If only the policeman would be willing to cooperate . . .

Their grief-stricken faces streaked with tears, the Jews pleaded to be admitted. Whatever hatred they felt for the men who, only hours earlier had helped load their loved ones onto the wagons, was now suppressed. Addressing the policeman in subdued tones, they wept quietly so as not to annoy the man in uniform. Those from whom the policeman was willing to accept a gift were fortunate indeed. For them, at least, there was some hope. But more often than not, all their pleading was in vain.

A Jewish policeman who sometimes accepted bribes happened to live in our building. Every night we would hear the pleading voices of the deportees' relatives. The sounds of their weeping would be accompanied by the irritated barks of the policeman ordering the visitors to leave. A few Jewish policemen refused to participate in the outrages of these roundups. But they resigned within a matter of days. All those continuing on the force, including those who had given assistance to one or two victims, were looked upon as enemies by the rest of the ghetto, as outcasts of whom nothing but the worst could be expected.

5. MY FAMILY IS DEPORTED

As the days passed, the deportations gathered momentum. Germans and Ukrainians joined the Jewish police in the grim roundups. Private Jewish factories were systematically liquidated and their workers deported. Some employment cards, including many of those issued by the *Judenrat,* were no longer recognized by the Germans. The cards I had obtained became worthless within a few days. Only persons employed in German factories were eligible to remain in the ghetto. All other Jews now were required to appear at the point of embarkation when ordered to do so.

Some letters from deportees were received in the ghetto which gave credence to the German assurances that those forced to leave had been given employment elsewhere. But, at the same time, it was rumored that the seemingly reassuring messages were in fact deliberate misrepresentations, in coded language prearranged between sender and recipient to circumvent the German censorship, conveying the most disquieting information about what was really happening.

Nevertheless, at this time very few believed that the Germans were forcing their victims to send cheerful notes to their kin at home when in fact they were about to enter the Treblinka death camp. All news was vague; it was easy to yield to the comforting hope that it was good. Optimism was encouraged by the appearance—on July 29th—of new posters calling on Jews to report voluntarily at the distribution center, where they would be rewarded with three kilograms of bread and one kilogram of marmalade.

"If the Germans are giving out bread, it must be because they need us," Jews consoled one another. "Otherwise they would not waste the flour." Many simply blocked out the suspicion that the loaves might be a lure to get them to the railroad cars. The lessening of hunger—no matter how briefly—and the prospect of work—diligently fostered by the German propaganda in the ghetto—were sufficient to dampen the doubts that nagged at them.

For those with neither confidence in the Germans, nor employment cards, the only recourse was to go into hiding. But that was no easy matter; the hiding place must be absolutely safe, since discovery meant death.

There was Baruch Zifferman. I had stayed in his apartment for a while after the ghetto was established, working together at night to prepare the underground Bund paper for the press. Zifferman had always dressed neatly; he had always been meticulous about his appearance. How different he looked when I met him again in the street during one of the brief respites from raids. Grimy and rumpled, his long face sallow, a blood-stained bandage on his head, he spoke in a dry, hoarse voice of his recent experiences.

The Germans had sealed off Nowolipki Street, where he had been hiding with his wife and young son in Birnbaum's house, whose massive iron door was very hard to open.

When the Germans shouted, "All Jews downstairs!" the residents had locked the door and stayed where they were. Then came the familiar loud banging to open the iron door. Crashing blows by iron bars came next, accompanied by commands in German to open the door at once. The five Jews inside huddled together, not stirring, wondering whether the door would hold.

The angry shouts of the Germans and the pounding on the door grew louder. At last, groaning and creaking on its hinges, the door gave way, and several scowling Ukrainians forced their way in, ordering everyone to put up his hands. After being searched and robbed of their valuables, the trembling victims were commanded to line up against the wall. Even with the guns aimed at him, Zifferman did not dream that the invaders would actually fire; he supposed they were only trying to intimidate the Jews. But the shots broke into his thoughts, and he fell to the floor.

When he regained conciousness, everything was quiet. The Ukrainians

Hanna and Shlomo Peltel,
the author's parents

Henia Peltel, the author's younger sister

In the Ghetto: (left to right) Moshe Kaufman, Abraham
Feiner, Feigele Peltel (Vladka), Marek Edelman

had left. His wife, his son, and the Birnbaums lay dead. Somehow, he managed to reach the courtyard, where other Jews found him and treated his wounds. Now he was walking about in a daze. His voice shook as he told me about Raizel Malinowski, who had also lived on Nowolipki Street. When the Germans surrounded her house, she had tried to hide in the attic along with several neighbors. The Ukrainians found them and shot them all, taking the watches from their lifeless wrists.

Every raid was now accompanied by indiscriminate shooting. In early August, the deportations had come under the direction of the infamous "Einsatz Reinhardt" contingent, which had some time before conducted the brutal "resettlement" in Lublin.

My family and I had planned to go into hiding with our neighbor, Mrs. Zacherman. She had three rooms, one of which we intended to block off with a cupboard. But just as we were about to begin moving the furniture, Mrs. Zacherman became frightened and canceled the arrangement. If we were resettled, she said, we might perhaps survive in another town. On the other hand, if we were caught here in our deception, we would almost certainly be shot.

As a result, we were left stranded, without employment cards or hiding place. My mother and brother had been hiding in the cellar of the public soup kitchen at 12 Nowolipki Street, where my sister was working. They happened to be elsewhere the day the hideout was discovered.

My mother had grown haggard; yielding to despair, she sometimes said, "We're bound to fall into their hands sooner or later. Maybe it would be better to give ourselves up to them now." Tormented by hunger, my brother was inclined to agree with her. Yet none of us could quite bring ourselves to leave the apartment. But some of our neighbors, especially the poorest, those who already had been uprooted once, did so, going voluntarily to the *Umschlagplatz* with their children.

Fear of the unknown destination of the railroad cars was the main thing that kept us from committing ourselves. We decided to hold out. Tomorrow—or the next day or the day after—we told ourselves, our situation was bound to improve. On August 2, it was rumored once again that our block was about to be sealed off by the Germans. Everyone there, including the families of the Jewish police, now lived in terror of the imminent roundup. The rumors had originated with the relatives of the police, some of whom had come rushing home that morning to warn their families. The news traveled quickly, leaving confusion in its wake. It was hard to find a safe hiding place; our own group of buildings had been raided several times, and its hideouts were no longer secret. Nevertheless, the bewildered Jews hurried to take refuge in lofts, in cellars, or wherever they could. Those who found secure hiding places refused to share the secret lest too many others take shelter in the same spot. They would share their good fortune only with their next of kin. Everyone tried to stay close to his own home, so that if he were deported he would at least have a chance to take along a few of his belongings.

My mother, my brother and I set out for the kitchen where my sister was employed. As we reached Karmelicka Street we saw the familiar police blockade, and retraced our steps. It was frightening to be out on the street even in broad daylight. The shops and stalls were closed. People hesitated to venture forth; only the Jewish police remained visible, along with a few *rickshas* and empty wagons. We breathed more easily as we neared home. I urged my mother and brother to come into my apartment at Leszno 72. Some friends were gathered there, because the atmosphere was less dismal than in their own homes.

An urgent restlessness, however, kept me on the move. I went to see Anka Wolkowicz, who was more familiar than I with the layout of the building, and therefore might know of some hideout. She did know a good place, she said, except that she could not reach it. Under the circumstances, it seemed best to stay in the third building, where there were empty apartments whose residents had been taken away a few days before. It was possible to squeeze through an open window of this house into another on Nowolipki Street. If there were a raid, we could crawl through to the other building—and perhaps elude death once more.

A score of Jews already were milling about nervously in front of the deserted building. It was unlikely that all would be able to push inside at the crucial moment. But they had no other refuge, so they sat, dejected, tense and frightened, on the steps, to be as close as possible to their only chance for safety. Now and then, one of them peered through the gate to see if anyone was approaching. At the first sound of a siren, the knot of Jews rushed for cover. When the vehicle merely sped by or turned off in another direction, the distraught Jews resumed their sitting or aimless milling about. They hardly exchanged a word with one another; fear had rendered them inarticulate. A few had bona fide employment cards.

Relatively confident of their own safety, they sought to give what reassurance they could to the less fortunate that they could rely on their own, not-so-genuine, cards.

The smell of soup drifted from an open window, where a few women had taken advantage of the lull to prepare a hot meal for their starving families. The savory aroma tantalized everyone's nostrils, giving an edge to the hunger we all felt. Few of us had tasted food since the evening before. The dwindling food supply permitted most of us to eat only once a day. My brother became increasingly restless. My mother tried to comfort him, "Just be patient; it will be night soon—and we'll pull through somehow . . ."

We decided that if one of us should be taken, he would try to stay at the detention center so as not to be among the first deportees. Whoever succeeded in escaping was to spare no effort to free the others.

The morning passed. The assembled Jews started back to their homes, reasoning that if there had been no blockade until now, none was likely to take place that day. My mother and brother went upstairs to their apartment. I remained in the courtyard.

Suddenly there was turmoil. Caught off guard, instead of hurrying along with the others to the little window, so as to squeeze through into the next building, I started to run up the stairs to my own room. Others shouted impatiently, "Move on—get out of the way!" The door to my apartment was open. I stood there trying to decide whether to enter or make a dash for the little window. Anka's sisters rushed in and were about to close the door. I squeezed inside, and scanned the scene through the window. It was too late; the Germans were already in the courtyard, their strident voices raised in the familiar cry, *"Alle Juden herunter!"* (All Jews downstairs!)

What was to be done? The knapsack that held our belongings was ready. No—better to lock ourselves in, and open only when ordered to do so. The invaders might overlook us during their inspection. The voices grew louder. Our neighbors' hurried footsteps echoed on the stairs.

My thoughts turned to my mother and brother, in their rooms, only three houses away. They would surely be taken in the raid. I berated myself for having allowed us to become separated.

But those of us in Anka's room now had to make our own decision. Moving on tiptoe lest by a sound we reveal our presence, we pulled on our coats. There were shots, the crash of falling glass, a confusion of hoarse cries. "Down! Lie down on the floor!" a voice warned. More shots.

From where we were, we could make out clearly what was happening on the opposite roof. A line of Jews was crawling along a catwalk on the rooftop, which was the sole link between one house and another. It was a hazardous venture. One slip, one clumsy move—and all would be over. The crawling Jews looked back furtively. One who had crouched behind a chimney was spotted by the enemy, and shot.

In our own house, we heard quick, heavy footsteps, first up the stairs, then at the door of our neighbor's apartment. Through the wall we could hear a sharp command, furniture being moved, a woman's voice pleading for mercy for an ailing father. A few minutes later, shuffling steps—undoubtedly those of the invalid—were heard in the corridor.

Now they were banging on our door. I looked at my companions—they sat as though frozen. One of Anka's sisters tiptoed to the door. Still without a word, the rest of us got to our feet. Rifle butts now were pounding on the door. We waited dumbly. After what seemed an eternity, the girl who had gone to the door opened it. Three Ukrainians, carbines at the ready, burst in shouting, "Downstairs, all of you, and be quick about it!" They rummaged through the household things, searched under the bed and table.

Gathering up our bundles, we walked out in numbed silence. "Hurry up! Hurry!" shouted another Ukrainian who had just arrived. In the courtyard, other groups of Jews, hugging their bundles, were emerging from the other buildings. Ukrainians, Germans, and Jewish police, now assembled in force, herded us towards the gates. The asphalt was spattered with blood; a feeble moan issued from a huddled form, lying face to the wall in a spreading pool of blood. A Jew holding some sort of certificate approached the Germans and began to plead with them, only to have a rifle butt brought down on his head.

Outside, the pavement was teeming with Jews. Everything was in confusion: a mass of parents, children, valises and bundles shifting in and out, and the sounds of muffled weeping. A little farther on, names were being called out. Men and women clung to one another for courage. Here and there someone fastened a belt or shoe lace—something there had been no time to do before—or tightened a bundle so as to make a good impression on the Germans. But the majority simply waited, gazing in speechless dismay at the haughty broad-faced officers, trying to guess what they would do next. Where was my own family? Would I find them in this welter? Where could I search? Almost suffocating in the crush of bodies, I could scarcely move a muscle, let alone go look for my mother and brother. Surrounded by fellow human beings, I felt alone and helpless. What were we, after all? Mere objects to which anything could be done. Dazed, I was carried along by the crowd, indifferent to the jostling, to the harsh German commands, to the kicks and trampling of feet. A sense of resigned fatalism took possession of my will: whatever was coming, let it come, and be over with.

"Have your employment cards ready for inspection!"

People became more alert. There was renewed pushing and jostling; everyone in possession of a scrap of paper was eager to be among the first. The Germans were already busy with the "selection." Standing at the curb, they glanced only cursorily at the outstretched cards.

"To the left! To the right! To the left!"

As each verdict was pronounced, two Jewish policemen escorted the victim to his appointed place. Those directed to the right found themselves on one side of the pavement; those ordered to the left found themselves standing in the middle of the street. The trembling, outstretched hands, the clutched scraps of paper, passed in rapid succession, until the rhythmic "Left! Right! Left!" became a meaningless refrain. The German officer in charge did not even bother to read the cards; a quick glance, and the holder's fate was sealed. After the sun had set behind the buildings, a sizeable crowd still stood on the sidewalk, waiting to be processed. Anka's sisters, one of them holding a child, shuffled by, holding bona fide employment cards.

"Left! Left!"

The child was a complication. The police escorted her to the middle of the street; she offered no protest, her face reflecting apathy and resignation.

Then came Julian Welikowski and his wife and child. He had been my teacher at the Yiddish language public school, the *Folkschul*, at Mila 51. He was devoted to his students, and they loved him for his good nature and fine voice. Since the beginning of the war, he had worked untiringly to organize illegal children's classes, soup kitchens, and clubs. Now he walked slowly, dragging his left foot, a large knapsack strapped to his back. With one hand, he led his four-year-old daughter; with the other arm, over which a cane dangled, he supported his pale, frightened wife. The three approached the German in charge, who had already been eyeing them. Waving aside the paper presented by the teacher, the German ordered, "Left!"

The trio stood there for a moment, uncomprehending. "Left! God damn it!" repeated the German. Welikowski slowly pulled his arm away from his wife, lifted his daughter and with a shudder hugged her to his chest as he let himself be escorted to the left. His wife followed in silence.

Some of those who had been ordered to the left tried to escape from the Jewish police. They wept and wailed and begged to be spared from deportation. They wanted to rejoin their families, from whom they had just been separated.

Inwardly, I too, though not yet caught up in the "selection," longed to find my mother and brother. My eyes sought them in the crowd, but in vain.

Another familiar face now confronted the German inspector. It was that of a neighbor who only that morning had shown me a document stamped by the German authorities, authorizing him to open a workshop. I had no doubt that he would get clearance, and evidently he was just as confident; he casually handed the officer his certificate, pointing to his wife and ten-year-old son, who were standing beside him.

"Man to the right! Wife and child to the left!"

The police stepped forward to carry out the order. The man held his ground, pointing again to his certificate, remonstrating with the officer. The German was adamant. The man clung to his wife and son, pleading tearfully with the Jewish police not to separate them; the woman and child huddling close, their eyes silently beseeching. The Jewish police clearly were too afraid of the Germans to help. With a final anguished cry, they were pushed into the mass of those about to be deported.

The "selection" continued rapidly. My turn approached. I had no employment card, only a small scribbled note that had been handed to me by my friend Kuba Zilberberg, authorizing me to go to Toebbens' workshop and register. Still, this was better than no document at all. A moon-faced German took the note and held it for a moment. With a skeptical glance at me, he asked ironically, "Is this *your* employment card?"

"Yes," I muttered, "it's my employment card from Toebbens." I had anticipated his verdict, and now was impatient to have done with it. The inspector threw me another piercing look.

"To the right!"

I could hardly believe my own ears—was I really among the lucky ones? The next moment, I was being escorted to the "safe" contingent. The crowd was thinner here and I could get a good view of the entire scene. I scanned the huge throng in the middle of the street, fearful that I might spot my mother and brother among those destined for deportation. But they were nowhere to be seen; not there, not among those who, like myself, had been spared.

The people around me, too, searched the middle of the street for their own families. Now and then, someone from among those spared would try to join the group of those about to be deported, but they were barred by the Ukrainian guards. Not a word passed among those of us safe on the sidewalk. We all watched the other group in silent anguish.

As the "selection" continued, trucks and streetcars began to arrive, cutting off our view. We could see only the vehicles slowly filling up with people. Ukrainians, their pistols drawn, guarded the entrances to the cars. Some Jews from our safe side made a last desperate effort to join their doomed relatives.

Our eyes were fixed on the cars, each packed beyond capacity as it pulled out, hoping and at the same time fearing to see a relative or friend.

"Faiga—Faiga . . ." I thought I heard my brother's voice. I strained to see through the streetcar windows, but it was difficult to make out the faces inside. A heavy Ukrainian hand on my shoulder held me back.

One by one, the cars and wagons disappeared into Zelazna Street. There was no tumult now, no sound at all except the harsh laughter of the Germans echoing in the deserted building. The middle of the street was empty. Sprawled near the curb were the bodies of two dead Jews. Tattered garments and shoes were strewn about. A small group of Ukrainians rummaged through a sack which one of the deportees had left behind: the Germans had already returned to their autos. The few of us who had been spared stood with blank faces, not speaking, staring down the street at the last of the vehicles bearing our doomed relatives away.

6. UMSCHLAGPLATZ

My loved ones were gone. What was I to do now? To whom could I, should I, turn?

With my sister, who was still safely employed at the public kitchen, I roamed through the ghetto, bereft and bewildered. We had already appealed to the Jewish policeman who lived in our building, consulted several acquaintances connected with the *Judenrat*, sought influence, wept, prayed and pleaded—all to no avail. Perhaps with American dollars or other valuables we might have been able to save Mother and Chaim. But we were penniless.

Woebegone, we prowled the *Umschlagplatz*, in search of news. Others there were similarly engaged. The tailor Mintz, a neighbor and acquaintance, was working on the night shift at Toebbens' shop. During the same raid in which our mother and brother had been taken, he had been seized, together with his wife and two sisters, and sent to the *Umschlagplatz*, where they had spent the entire night. Fortunately, his German supervisor from the shop had come that morning to intercede with the German authorities and a group of Toebbens' employees had been released, Mintz among them. But during that night on the *Umschlagplatz* he had seen my mother and brother, and had brought back from them a note—a scrap of paper on which my brother Chaim had scribbled a message in pencil.

They were lining up for their bread ration, Chaim had written. They were unendurably hungry and thirsty and had better hurry, lest the food run out and they would be thrust into the railway cars without a crumb to eat. That was all . . . and they were the last words to reach me from my mother and my brother.

I knew that they had been without food for two days, for I had gone back to the apartment after my release and had found a half-spilled bag of flour on the table and an empty plate with a glass of water alongside. My mother had started to fix dumplings for the soup when the raid had begun. She had never had a chance to finish.

I plied Mintz with questions: What was the spirit of the deportees? But he was too anguished to reply coherently.

"The place is teeming with people," he said, coughing. "Wherever you look, there are children and old people, men and women, all mixed together. A sea of people, yet each is desolate, absorbed in himself. Desperation . . . there's no one to talk to, to ask about anything. And no water—nothing, nothing . . ." He broke down in sobs. We joined him, weeping over our own misfortune.

Hoping to be able, still, to do something for my mother and brother, I ran to the *Umschlagplatz* for the second time with a small parcel of food. On the way I encountered our neighbor Mrs. Zacherman. The day before, during the raid on our street, while she was at work in Toebbens' shop, the Germans had taken her three small children away. With her own valid employment certificate, she had endeavored to reclaim the youngsters, but to no avail. Now burdened with parcels, she hurried down the middle of the street, staring straight ahead, as though she had seen something of interest in the distance.

I begged her to wait for a few moments so I might scribble a few lines, to be tucked into the food destined for my family—if they were still there. She looked at me puzzled, as if at a loss to understand me, then snatched the parcel from my hands, exclaiming, "Sorry, but I can't wait any longer! I must hurry—my little daughter must be crying there!" Tears welled in her eyes at the mention of her two-year-old child. Biting her lips, she tried to restrain herself, saying, "God knows whether I'll ever see them again." Raising her basket onto her shoulders, she asked, "And what about you?"

What could I say? Time and again, my sister and I had talked about joining our mother and brother and sharing their fate, But somehow we had hesitated, restrained by fear of the unknown. "I'll hang around here a while longer," I answered meekly. "Perhaps I'll find some way to get them out."

"You're wasting your time," Mrs. Zacherman commented with a wry smile. "I've tried that." And without waiting for an answer, she kissed me. "Well, we're not likely to see each other again." She hurried off.

I stood there as if stunned, my eyes following her past the ghetto wall. For the first time I grasped the awful truth: that not just kindly Mrs. Zacherman, but also my mother and brother had departed from my life forever.

7. "VOLUNTEERS"

Ten days since the deportations had begun—could it have been so short a time? We had been through so much . . .

Thousands upon thousands of Jews had already been deported and there was no reliable knowledge of their whereabouts. Some still thought the deportees had been assigned to some kind of work. One rumor was that they had been dispatched to the city of Smolensk, close to the Russo-German front, to dig trenches. But by now an ever-growing number of Jews tended to believe the horrible new rumors that all the German promises were false and that the so-called "resettlement" actually meant only one thing—death! We fought against accepting that grisly thought. Our loved ones were among the deportees. No, they must be alive; they surely must be alive . . . somewhere . . .

Throughout each day, while the raids continued, individuals and small groups of Jews, parents and children, trudged through the comparatively deserted streets, weighed down by bundles, baskets, and battered valises, their last pitiful belongings, towards the *Umschlagplatz*. Some walked slowly with heads bowed; others hurried along, as if pressed for time. No one detained them or barred their way; they were the "volunteers." The ghetto watched their mute, resigned march without surprise. In hiding places and workshops, hearts ached with silent admiration for the strength that had enabled these people to take at least this decisive step. My sister and I could summon no such courage.

Gloom pervaded the ghetto. There was no security whatsoever. Exhausted by privation, emaciated or bloated by hunger, crushed by the incessant fear of being trapped, many simply gave up the struggle. The Germans' diabolic tactics reaped their harvest. Hunger drove famished Jews to the bread line, where each received his three kilograms of bread—before being pushed into the waiting railroad cars. Three kilos of bread loomed very large in the eyes of a starving man. The temptation, even for once, to still that gnawing hunger eclipsed all other considerations, including the dread of the unknown, the destination of the railroad cars. In his tragic helplessness, the victim let himself be lulled by the Germans' soothing promises of an end to his daily struggle for survival. Perhaps it was true, after all, that there would be jobs waiting for them.

Yakub Katz, a barber from Kalisz, an intelligent man whom I knew from my work in the underground, had been driven in 1940, together with his wife and two daughters, from his home to Warsaw, where his family languished in the refugee compound at Leszno 14 for some time. Katz had worked hard, enduring hunger and cold, barely making ends meet, hoping that he and his family would weather the storm. I met him during the early days of the German roundups. Unnerved and starved, he informed me that his wife was ready to surrender to the Germans. "And you?" I asked, astonished. After all, Katz was familiar with the underground press. He knew better than to have any faith in the German promises. What had come over him?

"One can't go on starving forever," he answered gloomily. "We have no strength left to go on. We'll perish here anyway." His sallow, emaciated face and sad, sunken eyes underscored his words. The very next day I learned that he had left the ghetto.

The widow Chaveleh, whose husband had died in the war, came often to our home. She lived at Mila 48, gladly accepting a bowl of soup and a piece of bread in payment for her services as a seamstress. The evening after my mother and brother had been taken away, Chaveleh came to my mother's apartment while I happened to be there. A small, wizened old woman carrying a basket, she halted timidly at the threshold, inquiring after my mother. She had come to beg a few *zloty*—for the last time, she said, adding, "You see, I am about to go to the *Umschlagplatz* to get three kilograms of bread, and perhaps I'll find odd sewing jobs in some other town."

When she learned of our misfortune, her deadened eyes suddenly showed a strange gleam; she seemed jubilant. She had better hurry along, she said, if she wanted to catch up with my mother. It was easier to travel with friends.

Hunger was not the only reason for voluntary surrender. There were Jews who could have remained safely in the ghetto, who had bona fide employment cards, as well as jobs at German factories. They were not crushed by the trying conditions around them. On the contrary, they still harbored a strong will to live, to resist, yet they proceeded voluntarily to the waiting railroad cars. They did this for only one reason: they did not want to be separated from their families.

Abramek Bortenstein had been well aware of the fate that awaited the deportees, He worked at Roerich's factory at Nowolipki 74. He could have obtained an employment card and remained in Warsaw. But during the roundup on Mila Street, when his wife and year-old daughter were threatened with eviction, he had abandoned his job—the only secure place then—and had gone into hiding with his family. Together with a group of other Jews, they had hidden in a loft. The atmosphere in the attic was stifling and the baby whined. The others in the group, fearing that the baby's cries would give them away, forced Abramek and his family to leave the hideout. Meanwhile, out in the street, the Germans continued to "select" the inhabitants of the ghetto: idle Jews to the left, employed to the right. Abramek did not present his employment card, but silently followed his family to the left, rather than forsake them even in the face of death.

Yurek Blones, a classmate of mine, who was to be a participant in the ultimate uprising, was also taken to the *Umschlagplatz* along with his younger brother Lusiek. While some were being loaded into the railroad cars, other young men were singled out and sent back to work. Twenty-two years old and an able auto mechanic, Yurek would have been saved. But his little brother would not have been permitted to remain. Just then Yurek was spotted by a German fellow worker, who motioned him to step aside. "Your services could still be utilized in the factory," he said.

"But what about my little brother?" Yurek countered.

"He has to be deported," was the reply.

"In that case, I'm staying with him; he wouldn't be able to take care of himself."

Yurek and his brother were shoved into a freight car destined for

Treblinka. Somehow, Yurek cut a hole in the wall of the car and the two brothers jumped off the speeding train.

Miraculously, they survived and reached Warsaw. I met them shortly after they had smuggled themselves back into the ghetto. Eventually, the two brothers joined the ranks of the resistance organization and distinguished themselves in the Warsaw ghetto uprising.

My sister and I made a similar choice. Learning that the public kitchen on Nowolipki Street, where she was working, was scheduled for a raid, I rushed there to warn her of the imminent danger and pleaded with her to go into hiding with me. We were the only two survivors of our family, I said; we should at least stick together. Either both of us would escape or else we would go down the last road together. She listened attentively, then replied in a trembling voice: "I'm sorry, but I cannot leave my post."

To put my mind at ease, she tried to assure me that the Germans were not likely to bother a working crew. No amount of pleading on my part could dissuade her. That very day, the entire staff of the kitchen was loaded into one of the wagons for deportation. My sister went with them.

The Ghetto wall

One of the entrances to the Ghetto

Germans photograph one of the Ghetto workshops

Selection before deportation

8. IN THE WORKSHOP

I was alone now—my mother, brother and sister had gone to some dreadful unknown. My heart no longer jumped as much during a roundup as it had before. There was very little left to fear now.

A few people fortunate enough to escape from Treblinka had returned to the ghetto with their stories of their gruesome experiences. I refused to believe that my loved ones could be dead. Better not think about it, I told myself; they must be alive somewhere. I often felt sorry that I had not gone with them. Why should I be subjected to the constant anguish, the constant fear of deportation, when there was no way out anyway? I was depressed and apathetic, going mechanically through the days.

It was as if my heart had turned to stone, as if my will to live had dissolved. Had it not been for my friends, I would have been trapped more than once. They did not desert me in my time of need.

A few days after my family had been taken to the *Umschlagplatz*, Kuba Zilberberg came to see me. He arranged for me to get a job at his father's workshop at Muranowska 38. Riding with me in a *ricksha*, Kuba said that this workshop would be a branch of the Toebbens' factory and that he had already helped place several other friends there. But this unexpected promise of security had little effect on me; I was indifferent to everything. Kuba seemed to sense my thoughts and tried to comfort me, "All is not yet lost. We'll weather the storm." Three days later, while transporting another such friend to the workshop, he was himself taken away to the deportation trains.

The shop to which I had been assigned was still in the process of being

47

organized. Jews were bustling about in three huge rooms, furnished with sewing machines, tables, long benches and other paraphernalia. Employees talked at the top of their voices, pacing from one room to another. "When will we start to sew?" they kept asking the officials. Now and then the overworked owners, Zilberberg, Helfgot and Friedman—all former textile merchants—hurried by to plead with the supervisor:

"Either we get started, or there'll be a disaster."

While many applied for the jobs available at the shop, few were skilled tailors. During the first few days, many of the hired workers had to be shown what to do with a needle. Gray heads nodded attentively at the instructions of the young. Women lined up daily along the tables, waiting for a vacancy. No sooner did an operator leave his seat, than an eager claimant occupied it, demanding, "I want to sew, too!"

There was bickering and crying; some women had brought stools with them from home, but to no avail; those women still waiting for places had to be dismissed. The elderly were the most desperate of all; they were well aware that the Germans needed them least of all.

Eventually, the shop began operations, with most of the applicants placed in jobs. But shortly thereafter new clouds gathered: relations with Toebbens became strained, and the delivery of fresh cloth for uniforms was halted. The threat of a shutdown hovered over us; our very security was at stake. Seated grim-faced about the silent sewing machines, the idle workers repeated for the hundredth time rumors overheard from the office clerks: Toebbens was going back on his contract, demanding exorbitant sums of money, insisting on reducing the number of employees. Days passed without any work, yet everybody reported regularly at the shop. It was safer to be there than at home.

During one such idle period in the shop, the Germans held a roundup. We were alerted by a Jewish policeman whose wife was one of our co-workers at the shop. Each of us hurriedly seized some cut cloth and started to sew furiously. Elderly women applied makeup; younger ones brushed their hair. Mothers searched frantically for a hiding place for their children. Two young mothers in our room concealed their two children in a coat closet. Even the office clerks picked up cut cloth and pretended to be busy sewing.

We heard voices from the street. We were terror-stricken, but no one dared look up. "They're already in the .courtyard!" the Jewish policeman, our lookout, announced breathlessly. An eerie stillness settled over the room. We could hear doors opening, then heavy footsteps on the stairs. Moments later, the supervisor called out, "They're here! Don't look at the door! Keep busy!"

The sewing machines set up a clatter; my heart was pounding. Looking up furtively, I caught sight of several Germans and Ukrainians at the entrance to the room.

"Are all the workers here?" a gruff German voice demanded.

"Is no one hiding?" the officer followed.

"No, *Herr Offizier*," came the reply.

The Germans rummaged through the closets and the cut cloth. We dared not lift our heads; we dared not stop working. Finally, the door was closed. The Germans and their escorts had moved on to the next room. From there we could hear a child's cry, then a woman's scream. The hidden child had been discovered. "Keep working! Keep working!" hissed the supervisor.

But our hands were no longer sewing. We strained to hear the slighest sound from the next room. More footsteps. Our door flew open and two Ukrainians rushed back in, wildly searching under tables and machines, overturning the pile of cloth. Then they rushed back out again. We breathed more easily. Thank God they had not searched the closet. For several minutes we could hear a harsh German voice from the next room, but the words were indistinct. At last there was silence.

Patience! Don't move just yet! The Germans might return! At last, we heard the voice of the Jewish policeman: "They're gone!"

Bedlam broke loose in the shop. We wanted to know who had been taken, how many, and how. Several old people had been seized, and so had the mother and child. The shop officials were upset that the Germans had found a child on their premises. No good would come of it. Everyone was worried. "If workers can be taken from shops, then no place is safe," someone said apprehensively.

Before we could recover from this incident, our shop was besieged again. This time the Germans carried off one-third of the workers, mostly old men and women and children. I narrowly escaped. During the preceding few days, my feet had become so swollen from hunger that I had not been able to put on my shoes. I had found refuge for a few days in the home of Manya Wasser, wife of an eminent Bund leader, who urged me to stay in her house for a day.

It seemed that nothing could save us from our fate any longer, not even the German workshops, though they were the only places authorized to allow Jews on their premises. Yet one clung to the least shred of hope. "Perhaps a certain number of workshops will be spared, and I will be among them," each one hoped. It was the same in other workshops. But there was no time to brood; one had to be vigilant.

I spent an extraordinary night at Manya Wasser's. There had been rumors that the Germans would carry out a nocturnal roundup. Dragnets and deportations usually took place during the day, but this raid was scheduled for the night. Our group, which included Roma Brandes—Manya's sister, who had formerly taught in a Jewish school—did not go to sleep, but sat around a small lamp behind curtained windows so that the light should not betray us, waiting with bated breath. Would there be a raid, or was it only a rumor? Tensely, we listened for the slightest sound. A car passed by. The tramp of boots. Fortunately they did not stop at our house. Our hearts were pounding. The night magnified our fears. We sat transfixed in our chairs; the slightest noise of movement was likely to attract unwelcome attention, and so we just sat, staring at each other . . .

"I would like to tell you about a trip I once took to Vienna," Roma suddenly broke the silence.

"Tell us about what?" another voice asked, astonished.

"About Vienna," she repeated. She seemed lost in thought, her eyes somewhere else, glittering strangely in the gloom. She seemed completely calm, and even managed a faint smile. There was something definitely odd about her. How could she think of Vienna now, of all times?

"Never mind," someone snapped. "We must be completely silent, to listen for suspicious noises."

"And if the Germans do come, nothing will save us anyhow," Roma pointed out and, without waiting for anyone's approval, she launched into her account. No one interrupted her. At first we exchanged meaningful glances. The tension had affected her, we thought. We might as well let her unburden herself.

Gradually, her words took on meaning. She gave a graphic description of Vienna, where the Olympic games had been held, and described the festive appearance of the metropolis and of the jubilant young athletes. She told us about the parades, and about the hospitality of the Austrians. Little by little we became fascinated by her story. Her account, delivered with a strange fervor, was flowing and colorful. "That's enough!" someone broke in. "I can't take any more of this. How can you go on praising Vienna at a time like this? Where are they now, your noble-hearted Austrians?

These remarks had a sobering effect on us. Stark reality abruptly reasserted itself. Indeed, where were the Austrians—or anyone else? There had been no time or peace of mind in the ghetto to ponder the matter.

Roma would not be deterred. "Do you think that the whole world knows what is going on in the ghetto and is so cruel and bloodthirsty?" she asked.

"I don't know what to think nowadays. I only know the fix we're in," someone retorted bitterly.

A heated discussion followed. The group forgot about the lurking dangers. Our festering wounds opened up; we vented our disappointment in and resentments against our neighbors, against the world.

The wrangling grated on my nerves, and I took little part in the discussion. Vienna with its Olympic games seemed unreal and remote. But I felt that Roma's account reflected her faith in mankind.

She argued that our plight was entirely due to the fact that the whole world was now involved in a bloody war.

"Does such a war justify our total annihilation?" someone asked. "If the German people had been held to blame, perhaps they would have halted the carnage."

The discussion continued until dawn filtered through the curtained windows.

Shortly afterwards, during one of the sweeping roundups on Mila Street, Roma was deported to Treblinka. But her words—and perhaps even more, her faith in mankind—were to linger in my mind and heart for a long time to come.

At Gesia 13, from the window in the hiding place, I saw the march of the orphanage of Janusz Korczak. The children went silently, carrying blankets, walking hand-in-hand, surrounded by German soldiers and led by Dr. Korczak, a stooped, aging man. The noted educator, who had maintained his home and school for orphans of the ghetto against the greatest odds, was now accompanying his wards to their deaths. That day, the Germans "liquidated" the ghetto's remaining children's institutions. New ordinances were being issued by our tormentors. The "Little Ghetto" was to be "liquidated"; all Jewish inhabitants of the southern section, beginning with Chlodna Street, were ordered to vacate their homes within the 24-hour period between August 9 and 10, 1942. Only those employed by the Toebbens and Roerich firms were exempt. All those without employment, including relatives of those working for the German firms, were ordered to report to the *Umschlagplatz* on Stawki Street. Anyone without a job found in the Little Ghetto after the deadline would be shot on sight.

On the heels of this followed a decree   ordering everyone to vacate certain streets by August 20. German workshops were to be concentrated in certain sectors, where the workers would be provided with living quarters. Employees of German enterprises were not permitted to leave the areas assigned to them. If they were found elsewhere, they would be "resettled." That applied also to our shop. It was to merge with the other Toebbens units and move to the former Jewish hospital building at Nowolipie 69.

Confusion and turmoil ensued; families employed in different localities were broken up, while those without jobs were completely at a loss. Fights flared up over housing allotments. People occupied whatever quarters they could find, only to be ordered out by the Jewish police. The people of the Little Ghetto moved into the main ghetto; people hurried along pushing handcarts or carrying sacks and bundles. Small children were transported secretly; since they could not work, they had no right to be in the ghetto at all.

Every now and then some bewildered Jew stopped to ask, "Is it safe to go on?" Everyone was haunted by the fear of being trapped in a raid and deported. There was constant turmoil in the streets; wagons carrying shop equipment and machinery rolled by in a constant stream. During the morning and evening hours, when the roundups were temporarily halted, the streets were filled with Jews running with their most essential belongings. People had quickly become reconciled to the idea that they would have to abandon almost everything they possessed. All that mattered was to find a new place to live.

On the street, one stumbled over the bodies of Jews who most likely had been shot while trying to escape from a "blockade." The streets were strewn with broken furniture, torn bedding, old kitchen utensils—things to which no one paid any attention. There was no time to be lost now; one had to make haste, to meet the deadline for finding new quarters. At our destination there was much jostling and angry words over suitable quarters; latecomers had to move into rooms without windows or doors.

The transfer extended over two weeks, during which time the Germans ceaselessly continued their gruesome work, encircling whole blocks, trapping and deporting Jews by the thousands.

Our new quarters were in a ramshackle four-story building from which the Germans had evacuated nearly all the former residents. They had left behind reminders of their lives in these premises; tattered garments and bed linen, old shoes and glassware lay strewn about the floor and in open closets.

Our new workshop in the former Jewish hospital was set in surroundings totally different from our old place of work. It was a modern white structure with a small garden, long corridors and many doors and staircases leading to spacious rooms. Daylight streamed through the wide, high windows, dazzling our red, swollen eyes.

We felt lost and dwarfed in the large chambers. There was something incongruous about these glass doors and white interiors, out of character with our gloomy state of mind. We had felt much more at home in the grimy, cramped workshop on Muranowska Street, where we were already familiar with every nook and cranny, with the out-of-the-way passages, with the loft. There, in an emergency, one could run for cover to an adjacent house or disappear among other Jews. But the new workshop had been set apart by a barbed wire fence, restricting our freedom of movement to our assigned quarters.

In time, we became accustomed to our new environment. Like automatons, yet always filled with gnawing fear, we rose at dawn to march in a body to our places in the shop. The workshop would already be alive as workers were busy bartering the bread and sausage they had obtained from the Gentile smugglers or bargained over household belongings which they had brought along, or exchanged the latest war news and rumors.

"Salvation could come at any time—one can never tell," someone said hopefully. Others, however, spoke of the Jews who had been shot the previous day, of well-known individuals recently deported, or of the harassment to which the Nazis had been subjecting the Judenrat.

Fear of what the day might bring was our companion from the moment of awakening from troubled sleep. Each morning's nervous exchange of terse questions and tremulous replies, the bustling about to keep busy—these were only devices to contain our apprehensiveness.

A bell sounded. The bartering and trading ceased abruptly. In silence, we hastened to our work stations. The production quota for the day had to be met. Woe to the worker who fell behind and incurred the wrath of Herr Murmann, the tall, elegant, gray-headed German supervisor who, like his gleaming white starched collar, looked stiff and rigid. Nothing escaped his piercing eye. If a worker fell ill, he could only pray that Murmann would not notice his vacant seat and have a *Werkschutz* man visit the worker's home. A worker with a high fever, making him unfit for labor, was a likely candidate for immediate deportation.

Weakened by malnutrition, beset by aches and pains, and in constant dread, many collapsed at their machines, unable to meet their quotas. There were several such casualties.

Time dragged. The sewing machines clattered unceasingly. Heads heavy, tongues parched, eyes burning, we saw nothing but green cloth, guided under the needle, ten centimeters for the width, ten centimeters for the length. Squares upon squares, and these into larger squares—a universe of squares—squares, our only horizon.

We yearned for the end of the day, for our ration of a bowl of thin soup and escape from the day's toil and fear into exhausted sleep. If only we would not have to wake the next morning to the same chaos!

Even the night's short respite was sometimes denied us; the Germans' insatiable demand for production often forced us to toil for thirty hours at a stretch. On such days, Herr Murmann appeared just as we were about to line up for our soup ration, and harshly ordered us back to work—as punishment, we were told, for lagging behind our quotas.

By midnight, most of us were sick from sheer exhaustion. Yet no one dared to rest his head on his machine. Murmann was wide awake—and watching. He moved with almost feline quiet, riding-crop in hand, to stand unseen behind his chosen prey.

In our department, we had found a hiding place in the closet with the finished garments, where one might rest undetected. We took turns there every half-hour. Murmann had made the rounds of our section several times and failed to notice anything amiss, until one day, inspecting the finished stack of uniforms, he found a culprit in hiding. It was Raisel, a girl of 16, our youngest operator. With a fiendish "Aha!" he set upon her, beating her mercilessly, the crack of his whip drowning out her moans. Murmann's face was crimson with wrath; he literally foamed at the mouth.

None of us dared move; every blow of the whip whistled through the air like a shrill curse. Wearying, finally, he slapped the foreman across the face and strutted out.

As soon as he was gone, we rushed to the closet to revive Raisel, who was bruised and bleeding. Groans and cries from other departments told us that other unfortunates, too, had been discovered in hiding places like our own or had been guilty of other acts that provoked Murmann's ire.

Such was our life during the "tranquil" periods between one "selection" and the next.

9. IN THE CLUTCHES OF DEATH

During the most harrowing period in the ghetto, I shared an apartment with four others, among them my dear friend Yankel Gruszka. We had been together in the underground *Zukunft* Committee in Warsaw, had belonged to the same secret cells and had helped organize illegal children's groups.

Yankel had hardly any personal life. A zealous and ardent Socialist, he devoted himself completely, in the minutest detail, to whatever task was assigned him. His belief in justice and humanity was genuine and steadfast. He was a true idealist, whose view of reality was sometimes distorted by his vision of what it should be.

"He should have been born in another world, another era," a friend once said about him. But his friends all loved him for his kindness and devotion.

During the agonizing days of the *Aussiedlung* (the German euphemism for deportation), Yankel became extremely depressed, though it was not in his nature to be concerned about his own future. Haggard, emaciated, despondent, he spent whole days in isolation. He became indifferent to everything; a strange death-like apathy replaced his once sprightly animation. He even lost interest in the brush factory where he was employed.

"Of what use is all this struggle?" he often asked. He anticipated death and resigned himself to his fate.

Edzia Russ was entirely different from Yankel. I had been a schoolmate of this good-natured girl with auburn hair and brown eyes. She had yearned for life with all her being and could not be reconciled to

56

the idea of death. She braved the ever-present dangers and pitfalls, moving heaven and earth to stay alive. Her husband, Henach Russ, one of the outstanding leaders of the youth organizations, was master in the house. A lanky, vivacious man, with blazing eyes, a ready wit and a tone of authority, he held us all under his spell.

Schloima Pav, the fourth in our group, was an energetic Socialist, active first in Lodz and later in the ghetto. He was both intelligent and proud, But since the deportation of his wife, he had become a mourning recluse—the soul of resignation.

We helped one another to stay alive, to carry on, to endure hunger, to cope with the threat of deportation that hung over our heads.

Our collective dwelling space consisted of two dark rooms. The door between them was blocked by a huge closet in which we had made an opening through which we could crawl in case of emergency. At dusk, returning from a day's work, friends from nearby shops would gather there to await our arrival. Their number had dwindled. Some of them were employed in the brush factory on Swientojerska, others were in the Roerich shop on Nowolipki, or at Schultz's, while still others worked at Toebbens' shop on Leszno Street. It was strictly forbidden to go from one shop to another, but people were willing to take risks for the sake of learning the latest developments.

One day, several friends had appeared. All of us were delighted; seven had escaped death.

Little Moishe Kaufman, whom the Central Committee of the Bund in Wilno had assigned to work in Warsaw, reported a miracle. A roundup had taken place at Roerich's shop, where Moishe was employed. The Germans had come and taken several hundred men into custody. Together with six others Moishe had managed to go into hiding. But they, too, had been apprehended and along with thousands of others loaded into railroad cars. Moishe happened to be in the same car as Haika Belchatowska and Guta Blones.

It was twilight. The car was crowded to suffocation. The seven clung together, hoping somehow to escape the jaws of death. They succeeded in prying a slat from the boarded window of the car, squeezed their way through the opening and jumped out, defying danger. Moishe went first, followed by the girls. Velvel Rozowski helped them through the opening. He was the last to jump. The guards fired a volley, but the train sped on.

Those who had escaped, all of them unharmed, found one another on the railroad tracks.

Afraid to venture into the Polish neighborhood, they made their way under cover of darkness back to the ghetto, and to the shop where they were employed. Little Moishe got a hero's welcome. What luck! Seven people snatched from the jaws of death!

But our rejoicing was cut short by news of a fresh catastrophe. That day, Schultz's shop had been raided. Hundreds of workers had been arrested; hiding places had been revealed and many refugees ferreted out. Toebbens' workshop was marked for the same fate. The Germans had now turned their attention to the factories; the number of workers in the ghetto was to be restricted.

Once again, we were plunged into anxiety. Who knew what was in store for us? Would we, like little Moishe, be able to jump from a speeding train bound for the death camps?

One day we received a visit from Elie Linder, who had miraculously escaped from Treblinka. Though we were all consumed with curiosity about conditions in the camp and how he had managed to escape, we hesitated to question him.

"Well, tell us something! At least say something!" someone blurted out, breaking the oppressive silence.

Elie's narrow, normally sharp-featured face was haggard. He told us how, together with his wife Liebe and their year-old child, he had been removed from his job at the Jewish hospital. After arriving at Treblinka, they had been driven along with thousands of other Jews under a hail of blows to the so-called "showerhouse." They had been stopped at the entrance, where the women and children were ordered to one side and told to undress. The men were to wait their turn. More blows rained upon them as they begged to be allowed to stay with their loved ones. After taking off her own clothes and undressing the infant, Liebe had grasped her husband's hand and said tearfully, "Elie, we'll never see each other again!"

Elie paused, momentarily overcome by emotion. We hung in agonized concentration on his words. "Yes," he finally resumed, "those were her last words . . ." A German had separated them, and then pushed and prodded Liebe into one of the "showers" together with many other women.

Elie had known that the men's turn would come within minutes. His head in a whirl, he looked about in frenzy for any possible avenue of escape. He caught sight of a pile of discarded clothing. Perhaps he would be able to hide under it. But how? The place was teeming with Germans and Ukrainians.

"Strip—and be quick about it!" The German command was accompanied by truncheon blows and pistol shots. While he stripped, Elie edged his way toward the heap of crumpled clothes. Seizing a moment when all the Germans seemed busy with other victims, he leaped into the pile and burrowed into it. Trembling with fear, scarcely daring to breathe the fetid air that penetrated to the pile of tumbled clothing, he waited until the sounds of shuffling feet and shouted commands had died away. Emerging cautiously, he saw a group of Jewish prisoners nearby burying corpses. He joined them.

Later, while working with a crew sorting the clothing of victims, Elie again attempted to escape. Hiding in another mound of tattered clothing, he waited until nightfall. In the dark, he discerned the silhouette of a train against the night sky and wormed himself into one of its freight cars, hiding in the rags with which the car was loaded. Here he hid that night and the next day in mortal fear until the train at last pulled out of the depot.

Shortly afterward, some cars (including his) were detached from the train and switched to another track. Through crevices in the wooden car walls he saw fields, peasant huts and trees passing by the speeding train. By then the train was already far from the death camp. He was free from immediate danger.

Finally Elie Linder jumped out of the freight car. By stages he reached Praga, where he made the rounds of his Gentile friends in the hope of finding shelter, but all of them were afraid to accommodate him and he had to return to the ghetto.

Having told his grim story, Elie left us. No one tried to detain him. We were stunned. Though we had long suspected the fate that awaited the Jewish deportees, we had now heard our first eyewitness account. None of us uttered a word or slept that night. We tossed in our beds, thinking of Elie Linder and his miraculous escape.

"We must get identity cards." Henach was the first to voice a reaction. He was right; the usual employment card, which had been accepted before, was no longer considered valid. According to rumors current in the factory, those holding identity cards bearing the seal of the S.S. (*Schutzstaffel*—the Nazi Elite Guard) would not be deported; these cards were recognized by the Nazi authorities. Time and again we had applied to the shop management for such cards, but to no avail.

"The best thing is to apply directly to the *Arbeitsamt*," I ventured. Henach urged me to attend to the matter the following day.

For a while things at the factory followed the customary routine. Nothing unusual was anticipated. Nevertheless, one day I decided to make inquiries at the employment office across the street from our shop. I hurried through the factory corridor without being noticed by anyone, nor did I encounter any difficulty with the gateman.

Although this was during working hours, there was considerable activity at the *Collegium*. Hundreds of petitioners, mostly unemployed young men, were anxious to register for *placowkes*. Still others, like myself, had come for identity cards. Among them were *machers*, the wheeler-dealers who bribed and elbowed others out of the way. Everybody was pressed for time, anxious, desperate. Suddenly there was a panicked run for the stairs. "The place is surrounded!" someone near the door shouted. "The Germans are here!"

I felt dogged by bad luck. I had left the workshop for a few minutes only to fall into a trap. What could I do? There was no way of running back to the shop; the Germans were already at the entrance to the *Collegium*. But to remain where I was meant certain arrest. And there were hardly any places in which to hide.

The officials stopped working; all was turmoil and panic. I raced up the stairs to the sixth floor—the living quarters of the officials—where, breathlessly, I pleaded with one of the occupants to let me in. But the officials were frightened; this was their first German raid. Someone seized me by the arm and tried to drag me down the stairs. "Outsiders are not permitted here!" I pleaded with him, "I don't want to die in the gas chambers!" I struggled to break his grip. Where did I muster the strength to fight? Perhaps it was from Elie Linder's story.

Meanwhile, I could hear the voices of Jewish policemen ordering all the officials to hurry downstairs. I was left alone in a long narrow corridor with many doors. Below, I could hear sounds of a scuffle between some Jews and a Jewish policeman who was trying to prevent them from mounting a staircase. My head was spinning. I tried the doors and finally found one unlocked.

I found myself in a huge, deserted room, its furnishings consisting of two long benches, a desk, a chair, and two unlocked closets for storing medical supplies. I crawled into the closets. I could hear voices muffled by distance, whistling, intermittent gunfire. Then came a sudden, strange silence. My feet were numb; I was afraid to move lest I betray my hiding place. Time dragged on; there was no one in sight. Unable to think, I strained to catch any suspicious sounds.

Footsteps! Was it Germans, or was it people from the employment office? The steps were light and slow, so it was definitely not the Germans. Then the door opened and I heard a woman's voice, "We have never seen such hell before!" I emerged cautiously from the closets.

The Germans had been very thorough. They had arrested all the applicants as well as many of the officials.

Despondently I returned to the workshop. The employees had watched the scene at the *Collegium* through the windows on the street. For a while, they had been afraid that the Germans would raid the shop itself, but we were spared.

"How did you manage to escape?" my friends asked. But before I had a chance to answer someone whispered, "They're deporting a new group—this time from the Little Ghetto." We all left our machines, dropped our tools, and stared out the window in silence.

A tremendous churning black tide . . . There were *rickshas* carrying invalids; men, women and children, the young and the old, trudging along. Face after face passed below us, faces apathetic, agitated, terrified, some tense, others bereft of hope. We watched intently, searching for a familiar face among the thousands shuffling past. The sight made my head reel. All the faces blended in confusion; only bowed heads and bundles and bent backs, a single wave of humanity. The marchers were silent, the atmosphere stifling, only the sound of footsteps, all sorts of footsteps—the slow and nimble, adults and children . . . Its cadence pounding a final warning: "Remember!"

"You are fortunate," Edzia whispered, her voice strained and hoarse. Yes, I thought, I am indeed fortunate. I might have been among them.

10. THE GLOOMIEST DAYS IN THE WARSAW GHETTO

One September night in 1942, I was awakened by noises in the house. Could it be a night raid? Thus far the Germans had carried on their labors only during the daytime, but anything was possible. Cautiously I woke my friends. We crawled to our hiding place in the adjacent room. Then I slipped into the corridor. There were no Germans in sight. Why the uproar? What had happened?

A new edict had been issued. The announcements would be posted at seven in the morning. Throughout the six weeks since the deportations had begun there had been no end to the new decrees. Each new one made hearts sink again and awakened in each of us the obsessive search for means of escaping the dragnet, of avoiding capture and being taken to the *Umschlagplatz*.

The announcements posted the next morning ordered all Jews still in the ghetto—in the factories and workshops—to assemble in Mila, Wolynska, and Lubecki Streets, where those still eligible to remain in the ghetto would be designated. Any Jew failing to report at the specific place before ten o'clock would be shot. Everyone was to bring enough bread to last three days.

The prospect of a new "selection" of such magnitude utterly devastated our spirits. Elderly people hid in their cellars. Women put on make-up, girls their best clothes, hoping to make a good impression on the Germans and thus be spared.

I hastened to see my friends in another factory and find out how they were faring. They, too, were at a loss. Some of them were thinking of going into hiding, a choice appealing in its simplicity. More than once, we had hidden in attics and concealed rooms, holding our breath to avoid detection. Why, it was a daily occurrence, a commonplace! But the present situation was different. We might have to hide for days, and we might not be able to get out in the end! Some of us, therefore, decided to report in accordance with the German orders. After all, we were young; fortune might favor us.

By half past nine that morning, frightened Jews were scurrying about, lugging bundles and parcels and hunting for bread. No one seemed to have any reserves of food. I had a hundred zlotys and looked for one of the vendors—usually they were Jewish workers employed outside the ghetto—who occasionally smuggled in some bread.

I found one, surrounded by a quarreling, bickering group, like myself seeking bread. The vendor protested that he had none. On impulse I slipped him all my money and waited for the crowd to disperse. The fellow asked me whether the money was mine, then pulled out a loaf from under his overcoat. "As a matter of fact," he told me, "I was keeping this loaf for myself, but you can have it. I'll find another."

I hurried home to show my booty to my friends, after which we divided the bread and made our final preparations. Meanwhile, friends from other factories had arrived to bid us farewell. Silently, tearfully, we took leave of one another. Yankel Gruszka headed for his brush factory; Velvel Rozowski and Moishe Kaufman went to Roerich's; Henach, Edzia and I returned to our tailor shop. Pav decided to go into hiding. Who knew if we would ever meet again?

Henach, Edzia and I were probably the last to leave the house. The courtyard and streets were deserted. Doors and windows had been left wide open. Furniture, torn bedding, broken crockery and utensils littered the streets—the whole scene was reminiscent of a pogrom. An ominous silence hovered over the place which only a short time ago had seethed with life. Then the Germans appeared, smashing doors and shattering windows, prying into every nook and corner in search of hiding Jews . . .

We hurried to the factory which we found swarming with people, on the stairs, in the hallways, even at their sewing machines. All the workers were present. S.S. troops and Ukrainians were lined up at the entrance under the command of an officer and Herr Murmann, who held a whip in one hand and a packet of cards in the other—our passports to life or death.

We were lined up four abreast, ordered to turn about-face, sit down, then stand facing the gate. After their drill, we were lined up again and the selection was under way. There was considerable pushing and shoving; everyone tried to get out in front, fearing that there might not be enough cards to go around. There was shouting and weeping as workers took leave of one another. Women made their final preparations, combing their hair, wiping away tears, putting on smiles, and fawning on the German officer.

Not everyone managed to conceal his age, or to ingratiate himself with the officer. The air was rent with cries of despair from those who had failed to obtain one of the life-giving cards. I was borne along by the human wave, barely able to catch my breath. Everyone around me was pressing in the same direction . . .

Shots rang out. The mass of humanity halted. "It's nothing," a German voice said. "You Jews were in a little too much of a hurry. You have to be patient; everything will be taken care of. Take it easy!"

As my turn to confront the German officer approached, my terror grew. Would he give me a card that would mean continued survival, or would he refuse, dooming me to deportation and death? Trembling, I held out my hand. I turned my head away. My hand remained empty. I felt cold, my facial muscles congealed. Shoulders sagging, I lowered my outstretched hand and, as I did so, felt something pressed into it. A card! I was saved.

Henach and Edzia were still waiting their turn. I felt guilty—almost as if I had betrayed them. The thought of the still uncertain fate of my few dear friends brought on dejection. Did this coveted card mean only that I would be among the last to perish? Unable to control myself any longer, I wept.

But in the end my two friends shared my good fortune. Armed with the precious cards, we slowly walked together through the deserted streets. The glaring sun burned our faces; we were wet with perspiration and filled with misery. At the corner of Smocza and Gesia Streets, the site of the main "selection," squads of Germans, Ukrainians, and Jewish Police were watching as thousands of Jews surged through the streets, filling sidewalks and courtyards. We halted on Mila Street, where we had been instructed to stay for a second inspection.

Families and friends clung fiercely together. Once separated, they might never see each other again. Employees of each factory sought one another for companionship and mutual support, but not all Jews were registered in factories. I encountered several friends; we exchanged few words; greetings were exchanged and, in utter dejection, we parted without further speech.

Pav appeared. He wanted to go along with us, but since he had been absent from the factory, he had no identity card. We did not know how to help him. We ourselves were helpless, lost in a sea of helpless humanity. Pav moved away from us. Whether the coveted card could save us was still a matter of conjecture. At any rate, we were to be put through another selection.

Children and elderly people were sprawled out on the house steps or on the pavement, among the bundles and parcels. The old dozed fitfully. The heat and thirst were unbearable. Hardly anyone bothered about the children, who wandered about, neglected among the masses of humanity. Many of them had strayed from their parents, perhaps to give their elders a chance to escape. Anyone accompanied by children was doomed. Those small enough were hidden in knapsacks or concealed in bundles of warm clothing—but what of the eight- and ten-year-olds? They understood; they asked no questions. How wise and understanding they were, those little ones, trying to persuade their mothers to go on without them, insisting that they, the children, would somehow manage to escape on their own.

The wooden fence with the narrow passage on Zamenhof Street was lined with hundreds of S.S. guards, Gestapo officers, Ukrainians and Polish police. The officers were shouting, "To the left! To the right! To the right!" Families were separated, parents torn from their children. One had to hurry. The route to the left was familiar—it led to Treblinka. Hundreds of railroad cars stood waiting at the *Umschlagplatz*.

Behind me I heard a ten-year-old boy say calmly, "Father, I'm afraid we're going to be separated." The bewildered parent watched the gate. Children were being directed to the left. Clutching the youngster's hand, the father tried to allay his fears. After a whispered exchange, the lad disappeared but returned shortly. "Father," he reported, "they are no longer there." It seemed that the father had urged him to hide with some other group.

We lined up. All talk ceased. There was a burst of gunfire. The sea of compressed humanity heaved and undulated. Those of us standing in line fell to our knees. As the commotion subsided, we could hear the groaning of the wounded. Within half an hour, we got to our feet. The father and his son were still nearby.

"Father, I'll go. You try," the child said.

"Where will you go?" the man asked, in tears, holding the boy by the shoulder.

Unable to restrain myself, I whispered to the parent, "Why not put on your topcoat and let your son slip underneath? We'll cover you, back and front."

The next moment I regretted that I had interfered. The man only stared at us, dumbfounded. Our march resumed. The boy kept repeating, "Father, what are we going to do?"

"Quit stalling, friend," Henach became impatient. "Enough of this hesitation. You were advised what to do—now do it!" Swiftly, he helped the bewildered father tie the youngster to his waist with a rope, and we all helped him pull on his overcoat. Henach and his wife stood on one side of him and I was on the other. We anxiously approached the exit. If the ruse were detected, we would all be ordered to the left. We trudged along in silence.

At last we were at the gate. The employees of another workshop were still ahead of us; we were pushed back again. Crowded to suffocation, we waited for the command to advance. Here and there frightened individuals had withdrawn from the column after seeing that cards had been taken away from elderly marchers and turned over to younger people. The progress of the selection was watched from windows and balconies. It was best to avoid the head of the line. We lined up, exhausted and terrified, while life and death were decided.

Finally, it was our turn. In front of us, and on both sides of Zamenhof Street, stood rows of high-ranking Gestapo and S.S. officers. They examined the marchers cursorily, yanking some out of line. We went past them, our cards aloft in our hands, our eyes fixed on the swagger stick of the German commandant. Toebbens himself, the owner of the factory, was standing next to the German officer.

We watched the commandant's stick. It was pointing to the right! We managed to shove our bewildered friend into a narrow part of Mila Street. There we were safe. Pav was also there. Somehow he had managed to obtain a card at the last moment. The Ukrainians watched our every move as we marched along Mila Street (we were not allowed to halt). Our friend looked about him furtively, then loosened his overcoat and wept as he kissed the head of his son.

"Be careful. The Ukrainian is close by," someone cautioned him. "We'll try to keep the boy out of sight."

On the corner of Gesia and Zamenhof I caught sight of an old woman walking all alone. How had she gotten there? Probably she had been left alone in the house, and was now seeking a hiding place. I anxiously watched her halting steps. She was conspicuous in the deserted street. A young German in an automobile called to her to halt but she went on, unheeding; perhaps she was deaf. The automobile came to a stop. The young German, pistol in hand, got out, walked up to the old woman and almost casually fired two bullets into her. She collapsed, bleeding profusely. The German calmly returned to his car and drove away.

The incident had passed like a flash. The Ukrainians did not permit us to go near the dead woman. We passed by the corpse in silence.

The selection continued from September 6 to September 12. Special squads of S.S. and Ukrainian guards ransacked houses. Anyone ferreted out was shot at once. Jews died in their hiding places from starvation and thirst. An endless train of black wagons collected the corpses from the streets.

The inferno lasted a week. During that time some 60,000 Jews were deported; another 4,000 perished where they were, from starvation or by shooting.

11. "LET US RESIST"

They were gone now, our relatives and friends, co-workers in the shop, so many of them gone in the wake of the "selection" on Mila Street. Only the day before, they had been at work; now their vacant places and idle machines remained as mute testimony to the horror of the last few days. We sat numb and frozen at our places, the oppressive stillness of the room broken only by occasional sobs.

So we had survived. But for what? Why fool ourselves? Sooner or later we would all be deported—the Germans did not need our labor badly enough to want to spare us.

Murmann hurried about the shop, unnerved, slapping anyone in his way and screaming that if the machines stayed idle, he would close the shop and deport everyone. His threats were met by silence and apathy.

That evening I hurried to the area of Schultz's shop. The destruction had been widespread. There, too, the machines were idle, the apartments vacant. Many of my friends had been seized in the mass roundups: Bortenstein, his wife and child, Manya Wasser and her daughter, Anka Wolkowicz, Michelson, and Yankel Gruszka. They all had been ordered to the left.

I returned home. Another tortured night and another tedious day in the shop. Despite persecutions and despair, life seemed to go on, one foot dragging in front of the other, trudging onward, aware of the German deception, being driven to the same brink, the same abyss: Treblinka. All roads in the ghetto seemed to lead to Treblinka; there was no escape.

A spark had been smoldering even during the "peaceful" days of the ghetto. Now it began to glow, slowly, tentatively at first, then ever more fiercely:

"If it is our fate to die anyway, then let us die with dignity! Let us resist and make the enemy pay dearly for our lives!"

The thought of resistance had emerged in the wake of rumors of the extermination of Jews in the district of Wolyn, Lvov and Wilno late in 1941. The following March, Jewish representatives of various underground political organizations met to discuss the creation of a united military force to train the ghetto community for an active challenge to the German *Wehrmacht*. To some it was already apparent that the Germans' methodical extermination was not likely to be restricted to the Jews of eastern Poland; it was bound to extend to the ghettos of Warsaw and elsewhere.

Some representatives, however, considered such a venture premature. The idea of the total annihilation of Jews wherever they might be could be accepted only by assuming a punitive expedition on the part of the Germans. It was also argued that resistance could succeed only with the cooperation of the Polish underground. Although no definite agreement was reached at that time with the anti-Fascist bloc of Zionists and Communists, the Bund organized combat units of young men and women who were given military training.

A second attempt to reach an accord was made in July, 1942, after the deportation of Jews had begun in Warsaw. Once again the question of armed resistance arose, and again it failed to gain unanimous support. The Jewish leaders did not want to assume the responsibility of risking the lives of those who still hoped to survive. The prevailing opinion still was that no more than, say, 60,000 or 70,000 people would be deported and that the rest would survive. Under the circumstances, how could anyone find it in his heart to jeopardize the lives of the entire Warsaw ghetto for the sake of active resistance?

As the deportations continued, voices within the underground Jewish movement—including the Bund, *Hehalutz, Dror, Hashomer Hatzair*, and the Communist party—urged the Jews not to trust the Germans. They warned that deportation meant death, and counseled resistance. These admonitions went unheeded; the will to live blotted out the appalling reality.

"To fight the Germans is simply courting death," became the conventional wisdom. Having endured so much, were we now to invite immolation? Life had to go on, no matter the cost. The illusion that one was bound to survive drowned out voices of warning.

But on one occasion, we acted on our convictions. Our shop was suddenly surrounded by Germans and Ukrainians. Bedlam broke loose. In mortal fear of the imminent selection, the workers scurried to find hiding places. The few worthwhile hiding places were, naturally, taken by the supervisory personnel. The workers gave up and went back to their machines.

Pav, Henach, Edzia and I decided to stick to our posts and, even if faced with gunfire, resist being dragged out. Henach mounted a chair and addressed the other workers:

"You know where we'll be deported! To our doom! Remain here; when the Germans come, don't anyone move from your place! You hear me? Resist being dragged out!"

An ominous hush followed his words; the workers looked at one another in stunned disbelief. I, too, was astonished by Henach's daring; after all, ours was a mixed group. Some were utter strangers to us. From their silence, it was hard to know whether they agreed with Henach or not. There was some whispering. The four of us kept our places and waited.

The door was flung open and a frightened voice warned us: "The Germans have entered the building. Everyone is to go down to the courtyard!" After a moment's hesitation, the workers headed for the exits. We four hung back for a while before following the others. Fortunately, the German "selection" that day was limited to only one floor. But we had learned that even the faintest glimmer of hope for personal survival was more powerful than any fear of selection.

At the same time, cases of arson in the German warehouses in the ghetto were becoming more frequent. The fires were set by the various resistance groups.

More electrifying was the attempt on the life of Yosef Szerinski, commandant of the Jewish police, a man utterly detested in the ghetto. Israel Kanal, a member of *Akiba*, critically wounded him with two bullets, but failed to kill him. An attempt to kill Schmerling, a German collaborator of the Jewish police, also failed.

But the first signs of active Jewish resistance had emerged. One day in

October, upon returning from work, I found a message from Abrasha Blum. He wished to see me. I had not seen him since the beginning of the deportations, when he had given me an employment card. I had heard that he already had been dragged to the deportation wagons several times, but somehow had always managed to escape. Whatever he wanted to see me about was probably important.

Skipping my supper, I hurried out to join one of the groups returning from work outside the ghetto. It was the only way to be permitted out in the streets at night. Quickly eluding the guards, I slipped into one such column. The workers from each factory walked in a separate group. Workers from other factories were forbidden to join them. There would still be another inspection in the ghetto proper, at the corner of Zamenhof and Gesia Streets.

The former ghetto was now divided into three districts. The workshops and residential blocks of Toebbens, Schultz and Roerich were in one sector. Another was known as the "wild" or Central Ghetto, the home of the *placowkarzes*—those working outside the ghetto on the "Aryan side," as well as the unemployed, who were in hiding. The brush factories were in still another sector.

We marched through deserted streets—Smocza, Nowolipki and Zamenhof—their four-story buildings dark and desolate, their gaping windows staring blindly. A few weeks before, these streets had teemed with Jews, with activity of all sorts. Now they were deserted.

It was already dusk when I arrived at Mila 5, the home of Philosoff, a former Bund activist in Lodz. Several friends—the remnant of a group of young activists of the underground Socialist movement—were already waiting in the small room. I had not seen them for a long time; they were employed in other German factories.

Laibel Szpichler, trying to contain his elation, told Moishe Kaufman and Velvel Rozowski how he had managed to save the life of his four-year-old son. He had become acquainted with a Polish worker whom he had persuaded to conceal his child, for money. However, Laibel went on to say, the chances of finding asylum with the local Poles were rather slim because of their fear of the Gestapo.

Pulling down the window shade, Philosoff told of his own experiences with Gentiles. He, too, had been employed in a German shoe factory outside the ghetto. His Polish fellow workers had been friendly toward the

Jewish employees, shared their food, were helpful in the common tasks, and were of the opinion that not all Jews would be deported.

Pav and Grillak were seated in a corner reading a German newspaper which Philosoff had managed to smuggle into the ghetto. "If the Germans get bogged down in Russia during the winter, they will get what's coming to them," Pav remarked, but Grillak made no comment. Seated next to them was Marek Edelman. While the Nazi roundups went on, he provided friends with forged documents, which might at least occasionally save one from deportation.

Everyone was on edge, hurrying from one friend to another to compare notes. Such meetings of our underground group were rare during the period of the raids and those present were most eager for news and consultations about ways to keep alive. The next day might be too late.

The friendly atmosphere was heartening. I caught snatches of conversation that reminded me of pre-war days. Although they all seemed engrossed in their talk, one could sense their impatience for the arrival of our leader, Abrasha Blum. He appeared at last, his lanky figure taller than ever, his face paler, but calm.

Someone locked the door. Abrasha exchanged greetings with those present, who then found seats, some on the bed, some on the windowsill, others on the floor. After a brief silence, Abrasha began to talk.

His address was like a wave that both uplifted and engulfed me. At first I could not grasp the ideas he was presenting and had to ask those around me several times to explain certain points. Along with the others, I sat quietly as if in a daze, engrossed in what he was saying.

Abrasha reported that a Jewish Coordinating Committee had been formed in the ghetto. The aim of this committee, which included representatives of the various underground political organizations, was to amalgamate all the underground forces and to organize armed resistance.

"We must no longer submit to deportation," Abrasha said. "We must offer armed resistance. By now everyone knows where those freight cars are going.

"But one has to know even how to die," Abrasha told his spellbound audience. "A newly formed combat force of the Coordinating Committee is being organized. This force will lay the groundwork and direct military training for the planned resistance. The only question is: How many survivors do we still have left? Will such a small group of activists be able to accomplish anything?"

Then he answered his own question: "True enough, our number is small; most of our members and leaders have been deported. But we are not alone. Other organizations are also preparing for the fight. We must coordinate our efforts with those who are still left in the workshops. Wherever our people are employed, cells and circles should be formed with a view toward preparing for active resistance. We must obtain arms. Close contact must be established with any Gentile sympathizers. Also, we must remove women and children from the ghetto, as far as this is possible, to keep them out of the fighting."

I listened breathlessly as he spoke. More than once, since the deportation of my mother, my brother and sister, I had had to suppress the impulse to strike out at the Germans; a passion for revenge raged within me.

Now, preparations for direct action were underway. That ungratified desire for revenge which each of us harbored was now to be given outlet. The idea of death had become integrated into our outlook; we knew that all the roads led toward it. Our faces now bore expressions of grim determination. We exchanged glances, not daring to interrupt the speaker. Not one of us doubted the validity of Abrasha's arguments. The silence attested to the impact of his message.

There followed an animated discussion over how to establish the fighting units. Responsibility for the implementation of the various tasks was delegated: Edelman and Grillak were assigned to the brush factory, and Avrom Feiner to Schultz's shop. Moishe Kaufman and Velvel Rozowski would be responsible for Roerich's. Almost everyone present was entrusted with some task.

After the end of the meeting, the group excitedly discussed their impending duties. I had been the only one not given any definite assignment and felt somewhat let down in the midst of the excitement and anticipation. As I was about to leave, Abrasha drew me aside.

"You look like a Gentile," he said. "How would you like to cross over to the 'Aryan side'? You will be able to do something substantial there in connection with the plans you just heard."

"Of course I would," I replied, a bit confused. "But how do I do it?"

"No one must know about it. You'll get your instructions in a few days' time,'' Abrasha concluded. I asked no more questions and took my leave of him.

Was it really possible that I would get out of this ghetto inferno, quit the workshop and have done with the daily roundups? What was my next move to be? Who would be my contact? That night I lay awake mulling over the conference and Abrasha's proposition, as well as the events that were about to take place.

12. LEAVING THE GHETTO

One evening several weeks later, I heard a knock on my door. In the dim light of the corridor, I did not recognize the tall man asking for me, but I invited him in. It was Michal Klepfisz, an engineer active for many years in the Bund and in *Morgenstern*, a Jewish sports organization.

"Michal, what a pleasant surprise!" I exclaimed. "What brings you here? You've been away from the ghetto for quite a while. How are your wife and child?"

"I've come to take you away, Feigel," he answered. "Get ready; you'll be leaving the ghetto within two days. Meanwhile I'll prepare forged documents for you and try to notify some people in the Polish sector."

My heart seemed to leap into my mouth.

"Get ready," he repeated. "I'll wait for you by the ghetto gate at eight in the morning. You'll have to walk out with a labor battalion on the way to an outside work assignment; that's the best way."

"In case we should miss each other, leave me an address where I can find you," I suggested.

He hesitated. "I have no such address yet. I'm still living in someone's cellar. But I'll give you a temporary address, Gornoszlonska 3. Just memorize it; no written notes of any sort."

He could stay no longer, but hurried off to confer with Abrasha. I saw him out into the street, where he joined the last returning labor battalion and disappeared into the night.

I'd be leaving the ghetto in two days! I was aflame with excitement. My co-workers also had an air of secrecy; the first group of resistance fighters

75

had been organized at Toebbens' shop. My head was spinning. Now and then, beyond the ghetto wall running along Zelazna Street, I could make out the movement of adults and children, women carrying baskets, the rushing tempo of life. But here in the ghetto the streets were dead, life was at a standstill. Except for an occasional German patrol, there was seldom a soul in sight.

The thought of escaping from the ghetto kindled new hope among the workers. It seemed the only way to survive. But escape was easier said than done. For one thing, in order to slip across the wall one had to pay an exorbitant sum to the Gentile smugglers. Moreover, while one might bribe the German sentinel, one could never be certain that he might not decide to shoot his victim after all. To walk out with a Jewish labor brigade on the way to an outside work assignment was the only available alternative—but a most dangerous one.

A number of Jews with Aryan features—and well-lined purses—had already attempted to leave the ghetto. Some had been apprehended and either killed on the spot or deported. This did not deter others, and some succeeded in escaping.

Outside the ghetto lay an alien world where one had to seek refuge and contact Gentile friends who might help one obtain forged documents, prepare living quarters, and find a job. Above all, there had to be money—a great deal of money—to pay for every little service. Desperate Jews endeavored to contact Gentile acquaintances on the "other side of the wall," but most of the appeals fell on deaf ears.

Some of those who had succeeded in crossing into the "Aryan sector" returned to the ghetto a few weeks later. They had not been able to cope with the blackmail rampant there.

My way out would be by posing as a member of a labor brigade. No other means of escape was possible. The foremen of the labor gangs employed outside the ghetto were occasionally able to make substitutions for absentees. Such opportunities were rare and expensive. I paid.

I was to take with me the latest issue of the underground bulletin, which carried a detailed description and map of the Treblinka extermination camp. My roommates, aware of my preparations, advised me to hide the bulletin in my shoes. Our leavetaking was tearful. With sad smiles meant to be reassuring, we promised not to forget one another. We parted with handclasps. Would I ever see them again?

December, 5, 1942. At 7:00 a.m. the street was astir with people streaming to work. Brisk bartering went on as Jews traded their last pitiful belongings—a coat, a skirt, an old pair of shoes—to those working on the "Aryan side" for chunks of black bread. Later, the commodities would be smuggled out of the ghetto and sold to Gentile vendors.

After some searching, I found a Jewish leader of a forty-man labor battalion who for 500 zlotys allowed me to join his group. I was the only female in the unit. We marched in column formation to the ghetto gate, where we joined thousands of other laborers, men and women.

The morning guard, heavily reinforced, was busy inspecting the throng. People pushed and jostled wherever they could, hoping to elude the Gestapo scrutiny—to escape to the "Aryan side," to smuggle a few belongings out of the ghetto. The inspection had just started. We waited apprehensively, shivering in the morning frost. One never knew what the Germans might do next.

Some who had just been inspected were retreating, clutching bruised faces. They had been beaten up for carrying items the Germans considered contraband. One was hopping barefoot in the snow; the German had taken a liking to his shoes. Several others, half-undressed, stood trembling in the biting cold, as a warmly-clad German took his time searching them. An old man pleaded with a German trooper that he did not want to be separated from his thirteen-year-old daughter. "She's a regular worker, just like me! Here is her factory card!" he argued heatedly. The soldier rebuffed him brutally. In his despair, the old man looked about with pleading eyes, but no one dared to help him. His daughter was directed aside to a wooden shack from which she gazed forlornly at her father.

My detachment was the next to be inspected. Everything was going smoothly.

"How did you get this woman in here?" the German barked.

"She's employed in the factory kitchen," the group leader explained.

The trooper eyed me with disdain. "I don't like your face," he snapped. "Get in there!" He pointed in the direction of the wooden shack.

"I don't envy her," someone remarked. My blood ran cold at the thought that the underground bulletin might be found on me. In that event the entire labor battalion—not just I—would be detained. Consternation suffused the faces of those around me. A Jewish policeman appeared. The place was swarming with troopers and police; there was no chance of escape.

"Please let me slip out while the German is away," I whispered to the policeman.

"Do you expect me to risk my life for you?" the policeman snapped. "The German will be right back!" At the entrance to the wooden shack lay a man, bruised and bleeding. Off to one side was the young girl. I stood a moment, stunned. The policeman shoved me inside.

I found myself in a dimly lit room, its blood-spattered walls papered with maps, charts, and photographs of half-naked women. Tattered clothing and shoes were strewn about the floor. The only furnishings were a small table and a chair, in the midst of the tangle of discarded apparel—except for the knout that dangled beneath the little window. I stood by the wall and waited. A guard entered and began the interrogation. I fought for control over the terror that seemed about to engulf me.

"Full name."

I answered.

"Place of work."

I named the place for which the battalion was headed.

"I see! Now show me what you are carrying on your person." He pulled off my coat and dress and examined them closely under a light, searching the hems and pockets. My shoes! If he asked about them, I was lost.

"All right, now the shoes!" he demanded.

A chill passed through me. My mind was racing. I started unlacing my shoes slowly, stalling for time. Staring angrily, my interrogator ordered: "Hurry up—stop fiddling around! Let's have those shoes! Do you see this whip?"

As I continued to fumble with the laces, the Nazi seized the whip and started to advance on me.

At that moment, as if miraculously, the door flew open, and someone shouted, "*Herr Leutnant*, please come at once! A Jew has just escaped!"

The officer dashed out, slamming the door behind him. Left alone, I dressed hurriedly and walked through the door.

"Where are you going?" a guard stopped me.

"To the labor battalion," I replied, trying to sound casual. "I have already passed inspection."

The guard eyed me suspiciously for a moment, then waved me on. I was soon swallowed up by the throng on the "Aryan side," about to march out.

Michal Klepfisz was to have been waiting for me at the ghetto gate, but he was nowhere to be seen and I could not linger here, lest my German catch up with me. At last I located the group of laborers with whom I had marched out. They were delighted to see me.

"You're lucky," the group leader told me. "Hardly anyone ever gets out of there unhurt."

Soon we were in a wagon, rolling through the Polish streets. Our white armbands identified us as being Jews. The streets were familiar to me; very little had changed during the past few years. Several Poles chased our wagon, anxious to buy something; but none of us had anything to sell. We were nearing the work project. I racked my brains for a way to break away quickly.

The others, aware that I was on some sort of mission, urged me to discard my armband and jump off the vehicle. Acting on that counsel, I chose a moment when no passersby were in sight and leaped from the slow-moving wagon. I walked away briskly, then turned off into another street and slackened my pace.

Far from the ghetto now, I was free—but my sense of freedom was marred by a strange feeling of restlessness. I was in my own city, but seeing not a single familiar face. Here it was as if nothing had happened in the last two years. Trolleys, automobiles, bicycles raced along; businesses were open; children headed for school; women carried fresh bread and other provisions. The contrast with the ghetto was startling. It was another world, a world teeming with life.

Could the life that I had left behind have been only an illusion? I wondered as I walked the Warsaw streets. How strange and new everything around me was!

At last I arrived at Gornoszlonska 3—the address Michal had given me. I made my way to the cellar, and banged on the door. A blonde woman let me in. Michal was there, to welcome me, relief and joy evident in the warmth of his greeting.

"You're here at last! I was waiting at the gate for hours!"

Michal, along with his landlord, Stephan Machai, had waited at the gate for me since early that morning, and had just gotten back.

"I didn't expect you to venture out today; the guards were very strict," Michal said, after we had regained some composure and were sharing a cup of tea.

I took note of our surroundings: two small, low-ceilinged rooms inhabited by a family of four. Stephan Machai, a Gentile, seemed to like Michal. Before the war they had worked together, he as an unskilled laborer, Michal as an engineer. Now a *ricksha* pusher, the stocky Gentile considered it an honor to have the former engineer as his guest. An old, narrow bunk that Michal used took up half of the kitchen space.

Michal seemed depressed. I asked him what was wrong.

"My sister Gina died in the hospital," he told me quietly. "We're burying her today. If you wish, you can come with me to the cemetery."

I refrained from telling him of the ordeal I had undergone while leaving the ghetto. My experience paled in the presence of death. I had known Gina Klepfisz before the war, having worked with her in the *Zukunft* in a suburb of Praga, where she had organized a children's group. She had been both serious and kindhearted; children adored her. More recently, she had worked as a nurse in the ghetto. Her warm, sympathetic approach to her fellow men and the unique calm with which she met difficult situations had fitted her admirably for such tasks.

Now I had hardly stepped into the Aryan sector, only to hear that she was dead. Michal and I walked silently to the hospital, where he was to meet his wife, Ruszka Perczykow.

Ruszka was all in black, head bowed as she fought back her tears. A nurse led us wordlessly into the morgue. Gina's body was clothed all in white. My eyes were riveted upon this lifeless body—all that remained of the woman whom I remembered as vivacious and energetic, and who, as a hospital employee, had been instrumental in smuggling Jews out of the *Umschlagplatz*. She would steer doomed men and women across the barbed wire, under cover of darkness, at the risk of her own life. On one occasion she had been caught by a Jewish policeman. Her courageous stand had dampened his ire somewhat, but she was dismissed from her job. Thereupon, together with her brother, sister-in-law, and year-old child, she had crossed over to the "Aryan side."

The nurse signaled to us that someone was approaching. We made the sign of the cross, lest anyone suspect that Gina had been Jewish. As a patient, Gina had been registered as a Gentile, under the name Kazimiera

Juzwiak; the record had to remain intact. She was to be buried as a Christian.

A small funeral party awaited us at the cemetery. Among them were Yankel Celemenski and Hanka Alexandrowicz. Celemenski had been passing as a Gentile in Cracow—on the Aryan side. He had rescued the thirteen-year-old Hanka from the Cracow ghetto only a few days before. Zygmunt (Zalman Friedrich) was also present. A strange funeral indeed: of the ten mourners following the hearse, only Anna Wonchalska and her sister Marysia Sawicka, were Christians. The funeral was carried out in accordance with Roman Catholic rites. The grave was marked with a cross.

We took our leave of Gina Klepfisz, one of the few Warsaw Jews to be buried in a cemetery at a time when thousands of Jews were being gassed and cremated.

13. MY FIRST STEPS
AMONG THE ARYANS

My salient facial features were, indeed, "Aryan"—a rather small nose, grey-green eyes, straight light brown hair. But I lacked documents of identification. I had no place to live. For a few days I stayed in the apartment of the late Gina Klepfisz, but the other tenants began complaining that there were far too many newcomers frequenting the house. The landlady became frightened, and I had to leave. I moved in with Stephan Machai—in the cellar of Gornoszlonska 3, where Michal lived, but I could remain there only a few days. I was using an old passport made out to Wladyslawa Kowalska. Accordingly I had assumed the nickname of Vladka. I needed a certificate which would enable me to apply to any home for accommodation and legalize my residence on the "Aryan side."

I met my friends every day. None of them had found decent living quarters as yet. They had few contacts with Aryan families, and this made matters worse. Yankel Celemenski (Celek) was lodging with a young Gentile in a dreary room in a rooming house on Wspolna Street. Celek was not registered and his Polish speech was labored and heavily accented; he was sure to be recognized by the other tenants.

With ingenuity and effort and at considerable expense, Michal succeeded in obtaining a birth certificate and identity card from a building superintendent. It was in the name of Tadeusz Metzner, currently employed in Germany. Delighted, Michal immediately registered as a resident at Gornoszlonska 3 and a native Pole.

Early one morning while he was still asleep in the kitchen, an elderly Gentile woman came to the apartment, asking to see Tadeusz Metzner. She said he was her long lost son. Fortunately, the landlord instantly assessed the situation and informed the visitor that her son was away on a trip. Michal, by then wide awake, held his breath for fear that the old woman might insist on looking for him. She finally left, but she came back often to find out why her son was avoiding his own mother. Michal was forced to look for new lodgings, for fear that the persistent old woman might 'stumble upon him and expose him as an impostor.

Zygmunt was the most successful among us in settling down in his new environment. He had been living in the Polish zone for a long while, had some acquaintances in the neighborhood, and was registered as lodging with an Aryan family. His wife had also found refuge with an Aryan family, and their five-year-old child, Elsa, was in a Polish church orphanage in the suburbs of Cracow. Zygmunt had been fingered several times by informers but had managed to elude his captors and, at the moment, was the leading activist in the underground. He could move about freely and was in a position to carry out various tasks.

Stefan Machai was well aware that all of us were Jews; he only insisted that we should stay out of the building during the day. He was afraid that other tenants in the house would discover our presence and report him to the authorities. All day, therefore, regardless of the weather, we wandered about the city, careful not to be caught without proper documents. We were able to return to the cellar only after nightfall, exhausted by the walking, to report on our experiences during the day.

One evening we learned that Zygmunt had had a narrow escape. He had barely managed to shake off his pursuers, and would have to go back to the ghetto to hide for a while. Now there were only three of us left on the "Aryan side"—Michal, Celek, and myself. We met several times a day and lived only for news of the ghetto.

Then, my own luck took a turn for the better. With the help of his Gentile friend, Wanda Wnorowska, Michal found a job for me as a seamstress. Wnorowska was aware of my Jewish identity, and received me warmly. As a result, I had a refuge during the day, was earning my keep, and was provided with an identity card. Time passed; I made acquaintances among the Gentiles, and bit by bit got to know my new environment.

After a fortnight, Michal informed me that Mikolai Berezowski (his original name was Dr. Leon Feiner) wanted to see me. He was the Bund representative of the coordinating committee on the "Aryan side," and the central figure in the Jewish underground, and our liaison with the Polish underground. I had heard his name so often in my dealings with Celek and Michal that, although I had never met him, I thought of him as a sincere and devoted friend.

I was to meet him at Sewerynow 6, between two and three in the afternoon, in a convent, which had a restaurant open to the public. It served as a rendezvous for our small circle of underground activists. Since our group had no steady meeting place, we had to use quiet public sites, and could not meet too often in the same locale.

Michal accompanied me to the convent, which was on a quiet lane where people rarely passed. Next to the kitchen were a small waiting room where one could smoke, a cloakroom, and two spacious halls. Our group usually lunched in one of these halls, which was screened by old green palms set near the window. A rare serenity prevailed here. The diners were predominantly office clerks and impoverished middle class people. Compared to other public kitchens, the prices here were very moderate.

Michal guided me to a small vacant table, whispering instructions. Two men were dining at a table to the right. One of them was about forty years old, with a crop of black hair, a somber face and unassuming black clothes. He looked like some minor Polish government official. This was Borowski (Dr. Adolf Berman, representative on the Aryan side of the Jewish National Committee, and leader of the Left Poale Zion). Beside him sat a blonde gentleman with a well-groomed moustache, calm and confident in bearing. This was Henryk (Salo Fishgrund), who had been a Bund activist in Cracow prior to the war. Our own Celek was sitting by himself at a table opposite.

Shortly, a tall, elegant elderly man with silvery hair and an upturned moustache, bright eyes, and rosy cheeks—the image of a Polish country gentleman—entered. Like Henryk, he had an air of self-confidence. This was Mikolai. He took in the scene at a glance and, catching sight of Michal, joined us.

After exchanging pleasantries, we ordered our meal. Even-tempered, with a faint smile, Mikolai spoke to me with fatherly warmth. Though he had already heard about me, he was eager to learn more about my personal life. I gave him a brief account and he concluded that, being a woman, I would have more freedom of movement and would not be as conspicuous as a man.

"Our task is to get more volunteers," he remarked. "But we must be very careful; if we make one mistake, we can get a lot of people into very bad trouble."

"What will my assignment be?" I asked.

"As you are doubtless aware, our main tasks are to establish contact with Gentiles, find living quarters for women and children, assist Jews who are in hiding, and, in particular, to find sources of arms."

Michal and I listened closely, as Mikolai continued his instructions in a low voice. "As far as possible, each of us must create his own tasks; that is, try to cultivate new friendships, but he must do so with the utmost caution. Keep me posted on any new contacts and any newly-acquired lodgings or weapons."

As the waitress approached, we stopped our discussion. After she had left, Mikolai asked me whether everything was clear to me.

"Yes," I replied, "it is all clear. But whom am I to contact? With whom must I keep in touch?"

"For the time being," he replied, "keep contact with Henryk and myself." Then, after a moment's pause, in a louder voice, "I believe you'll be able to handle the situation."

Again, for the benefit of the waitress, we changed to comments on the weather and our delicious meal. When she had gone, we agreed that I would meet Henryk and Mikolai at this convent every day for lunch. All issues would have to be settled at this meeting-place. On special occasions, however, I was to visit Henryk at his home at Senatorska 9. Michal then disposed of a few odds and ends and the meeting was over.

This quiet conversation over lunch in a convent kitchen marked a turning-point in my life and activities. From now on I was to be an integral active part of the underground.

I started a new life. We carried on our activities in accordance with the quiet conversations we had had in the convent refectory where practically all the activists who could move about in public because of their Aryan looks converged.

It was shortly after my first meeting in the convent that I chanced to meet Aryeh Wilner (Yurek). I was in our cellar at Gornoszlonska 3 when a young man in his twenties, well-dressed, with a ruddy complexion and a snub nose—obviously not Jewish, I thought—delivered several wooden crates. Because our landlord owned a cart, parcels were occasionally brought to him for delivery to various addresses. I was not at all surprised by the stranger's visit, but I found it odd that Michal should give him such a warm welcome and appear so pleased with the transaction. Perhaps it was a friendly Gentile, I reasoned. The landlord set a price and, as usual, inquired about the contents of the crates.

"Nails."

After some bargaining the deal was made. Michal was to give instructions as to the time and place of the delivery. The landlord went off to stow away the crates. The young Gentile exchanged whispers with Michal and, as he left, observed cheerfully, "May we have many more such transactions."

When he eyed me suspiciously, Michal reassured him and introduced me. "This is Vladka—one of our group. She recently got out of the ghetto."

The deliveryman smiled. "Very good—lots of luck!"

Later I learned that the deliveryman was Aryeh Wilner, of *Hashomer Hatzair*, who represented the Jewish Fighting Organization (*Zydowska Organiacja Bojowa*) on the "Aryan side," and that the crates contained not nails but the first ten revolvers to be secured from the Polish underground (*Armja Krajowa*) after prolonged negotiations.

I became a participant sharing the secrets which were to usher in a new chapter in our lives. Day by day I was being drawn deeper into a perilous undertaking and was in close contact with the most important underground leaders.

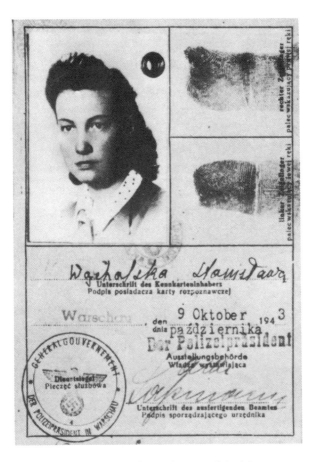

Vladka's identity card as a Polish girl

Roundup and deportation

14. BLACKMAILERS—SZMALCOWNICY

I had expected that on the "Aryan side" there would be an intense interest in the life of the ghetto, that the Gentiles, who lived so close to the wall and could observe through their windows the horrifying events in the ghetto, would be haunted by what they saw. I had thought that the Poles were eager to aid their Jewish acquaintances and neighbors. After all, they had worked side by side with them, reared their children together with the Jewish children and shared both joy and sadness with their Jewish neighbors. Now, when Jews were so relentlessly exterminated, it would be only natural for the Poles to show some human compassion and a desire to help the Jews.

But before long, something happened that shattered my illusions. One Sunday I was strolling along a Warsaw street in the "Aryan sector," not too far from the ghetto wall. There was a playground on Krasinski Square opposite the wall, and that Sunday it was crowded with youngsters and adults engaged in sports, dancing and games. The small cafes were bursting with young men eating, drinking and having a good time. I paused at some distance and took in the scene, then turned left. The ghetto wall was only a stone's throw away. Two different worlds on the same street.

Suddenly, a volley of gunfire rang out on the other side of the wall. There were anguished screams, then silence. The Germans had claimed another victim in the ghetto.

I looked toward the park. Had the people there heard the gunfire? Some of them had looked over their shoulders, startled and alarmed. But one of them pointed toward the wall, and with his other hand made a motion indicating that there was nothing to worry about.

"That is just for the Jews," a youthful Pole remarked with a grin—and returned for a second ride on a swing.

It was a sunny winter day; the avenue was filled with families taking their Sunday stroll. I watched the well-dressed Gentiles moving along at a leisurely pace, the little children running ahead of their elders. But in my mind's eye I saw my people in the ghetto and a swagger stick pointing this way and that while a rasping voice dealt out death and temporary reprieve, intoning incessantly, "To the left! To the right! To the left! To the right!"

A clamor ahead brought me back to reality. Two elderly Poles were dragging a pale, poorly-clad young man between them. His terrified eyes frantically sought help from the onlookers. From time to time he pleaded with his captors but they pulled him along, shouting, "Jew! Dirty Jew!" The two no doubt had seized him on the street and now held him captive. In all likelihood he had no money to buy them off.

Following at some distance, I saw a Gentile run off and then return accompanied by a German guard. The Jew, apparently resigned now to his fate, ceased struggling.

The German hailed a passing taxi, roughly pushed the young man in, then climbed in himself, followed by the two Polish informers. So much for the unfortunate Jew . . .

A large crowd had gathered. I studied the faces and gestures. The Gentile onlookers were not especially proud of what they had witnessed. Some shook their heads, others smiled wryly. But none interfered or protested. They resumed their Sunday stroll as if nothing had happened.

How could the Poles remain so indifferent? For the rest of the day I wandered about in great distress. I could not go home as yet; my landlady was expecting some relatives and didn't want them to know that she had a lodger.

When I finally ventured home, well after dark, I found Ania (Hancia Werkzweig Ellenbogen) waiting for me there. Ania had worked with her husband Bolek (Hayim Ellenbogen) in the Medem Sanatorium for children until the Germans had liquidated it in August. Miraculously, they had managed, together with Bolek's sister Perele, a teacher, to escape to the "Aryan side." Ania was living with her husband in the home of some poor Gentiles, working as a seamstress. Things so far had been quiet, but today she seemed distressed.

"Yesterday, as I was about to get off a trolley car," she told me, "someone tapped on the window and motioned to me. It was Bolek. He looked very much upset, but seemed glad he had finally found me. He had been waiting at the trolley stop for hours to warn me not to go home. The *szmalcownicy* (blackmailers) were lying in wait for me."

Ania paused uneasily, then continued, "It seems that some Gentile had recognized Bolek as a Jew and followed him into the house, demanding money and carrying off whatever he could lay his hands on. But this was not enough for him. He decided to take Bolek along and turn him over to a German sentry. Two hooligans joined the *szmalcownik* on the way, but Bolek somehow managed to shake them off. Now he was afraid that they would return to our lodgings and find me there, so he had waited at the stop to warn me."

She paused again, breathless and tearful, then burst out: "Last night a woman took us in for a few zlotys, but now we have no roof over our heads."

"I'll talk to my landlord," I tried to comfort her. "Maybe he'll be able to arrange something for you."

Stephan Machai was slightly drunk. When I asked him for help, he kept beating around the bush, shifting from "yes" to "no." Finally, he agreed to let them spend just two nights in his house, the rent to be paid in advance.

Well, at least we would have a two-night breathing spell. After that, we would see.

Finding living quarters was difficult, not only for newcomers, but even for those Jews who already had been on the "Aryan side" for some time. It was not easy to maintain the pretense of being a Gentile. One had to be wary of each movement, each word, to avoid giving oneself away. The Poles had no difficulty in recognizing Jews. Lately, having become aware that some Jews were escaping from the ghetto, young Poles had lost no time in capitalizing on this knowledge through *szmalcowe*—blackmail. The moment they came upon a Jew, they demanded money and, if they failed to find enough, stripped the victim of his overcoat, shoes, or anything else of value he happened to have on his person. Such a character had helped himself to Celek's overcoat. These *szmalcownicy* were to be found everywhere. They haunted the residential quarters, prowled the streets and factories, looking for victims.

The Jews in the "Aryan sector" lived in mortal fear of the Germans, and consequently would sacrifice whatever they owned to avoid being turned over to them. If a Jew turned out to be destitute, the blackmailers would hand him over to the Gestapo, who had set a price of 100 zlotys on every Jewish head. Without these Polish informers, the Germans would never have caught as many Jews as they did. Of course, not all Poles were of this sort. Some even showed compassion, but these were few in number and their assistance was meager.

Michal had already been blackmailed. He was tall, fair, and blue-eyed, but his Jewish-looking nose gave him away. He tried to avoid being seen.

I, too, got a taste of blackmail during the first weeks of my activity in the "Aryan sector." We had received word from the ghetto that what was especially needed at the time were metal files. These files were intended for the use of Jews who had been rounded up and put aboard trains bound for Treblinka. Their only hope was to escape from the speeding train. Armed with a file, a prisoner could make a small gap in the window bars and try to jump to freedom. Success meant survival, at least for the time being.

The task of procuring such files was assigned to Michal and myself. One frosty afternoon found us near the German factory at Chmielna 2. We had already obtained some files and were now seeking to establish contact with the Jewish group leader employed there, hoping he would take one of us along when he and some of his men returned to the ghetto.

Michal went up to the locked factory gate while I acted as a lookout, scanning the street to be sure no Germans were around. At my signal, Michal rang the bell at the gate. I saw him slip a something into the hand of the guard who answered. He entered and the gate closed behind him.

Alone, I waited, suspense and apprehension building steadily. At last, the gate opened and Michal emerged. Even before we had exchanged a word, I knew from the slight sag of his shoulders, the heaviness of his step, that he had not achieved our objective.

The Jewish workers had not been reporting for work during the past few days. The all too familiar roundups had been resumed in the ghetto, and Jewish labor brigades employed on the "Aryan side" were now undergoing "selections."

We left the factory, discussing possible ways of smuggling files into the ghetto. Suddenly, we were aware of footsteps behind us. Three Gentiles were trailing us; obviously, they were *szmalcownicy*, and they were not likely to let us go. We quickened our pace; they quickened theirs.

We had no money to speak of; I had 10 zlotys on me, and Michal had about 50—a mere pittance.

Just then a trolley passed by. We both tried to jump on it. Michal succeeded and was carried off, leaving me running after the trolley breathlessly, though I knew it was useless. Seized roughly from behind by strong hands on my shoulders, I was twisted about to face the three ruffians who had been trailing us. The one holding me was tall, with bleary eyes. He released me, now that his two companions were there to thwart any effort on my part to escape, and, with a mock bow, smirked, "You tried to get away, but you won't be rid of us so easily."

"What do you want from me?" I asked, pretending puzzlement.

"You mean to say you don't know who we are?" the man who spoke was puny and emaciated, with black piercing eyes. "We know you, sure enough! Why were you snooping around the factory where they employ Jews?"

"I was looking for a job," I replied. It was the only plausible answer that occurred to me.

"Don't try to put anything over on us," snorted the tall one. "You are from the ghetto, and the one who got away is another Jew."

A curious crowd had begun to gather. Desperation prompted me to gamble on a ruse. Faking a calm smile, I invited my pursuers to accompany me and started walking. They followed.

"If you want us to let you go, let's have three thousand zlotys—one thousand for each of us. Then you'll be on your own."

Three thousand zlotys! I had less than fifty on me, but my captors did not know that. I decided to trade on their cupidity as long as possible. I kept insisting that I was a Gentile and at a loss to understand why I was being harassed.

Apparently they had decided to call my bluff. They closed in menacingly. The tall one spoke again.

"Do you expect us to stroll along with you for pleasure, you Jewish bitch? Hand over the money, or else we'll take you straight to the Germans; they'll settle accounts with you!"

I knew that if they did this, it would be the end for me. I would have to make my bluff work or else.

"Very well, let's go," I said with a shrug of anger. "You will be called to account for casting suspicion on me and for your attempts to blackmail me."

Evidently shaken, my companions were whispering among themselves. I strode ahead, unheeding. I had to find a way of escaping them before we approached a German sentry.

They followed me for a while, but the sound of their footsteps behind me grew fainter and at last subsided. I crossed to the other side of the street and cautiously looked back. They had stopped, still watching me. Evidently they were still not sure whether I was a Jewess or not. This was not the time to make a run for it; the best thing would be to stroll along as if nothing had happened. I mingled with the throng and little by little outdistanced my pursuers. Finally, I found myself in a narrow street with no one in sight. I boarded a trolley and for several hours transferred from trolley to trolley until I was convinced that no one was trailing me.

Large numbers of Jews were not so fortunate as I. While the *szmalcownicy* did not kill Jews outright, as the Germans did, they deprived the Jews of those last meager possessions without which it was impossible to find refuge on the Aryan side, thus driving many of their victims to despair and often death.

Mrs. Brzeska, a friendly, upright, compassionate Polish woman, who lived at Topeil 8, had given shelter to five Jews in an emergency. Her first Jewish lodgers had been a mother and her son, a former member of the Jewish police. Both had typically Jewish features and consequently had to keep well out of sight. They were often visited by some of the Gentiles who had recommended them to Brzeska as lodgers.

One day *szmalcownicy* appeared and, evidently well informed, went directly to the room where the old woman and her son were staying. The robbers took money and jewelry from the two and assured the frightened landlady that they would never come again; the Jews could safely remain where they were.

What were the mother and son to do? No other living quarters were available and all their money was gone. They begged to be allowed to stay a little while longer, so that they could sell their last possessions and try to find another hideout.

Several weeks later, the *szmalcownicy* returned. They seized whatever rags and cash their victims had left. By now the landlady was in mortal fear, but she did not have the heart to turn her lodgers out. Both the mother and the son kept talking about committing suicide. The mother insisted that her son would survive if he were not burdened with her.

Another friendly Polish woman accommodated the pair, but soon afterward the mother took cyanide; she did it not at home, but on the outskirts of the town, so that, even in death she would not be a burden to anyone. The son disappeared without a trace.

Our Jewish underground tried to combat the blackmailers. We even appealed to our supposed allies, the Polish underground, to launch a campaign in their secret press to make the Polish populace regard the *szmalcownicy* as criminals and as German collaborators and to deal with them accordingly. Unfortunately, our appeals fell on ears afflicted with a deafness to the supplications of Jews. The blackmailers went right ahead with their diabolical work.

15. FINDING WEAPONS

The main objective of our mission on the "Aryan side"—the goal for which we endured constant danger, hid like frightened animals, assumed false identities, moved from dwelling to dwelling to escape detection as Jews—was to obtain arms for the resistance in the ghetto. It was an effort that commanded the unreserved collaboration of all the groups and elements in the ghetto, a collaboration that overbore differences of ideology and doctrine, uniting all of us in the common fundamental passion for vengeance upon our tormentors, the murderers of our friends and kin, the enemies of our Jewish people.

Gradually, our "Aryan" contingent was enlarged, as new couriers from the ghetto joined us. We continued to meet from time to time in the basement of Gornoszlonska 3, where our conversations invariably centered on the crucial question: How? How, as strangers among the Poles, in the guise of ordinary Polish citizens, were we to conduct traffic in such forbidden, scarce commodities as weapons and explosives? Every time my co-workers in the underground heard that I was to meet Mikolai, their invariable plea to me was to find out from him how his efforts at arms procurement were progressing.

We knew that the Polish underground had secret caches of weapons. Mikolai was in touch with the leaders of the Polish underground. "They keep making promises!" he told me again and again. We were urged to be patient. Often, we wondered why, in spite of our willingness to pay generously, the underground refused to help us. However, our contacts with the Poles were tenuous and often came to grief; many times we were sold out.

Yurek (Aryeh Wilner) had succeeded in buying a considerable quantity of revolvers and hand grenades from a Gentile woman. But as soon as he had brought the valise with the "merchandise" to his apartment, the Gestapo swooped down on him, found the weapons, and arrested Yurek together with the other tenants of the house. We were convinced that he had been sold out by the same Gentile woman who had sold him the weapons. When Yurek's close friend, Tosia Altman of *Hashomer Hatzair* told us the news, we were stunned. There was no escape from the clutches of the Gestapo. But Tosia was not to be deterred; she had come seeking advice from Stephan Machai; perhaps he knew someone who could be bribed.

Several months later I learned that Yurek had been tortured by the Gestapo. His hands and toes had been beaten to a pulp, yet he had not betrayed his co-workers. Through an error of the prison administration, Yurek was transferred from the Pawiak Prison to the Kawenczyn camp near Warsaw. From there he succeeded in contacting the Jewish underground, which managed to smuggle him out. Eventually, he made his way back to the Warsaw ghetto, where he was hospitalized for his injuries. Yurek was to die at Mila 18 during the ghetto uprising; he perished together with the staff of the Jewish Fighting Organization, including Mordecai Anilewicz, the heroic commander of the ghetto revolt.

The loss of Yurek was a severe blow to the "Aryan sector" of the Jewish underground. He had been an energetic and fearless activist. Michal succeeded to his post.

It was a great event for me when I managed to procure my first revolver, bought from our landlord's nephew, Heniek Dubiel, for two thousand zlotys. I turned the weapon over and over, pretending to inspect it, though I had not the faintest idea of how it worked. I bought it, finally, confident that my friends would know how to repair it if necessary. I hurried off to our cellar to show my new treasure to Celek and Michal. In the cellar I found the two men conferring with Bernard Goldstein, a member of the Bund's Central Committee. I had not seen Bernard in a long time; he had gone into hiding in the ghetto, and the Gestapo was on his trail. On the "Aryan side," he rarely appeared in public. He was an expert on weapons. I showed him the gun I had acquired, and he assured me that I had not been cheated. The next move was to make contact with the ghetto.

Although the ghetto was not supposed to have any contact with the "Aryan side," there were a few telephones in the workshops through which the entire city could be reached; one of these telephones was in the office of the brush factory. Twice a day, at specified times, one of our comrades would be stationed there, to receive any messages that might come from the "Aryan side." We telephoned there only in case of emergency. As a rule, we made our calls from pay telephones, using code language only the initiates could understand. Whenever the central telephone office interrupted, as often happened, to ask for our number, we hung up and hurried away.

We arranged to smuggle the revolver into the ghetto through a hole in the wall at the corner of Swientojerska and Bonifraterska Streets, between eight and nine that evening. Some smuggling went on there almost every evening, because the Polish sentry there was amenable to bribes and one could climb over the wall. We packed the gun in a box to look like an ordinary parcel. Our landlord handed the box through the hole, unaware of its contents, and received the usual fee of 75 zlotys.

Celek managed to obtain quite a few weapons. He struck up a friendship with a Polish Socialist named Yanek, who provided him with lodging at his mother's home at Browarna 20. Yanek had promised Celek three revolvers and four boxes of dynamite for 6,000 zlotys. We were overjoyed at the prospect; such an acquisition was a windfall. But we still were faced with the problem of how to smuggle our purchase into the ghetto.

I hastened to our usual meeting place in the convent to inform Mikolai, who had to confirm the purchase and supply the money. Mikolai gave his approval and granted the required sum.

"Can you trust this Gentile?" he inquired.

That was a hard question to answer. Celek's acquaintance was a member of the Polish underground. Moreover, one of the Polish Socialist leaders had vouched for him. Everything seemed in order, but no one could guarantee how he would act under unforeseen circumstances.

Mikolai left the room for a few minutes, then returned and placed a pack of cigarettes in front of me. This was our currency. As I dropped the pack into my handbag and took my leave of him, I could feel Mikolai's eyes follow me with fatherly concern.

Later, Celek introduced me to my contact, Yanek, a short, pleasant young Gentile. He seemed to boast a little too much of his exploits in the Polish underground, but he struck me as basically trustworthy. He even promised to help smuggle the arms into the ghetto.

I passed the money to him in a small cafe at Radna 18, where we drank a toast to him and some of his friends, who happened to be present. We then agreed on a time and place for the pickup.

Yanek arrived at the appointed hour but, to our deep disappointment, with no revolvers and only three small packages of dynamite. He explained that the revolvers had been lost; one of his friends had been taken into custody with the weapons on his person.

The money paid for the revolvers was gone. We consoled ourselves with the thought that at least we had the dynamite, which would come in handy in the ghetto.

One of our most adept arms procurers was Tadek (Tovye Shaingut) of *Hashomer Hatzair*, a newcomer to our ranks. A sturdy, towheaded young lad, he wore heavy high boots and a farmer's long overcoat and had the looks and ways of a peasant.

Tadek first appeared in our cellar after Yurek's misadventure. He visited us frequently, and in fact, when he lost his lodgings, he moved in with us. Before long, Tadek made friends with our Gentile companions and began to do business with them. He was frequently in Yanek's company and trailed Heniek Dubiel and others. We were somewhat irked to learn that Tadek was secretly buying arms from our own sources. Why hadn't he told us about it? We never learned the reason; that was just the way Tadek operated. He was both shrewd and fearless, undeterred by obstacles. He always carried a revolver, and declared that he would never be captured alive.

He must have had a premonition. Several months after he joined us, he made contact with certain Gentiles in Praga, where he was to obtain a shipment of arms. Together with Kazik (Rotheiser), another ghetto fighter, Tadek went to Washington 80 to pick up the promised arms.

Everything seemed to be in order as he entered the house. But they had hardly begun to examine the weapons when there was a wild banging on the door, and the next moment the Gestapo broke into the house. The only way of escape was through the window. Clutching their revolvers, our comrades edged their way towards it. Shots were exchanged. While bullets whizzed over their heads, the two leaped through the window. Kazik was fortunate enough to escape, but Tadek was hit by a bullet and died instantly. It was as he had predicted. The Germans had not been able to take him alive.

16. SMUGGLING ARMS

Getting the arms, once acquired, into the ghetto posed its own problems and hazards. Getting back into the ghetto, even without contraband, was no easy matter. However, if one was empty-handed, one could mingle with a Jewish labor gang returning from the "Aryan side." But if one was carrying something, one was likely to be searched and arrested at the ghetto gate. Safer routes had to be found.

Michal himself had succeeded in smuggling into the ghetto a revolver he had acquired from Fishgrund. He had contacted a Gentile smuggler, a railroad worker employed in the ghetto, and had agreed to meet him at nightfall. When the Gentile failed to appear, Michal decided to proceed on his own. He had learned from passing Poles how to worm his way into the ghetto.

He had to traverse a section of the *Umschlagplatz*, where the Germans searched every suspicious passerby. Michal kept a firm hold on the revolver in his pocket, ready to use it in self-defense if anyone stopped him. Fortunately, he succeeded in completing his mission. But we had to find more reliable means of smuggling.

The ghetto wall extended along Okopowa and Dzika, parallel to an alley called Parysowski Place. Entrepreneurs had bribed the guards at that intersection and developed a thriving smuggling operation. Enterprising Gentiles scaled the ghetto wall to purchase wearing apparel, underwear, shoes, sewing machines, and other items from the Jews who, in their desperation, parted with their belongings for ridiculously small sums. There were also the "brave lads" who ransacked deserted Jewish homes, dismantling chests, beds, sideboards and other furniture and hauling their loot over the wall to reassemble on the other side. For a time, black marketeering and indiscriminate looting of Jewish homes flourished near the wall. But ultimately the German authorities unearthed most of the smuggling routes and shot some of the smugglers. Getting in and out of the ghetto became more difficult every day.

Michal was the first to direct me to the smuggling area at Parysowski Place, the route by which he and Yurek had smuggled in their first lot of arms, some ten revolvers which the representatives of the Jewish Coordinating Committee on the "Aryan side" had acquired from the Polish underground. The revolvers had been placed in small cartons, covered with nails, and trundled on a handcart by Stephan Machai. Michal and Yurek, both armed, followed at a discreet distance. Everything went well until the three were stopped by a Polish policeman, who asked to see their license for transporting merchandise. Fortunately, a few zlotys satisfied his curiosity, and he allowed them to proceed.

Some comrades of the Fighting Organization waiting on the other side of the wall heard Michal's password. One of them clambered up the wall, took over the cartons of "nails" handed to him by Michal, Yurek, and Stephan, and lowered them to his companions. Had any one of their group of combatants been intercepted they would have opened fire. No one would have permitted the anxiously-awaited revolvers to fall into the hands of the enemy.

Later, I, too, resorted to this route. The first time I visited the area with Michal was to transmit a package of steel files for the Fighting Organization. We arrived at the wall dressed like peddlers. I carried the package while Michal entered the ramshackle building opposite the ghetto which served as the headquarters of the Gentile smugglers. After paying their agent for the privilege of being allowed to climb over the wall, we waited a considerable time. Then, on a signal by a young Pole, Michal scrambled to the top. I handed him the package; he seized it and jumped off the wall into the ghetto. The assignment completed, I went home.

On the second occasion I went to Parysowski Place alone. This time I had been commissioned to transmit three boxes of dynamite. A deathly silence hung over the area; the smugglers were conspicuously absent. My suspicions aroused, I called to a passing elderly woman, asking her why the place was so quiet.

"They shot two smugglers this morning," the old woman replied. "A couple of them were arrested. The patrols have been reinforced."

What now? Delay was unthinkable; the dynamite was desperately needed in the ghetto. Undoubtedly my comrades were waiting on the other side of the wall. I telephoned the ghetto, asked about the new state of affairs, and said that I intended to smuggle the package through Feifer's factory. I would call back later.

The factory was situated on Okopowa Street near Gliniana, adjoining the ghetto. Jews occasionally escaped to the "Aryan side" by this route and our underground had used it to smuggle things in. There was a slight complication, however, because a German sentry stood facing the factory gate, keeping a sharp eye not only on the Jewish cemetery which was parallel to the other side of Okopowa, but also on Feifer's workshop. I rang the bell, and the watchman opened the gate. The dim passage was deserted. I dickered with the elderly Gentile to let me smuggle a small package into the ghetto. The old man hesitated, but finally was persuaded by some cash and a bottle of vodka. Delighted, I telephoned my comrades again, telling them to be on hand near Feifer's tannery at six o'clock.

I returned at twilight to an almost empty Okopowa Street. Keeping out of sight, I watched the sentry, who did not seem to budge at all. Rather than risk being seen, I decided to lie low until it was fully dark. Finally, after what seemed an eternity, the sentry turned away to light a cigarette. Hurrying to the gate, I rang the bell. The watchman let me in, then led the way quickly through various workrooms and up and down stairways until we came to a cubbyhole crammed with boxes and crates. I scanned the room, trying to find the passageway that led to the ghetto. The watchman pointed to a corner. "Get ready," he said, and turned off the light. I heard something stir in the darkness. Gradually the outline of a small, grated window became visible.

"Hurry and get rid of your package!" he urged me.

I tiptoed over to the little window and strained my eyes and ears. Not a sound. Was it possible that my comrades had left? I called out in a very faint voice, "Yurek! Yurek!"

"At last you are here!" someone whispered in answer.

A silhouette appeared at the little window. It was Yanek Bilak, a member of the Fighting Organization and the *Zukunt*. A man who knew no fear, he always seemed to take on the most dangerous missions of his group, which was based in the brush factory. I tried to pass the package of dynamite through the grating, but the package proved too big. How was I to repack it fast enough to keep the watchman from observing its contents?

"Hurry!" Yanek whispered from outside.

"Please be patient—I must repack." I asked the watchman to leave me alone for a few minutes, but he answered frenziedly, "Let me help you."

I had no choice. Together we tugged and fumbled, untying, emptying, repacking, retying. It seemed to take hours. The watchman was trembling like a leaf. Why hadn't he advised me to divide the package into smaller units to begin with? The voices outside kept urging me to hurry. What did they think I was doing?

At last the task was finished. Breathing hard, heart pounding, drenched in nervous perspiration, I thrust the dynamite through the grating. The watchman banged the window shut and switched on the light. He was flushed, open-mouthed as if gasping for air, sweating profusely. I gathered up the surplus wrapping and some spilled dynamite dust.

"See," I reassured him—and myself—"there was no cause for alarm. Everything went off all right."

"I'll never take such a chance again," the watchman mumbled. "I was scared to death."

I thrust 300 zlotys and a flask of vodka into the old man's unsteady hand and bade him goodbye.

"Tell me the truth: what did you have in those packages?" he suddenly asked me.

"Nothing special," I told him. "Just some packages of powdered paint."

"Was that all?" the old man asked, eyeing me suspiciously.

"Yes, that was all," I answered and left.

Such were the routes along which our "paint" and "nails" and similar merchandise were transmitted to the Jewish Fighting Organization in the ghetto.

17. THE GHETTO REVISITED

While buying arms on the "Aryan side" and smuggling them into the ghetto, we maintained close liaison with the underground inside the ghetto. Michal, Celek, Tadek and others crossed the wall at intervals to bring in illegal literature and correspondence as well as weapons, and to bring out instructions and directives for those of us working on the "Aryan side." On one such mission, I was assigned to smuggle a sum of money, some letters, and illegal Polish literature into the ghetto for delivery to Abrasha Blum.

By six in the morning, I had reached Parysowski Place, where I paid the then going rate of 75 zlotys to the chief smuggler and waited my turn. A stepladder was placed against the ten-foot ghetto wall. I mounted it quickly and dropped to the ground on the other side. At once, I tied a white handkerchief around my right arm as a substitute for the armband that all the Jews of the ghetto were required to wear. No one paid any attention to me. The few Jewish smugglers hugging the wall were used to dealing with Gentile traders. I hurried to the brush factory at Franciszkanska 32, where I was to meet Abrasha.

As I walked away from the ghetto wall I caught sight of Abrasha's wife, Luba Bielicka. She was wearing the white uniform she had worn before the war as director of a Jewish nursing school. She had remained at her post, even through the period of the deportations.

She was now talking with Zygmunt, who had been the first in the underground to break the news of the horrors of Treblinka. Accompanying a Gentile railroad worker on the Warsaw-Malkin line, whom he had befriended, to the town of Sokolow, he had had to stop over because the line branched off at this point and civilians were barred from traveling on it. He had learned from other passengers that, day in and day out, trains packed with people passed along the spur line toward the Treblinka station. As a rule, these trains came back empty.

The next day Zygmunt met an eyewitness who had just fled Treblinka, Azriel Wallach, a nephew of the Soviet diplomat Maxim Litvinov. It was from him that Zygmunt first learned the terrible facts about Treblinka. He then brought the news to the Warsaw ghetto.

Later, on the "Aryan side," he had come under such harassment from the *szmalcownicy* that he returned to the ghetto.

A little girl of five was clinging to Luba. I hesitated to approach them until Zygmunt saw me and motioned me to join them. We exchanged greetings.

"Are things quiet on the 'Aryan side'?" Luba asked me.

"Fairly quiet," I answered.

"As you can see, we want to get the child over there," Zygmunt remarked.

"How do you intend to arrange that?"

"The guard has been bribed today; we also bribed a friendly Gentile to accompany the litle girl to some out-of-the-way street in the 'Aryan sector' and leave her there. If a stranger sees her wandering about there, a child alone, he'll be likely to take her to an orphanage. Our Gentile friend will watch from a distance to see where the child will be taken," Zygmunt explained.

"The little one speaks Polish, and she knows how to behave. Perhaps that will save her," Luba added.

What could I tell them? There was no place in the "Aryan sector" where the child could stay. I remained silent as I watched the little girl, who listened attentively to our conversation. Every so often she lifted her dark brown eyes to Luba, who patted her head.

The Germans had taken the child's parents, and Luba had been taking care of her for a long time. But the hospital in which Luba had been staying was about to be liquidated. On the "Aryan side," the child would have at least some chance for survival.

Luba, Zygmunt and the little girl were waiting for a signal from the smuggler. The child did not make a sound; her eyes shifted from

Zygmunt to Luba and then to me. Did she realize her tragic situation? I bade a silent farewell to my friends and the little girl. I kept thinking about them for a long time. Perhaps their plan would work, after all.

Few people were to be seen in the ghetto; the streets were desolate and dismal, the houses vacant and void. Furniture was strewn about, together with torn bedding and blankets. No one had any need of it. Each brick, each door, each house seemed to testify to the appalling events that marked each day.

The somber, stilled ghetto streets were dearer to me than the cheerful bustle of the streets on the "Aryan side." The ghetto was a dreary place, but it was my own, real world where I could be myself. Here I had no need to maintain the forced smile I wore before my Polish neighbors. Here I did not have to listen to snide remarks from the Poles that the Jews had had it coming to them and that Hitler was purging Poland of the "Jewish plague." Here I did not have to live in constant fear of being unmasked as a Jewess. I was among my own.

During the day, only those with special permits were allowed on the ghetto streets. German patrols made the rounds; now and then I had to seek refuge in some house. I came upon several frightened and haggard Jews with sacks over their shoulders. Nearly all Jews lugged such sacks, wherever they went. During the first days of the *Aussiedlung*, when the Jews still believed the German lies about the labor camps, every Jew had carried on his person at all times a few things he would need— a skirt, a towel, a shirt. By now, everyone knew what was going on at Treblinka; yet they still refused to part from their sacks. A Jew could be picked up at any moment—and the sack could come in handy, in any event.

From time to time, I was offered some item of clothing or bedding—an old skirt, a shirt, a worn pillow case—for a pittance. The desperation of the vendors tore at my heart, but I had to hurry on.

Half a block away I saw a boy of fourteen or so, clothes in tatters, hair disheveled and bristling with feathers, face grim and eyes bulging. He was searching the pavement and gutter, looking up every few moments, then going back to his rummaging. At intervals, he found something, wiped it off on his rags and bit into it. What could he possibly find in the ghetto streets now, when people hardly ever discarded anything?

"They're coming! They're coming!" a child suddenly called out.

People fled in every direction. One could never be too careful.

The Germans moved on. Suddenly I noticed Luba behind me. It would take a little while before the child could get out of the ghetto, she said. So she had left the little girl with Zygmunt, not far from the ghetto wall. She asked me to accompany her to her home at Gesia 6, in the block where the Jewish Hospital was located; I might find Abrasha there. Walking with Luba was safer for me than to walk alone. Her white nurse's uniform was a protection of sorts.

The hospital was in turmoil. Bundles of packed knapsacks showed that both the staff and the inmates were ready to move at a moment's notice. Abrasha was not there. I left and continued toward Franciszkanska Street where he was to meet me. I had to be more cautious than ever as I neared the brush factory, because there were additional German patrols. To elude them I passed through a series of gates, alleys and lanes. At last I found myself on Franciszkanska Street. It was much more alive than the other streets in the ghetto, filled with Jewish peddlers and workers hurrying home. The Jewish police, however, were the most numerous and conspicuous. They were everywhere. Now and then one of them would stop a passing Jew to examine his identity card. If documents were found to be not quite in order, haggling began over what amount would be proper as a bribe. The Jewish law enforcement agents liked money. From time to time a German patrol appeared; and then the Jews scurried away.

Here I met Lusiek Bloness, younger brother of a former schoolmate of mine. He was thirteen years old, the youngest member of the Fighting Organization, a small lad, scrawny, but both shrewd and brave.

"Are you headed for our group?" he asked with obvious pleasure.

"Yes," I told him.

"Come along, then."

Lusiek knew all the ins and outs of the brush factory; I trailed after him, crawling through lofts, up and down stairs, and in and out of holes. Quite a few Jews followed this devious route; it was safer than the streets.

Bruised and grimy, we reached our destination, a run-down, fourth-floor flat. Here a group of the ghetto Fighting Organization was being trained in the use of firearms for the final challenge to the Germans. I knew almost all these people. They had been my comrades in *Skif* before the war. I had been to school with some of them. They welcomed me warmly. All were anxious for news from the other side of the wall. Abrasha Blum was with them; there was real warmth in his handshake.

There was little time for small talk. Abrasha led me into a vacant room littered with lumber, nails, and paper. The door was shut; I took out the letter, some American dollars, a batch of underground literature, and handed it to Abrasha. Delighted, he asked me, "Did you have trouble getting here?"

"None at all," I told him.

I watched him as he read the letter in silence. His face, grave as ever, and even more pale and haggard than I remembered it, seemed to sag, to lose the mask of calmness that it habitually wore.

"Well," he finally said, in a strangled voice. "It's clear enough. From now on, we are on our own."

I spoke of the difficulty of procuring arms in the "Aryan sector," especially with our meager resources.

Abrasha was aware of all this. The ghetto also was trying to acquire arms on its own. The arms traffic flourished in the ghetto; one could obtain revolvers from Gentile and even Jewish smugglers—at a price. But the arms obtainable from this source amounted to a mere drop in the bucket. We had accomplished so little, measured against the need.

There were rumors that the Warsaw ghetto would be cleared of all Jews by the Spring of 1943. Abrasha discussed the possibilities of resettling Jewish women and children on the "Aryan side." We must try to find as many hiding places as possible, he said; only on the "Aryan side" could there be any chance of saving some of the Jewish children.

"What are the possibilities?" Abrasha asked.

"It's very difficult," I explained. "The Poles are reluctant to take risks. And if one of them does agree to give shelter to a Jew, he demands an exorbitant sum."

Abrasha sighed. "Yes, the world doesn't want to hear about what's happening to us. There is little hope of help from outside. The ghetto is as good as isolated."

I told him of some of our activities, the hardships we endured, failures and rebuffs.

He listened, but then seemed to be talking to himself: "The people in the ghetto, too, must take extra precautions. The Germans have an inkling that there's something in the wind; they are searching . . . The boards and planks in this room have been arranged so that people can hide behind them if the Germans stage a raid."

We moved into another room where we found some more trainees. Romanowicz and Dunski, two swarthy lads of about twenty, were tinkering with a revolver.

"This thing seems to be jammed," Dunski remarked.

Lusiek's brother, Yurek Blones, was there, too, oiling a revolver. His sister Gutta Blones, three years older, dark and attractive, was the only girl in the group. She was busy preparing some food.

I was anxious to get back to the "Aryan side." It was easier and less dangerous to sneak over the wall by daylight. But I lingered, infected by the high spirits of the young men as they compared notes, interrupting the talk every so often to urge Gutta to hurry up with the food.

"The bread over here is supplied by the baker especially for our group." Yanek Bilak told me. "We get it free of charge."

Yurek interposed: "The little money we have must go for arms. Yanek and I explained the situation to the baker, and he agreed to provide us with bread every day."

"Do the people in the ghetto know about the Fighting Organization?" I asked.

"I should say so!" one of the men replied. "Ever since Laikin, that son-of-a-bitch commandant of the Jewish police, got killed. Everybody knows we did the job."

"The Jewish informers in the ghetto are in mortal fear of us," Gutta broke in.

Marek Edelman entered the room. He was the commandant of all the resistance groups in the factory area, and also the Bund's representative in the General Command of the Fighting Organization. He was accompanied by Berlinski, another member of the General Command.

"We're glad you've come," he greeted me. "We want to give you some jewelry to sell on the 'Aryan side'."

"Where did you get the jewelry?" I asked in astonishment.

Marek explained, matter-of-factly, that the Fighting Organization had been levying "taxes" on Jews in the ghetto who were known to be wealthy, particularly those who had prospered since the ghetto had been set up. They were informed by letter of the time and place at which specific amounts of money were to be deposited for the Fighting Organization. Prior to dispatching such a letter, the resistance groups investigated carefully whether the addressee was really in a position to make a contribution. A tax was levied, as well, upon the *Judenrat*. The collection of these taxes was a dangerous business. One never knew who might be waiting at the designated payment site. Hence, the collectors were fully armed. Not all Jews yielded voluntarily; many had to be pressured into handing over the levy demanded by the Fighting Organization.

Marek drew a small packet from under the mattress, then handed me some pieces of jewelry. We were to sell these trinkets on the "Aryan side" for as much as we could get for them, then remit the proceeds to the Fighting Organization.

I shared a plate of potato soup and a slice of bread with the group. Then it was time to leave. We shook hands silently; I was too moved to speak. This may be the last time I will see any of you, I thought, as we parted.

"Be careful when you go over the wall," Abrasha cautioned.

Yurek accompanied me to the ghetto wall. We walked quickly through the darkening streets, passing Jews going home from a day's work at the German shops. At the wall, Yurek went to check with the smugglers to see whether it was safe to cross over now. He was told that it was not; we would have to wait until the German patrols had gone. We picked a deserted building on Szczensliwa Street, where we settled down near a broken window to watch and wait. The smugglers appeared one by one. Now was my chance . . .

"Wait a while," Yurek held me back. "You don't have to be first."

Through the window we saw one woman, then another climb over the wall. Suddenly there was gunfire. We drew back from the window. Then there was total silence. The street was deserted, except for a woman lying in a pool of blood at the foot of the wall. Had Yurek not restrained me, I would have shared her fate. We waited; it was dangerous to step outside.

The ominous silence remained unbroken for an hour. Then, people began moving about. Two men went to the dead woman. One of them shook his head mournfully. Some others passed the body over the wall, where the smugglers were already busily at work.

"Well, good-bye, Yurek. I'm going to try it now." I removed the white band from my arm. We hurried down the street towards the wall. Yurek helped me climb the wall. I jumped down on the other side and was once more on Aryan soil. Immediately, a Polish policeman came up and grabbed me by the arm, but for a small consideration he let me go.

Again I was a stranger in a strange and alien world.

18. JEWISH CHILDREN ON THE "ARYAN SIDE"

One of our tasks as underground couriers operating outside the ghetto was the rescue of Jewish children. The relentless program of extermination carried on by the Germans had left very few children in the ghetto. Of those still surviving, only a small number had been smuggled over the wall, for it was hard to find Poles who would shelter Jewish children.

During the winter of 1942-1943 the Poles had given a compassionate reception to the first trainloads of Polish children evacuated from the eastern section of the Zamoscz region. Women had run to the sealed railroad cars with bread and clothing for the hungry, shivering youngsters. But the same Poles remained utterly indifferent to the fate of the children of their Jewish neighbors in the ghetto. Few of them were willing to harbor a Jewish child, even for money.

We spared neither effort nor expense in trying to persuade Poles to hide Jewish children in their homes. Two new Jewish couriers joined us for that aspect of our mission. They had been recommended by Marek Edelman for work in the "Aryan sector" after they had escaped from the ghetto and offered their services to the Jewish underground movement. Marysia (Bronka Feinmesser), a young woman of twenty-four years, had formerly been a telephone operator at the Jewish children's hospital. Inka Schweiger had been a pediatrician in the same hospital.

The mothers who entrusted their children to us were close to tears. How hard it was for them to part with their little ones after having seen them safely through so many dangers. Would they ever see them again?

Yet, the anguish was mitigated by the hope that perhaps, on the "Aryan side," the children might have a chance to survive.

Some mothers could not bring themselves to part with their children. Once, Abrasha and I were chatting with Manya, the wife of Arthur Zygielbojm.

"Manya," I told her, "we could take care of your Artek on the other side. But the trouble is that we cannot as yet provide shelter for both of you."

Manya blanched, then thought for a moment before answering, "I can't do it, believe me, I can't part with Artek. My son has no one but me now. I guard him like the apple of my eye. Together we have endured all this misery and misfortune. Without me, he would perish."

What could I say to Manya? What assurances could I offer? I wanted to persuade her that Artek would be safer beyond the wall than with her in the ghetto. But I could not speak. Abrasha, more composed than I, tried to persuade her that the ghetto was becoming more dangerous each day, that it was on the verge of a bloody battle. He urged her to think the matter over and send her son over the wall, where he would have a good chance of surviving.

Manya heard him out in silence, the battle between emotion and reason mirrored in her pale, drawn face. I tried my best to describe the place we had found for her son, with an honest, trustworthy Polish railroad employee who had been recommended to us by a co-worker.

"No, I cannot do it." The decision seemed wrenched from her by a force she could no longer fight. "Whatever my fate, it shall also be the fate of my son. We've been through so much together. Perhaps we'll succeed in surviving after all. If not, at least we'll perish together."

And so, Manya Zygielbojm did not part from her son. Both of them were to die in the ghetto uprising.

The truth was that we could never be sure of what would happen to the children we smuggled over the "Aryan side." There was always the danger that they would say or do something to give them away, or that the Poles who had agreed to take them in would go back on their promise at the last moment.

Nellie and Vlodka Blit, a pair of twins, ten years old, had gotten safely over the ghetto wall. Michal had placed them with a family named Dubiel, in a small house near the factory on Czerniakowska Street, where

Michal was then staying. Mrs. Dubiel, a kindly old Pole, had been somewhat disappointed; she had expected children with Aryan features, not brown eyes and dark hair. Nevertheless, she took them in. The two girls spoke Polish perfectly and were careful never to mention the ghetto.

Both girls were greatly distressed at being separated from their mother. They stopped eating, would not speak to anyone and hid in corners. But though they sulked in the presence of strangers, they perked up whenever I appeared. They hoped that I would have messages or letters for them.

"Have you brought us anything from over there?" they would ask the moment I crossed the threshold. If I brought them a letter from their mother, they went into transports of delight.

"Tell us, tell us—what does Mama look like now?" they would plead with me. And I would recount in detail my conversation with their mother, Fella Blit, who had been a teacher in the *Cyszo* schools. I used to meet her on my missions to the ghetto.

The children calmed down somewhat when the Dubiels moved to new quarters on Swientojerska 21, which ran parallel to the ghetto wall dividing the street into a Polish sector including the Krasinski Park, and a Jewish sector bordering on Wolowa Street. The windows of Dubiel's new residence faced the street.

On one of my visits to the children, they ran to meet me crying, "Quick! Quick! Come on in, we've got something to show you!"

They pulled me to the window and pointed to a woman walking about in the ghetto. It was their mother! But we could get only a brief glimpse of her because just then the Ukrainian sentry noticed us and aimed his carbine at us. We withdrew hastily into the room. The Germans did not permit anyone on the Polish side to get close to the ghetto—not even to peer through a window. The little girls told me that they saw their mother every day.

"How did your mother discover your window?" I asked in astonishment.

The elderly Mrs. Dubiel explained that her husband had happened to work in the ghetto for a few days. One day the children that he was hiding had brought him bread and milk and begged him to try to locate their mother and take some food to her. Mr. Dubiel had found their mother and had shown her the windows of his house. Thereafter she had haunted Wolowa Street every day and, making sure she was not being watched, she would walk slowly up and down, looking up intently at the closed windows of Dubiel's house. The little girls would wait for her and peep through the curtained windows.

"And when the Ukrainian sentry is off on a patrol we exchange a few words across the wall or even drop a note," Nellie told me.

Of course, this was a dangerous thing to do. Someone might notice what was going on and report it to the Germans. That would seal the fate not only of the mother but of the daughters and of the Dubiels as well. The girls accepted my warning in silence and without objections, but their dark eyes looked at me in sorrow. I bowed my head with a sense of guilt; why did I have to be the one to cut off the only source of joy left to these children and their mother?

The children survived, but their mother was to perish in Maidanek.

Olesh Blum was six when his mother entrusted him to me. He, too, spoke Polish perfectly, knew that he must never mention the ghetto, and remembered that his name was now Olesh Kowalski. He calmly said good-bye to his mother, but the moment she was out of sight the youngster lost his self-control. In contrast to the drabness in the ghetto, he was suddenly confronted with the hustle and bustle of Warsaw. Like other children, he babbled and kept asking questions:

"Why are there so many cars and trolley cars here and none there? Why are there so many stores with fine things here, and none there? . . ."

Olesh and I boarded a trolley to go the home where he was to stay. I was disturbed by his incessant questions. The passengers began to smile and exchange meaningful glances. I had to get off with him. I was afraid that the youngster would give himself away by a word or act. The child's innocent babbling could bring disaster to us both.

Olesh's new home was the flat of Marja Barkowska at Krochmalna 83, where two elderly Gentile women shared one small room. But Olesh stayed with them only a few days, because they were apprehensive about having him around. The little boy did not cry, but he kept to himself and hardly uttered a word. Neither toys nor candy aroused his interest. He sat quietly, staring into the distance, longing for his parents. When I presented him with a toy, his little brown eyes lighted up for a moment and then sank back into apathy. He often asked, "Will I have to wait much longer to see my mother and daddy?" He never protested or wept, but grew paler and thinner all the time.

New quarters were found for little Olesh with an intelligent Gentile couple who lived on Zoliborz at Wilson Square and who had a six-year-old son of their own. They had consented to accommodate little Olesh for a short period at the rate of 2,500 zlotys a month. There, in the company of a new Gentile playmate, Olesh came to life again, but occasionally he awoke at night crying and ran to his hosts. His mother eventually managed to escape to the "Aryan side," and Olesh's hosts agreed to let her see her son from time to time. The little boy became adjusted to his new life. But it was again disrupted not long after, when the Zoliborz area was raided by the Germans. The boy's hosts became frightened, and he was transferred to a new home in the suburbs. However, he survived.

The case of year-old Krysia Klog was much simpler. She had been placed with a poor Polish family in Pludy, a suburb of Warsaw. Barefoot, unkempt, unbathed, the toddler wandered through the dirty, almost empty rooms. The downtrodden, feeble Gentile landlady paid little attention to the little Jewish girl, since she was hardly able to care for her own children.

The woman distributed all of Krysia's belongings among her own youngsters. No matter how many dresses and shoes were supplied for Krysia, she was never seen in shoes, or in anything but rags. She also looked more undernourished than the other children, although the woman received 2,500 zlotys every month without fail for Krysia's upkeep. Nevertheless, Krysia seemed to feel at home. No matter how she was mistreated, she always reacted with a meek smile and quietly sought a corner in which to hide.

Though aware of the child's wretched surroundings, we had to keep her there—it was still safer than the ghetto. Krysia's parents managed to escape from a train headed for Treblinka. The landlady permitted them to join their child, but it proved to be a shortlived reunion. They were reported to the Gestapo and taken away. The child happened to be out during the raid and was thus saved. We succeeded in finding another home for her. She, too, survived the war.

Six-year-old Else Friedrich and one-year-old Irena Klepfisz—the daughter of Zygmunt and Michal—were placed through a Catholic church. The nuns accepted the little girls without knowing their origin. Orphanages and churches were the safest asylums for Jewish children. The nuns generally could be relied on not to report the Jewish children even when they learned that they were Jewish. There was no fear that the youngsters might be turned out if there was no more money for their support. However, it was difficult for us to place our children in religious institutions. Such placements had to be made by "pure Aryans" who were on good terms with the nuns, and such friends were painfully few.

Great misfortune befell twelve-year-old Mika Perenson. In return for a substantial sum of cash the occupants of Dubiel's house had agreed to take four more Jews, including Paula Flinker, Friedrich's wife, Ruta Perenson, and her son Mika. Both Mika and his Gentile guide, Dubiel's own son, had safely climbed the ghetto wall and were hurrying towards the hideaway when two Polish policemen seized them and put them in prison.

For several days we lived in mortal fear that the two prisoners might break down and betray us, thus jeopardizing the security of the new hideout as well as the Dubiel residence, where the two little Blit twins were staying. Several days later we managed to bribe a policeman to transmit food packages to them.

The first news from the prison was profoundly distressing. Ten revolver bullets had been found on Mika. The child had been tortured to make him reveal the source of the bullets, as well as his address in the ghetto, his mother's name, and where he himself had been going. The Polish prison officials were amazed that a Jewish boy could be so brave.

At first we were at a loss to explain how Mika had acquired bullets; perhaps someone had deliberately placed the ammunition among his things. At any rate, Mika refused to give in; he did not betray his secret. His mother sent us desperate messages begging us to rescue him. But we were helpless; we had no contacts with the police. Only when Stephan Machai happened to meet a police detective he knew did a ray of hope appear. There was a possibility that Mika could be saved by a substantial bribe. There followed days and weeks of negotiations, of promises, of hush money payments and of anxious waiting.

Meanwhile, Stephan Machai and his friends in the secret police kept quenching their thirst on vodka and *shnapps*. Stephan had changed a great deal. He was no longer the kindly person who had collaborated with us for so long, no longer the friendly host who had rendered us great service. He was hobnobbing with underworld characters. Nevertheless, we did not break off our relations with him. After all, Stephan was in touch with the fixers, the shady characters who had Mika's fate in their hands.

At long last we succeeded in saving Mika and his Gentile guide for an exorbitant sum. It turned out that the bullets had belonged to Dubiel's son who had escorted Mika over to the "Aryan sector." It seemed that the young Gentile had panicked and dropped them into Mika's pocket. Shortly before the ghetto revolt, a Polish policeman brought Mika to the ghetto. There he shared the fate of many other Jewish children.

I was particularly upset by my visit to *Centos*, the Orphan Care Center (*Centrala Opieki nad Sierotami*) at Dzika 3 in the ghetto. It was winter. Just before I had set out on one of my missions into the ghetto, Bolek had come to ask me to take a small package of food to his ten-year-old brother, Luzerel, who was living in one of the *Centos* orphanages. Luzerel, together with his brother, had haunted the streets of the "Polish sector" for a time. The unfortunate youngster had hidden out in attics, lofts and among Gentiles, but these refuges always proved temporary. For some reason he could find no permanent shelter and had returned to the ghetto. Finally, he found himself in the *Centos* orphanage. That is where I went to see him.

There was a sort of truce in the ghetto at the time. Some of the German shops were open, and some of the Jews who were still in the ghetto tried to comfort themselves with the illusory hope that for some reason the deportations had come to an end. They still had a strong will to survive. The merest hint that the Germans were relenting in their war against the Jews was enough to rekindle the hope of survival. In order to lull the Jews even further into this self-deception, the Germans had at that time permitted the opening of *Centos* which offered relative security to children whose parents had been deported or youngsters who had returned from the "Aryan side" because they found themselves in danger there, too.

My visit to the *Centos* orphanage left me with an aching void. The street was desolate; there was no one in sight. Moreover, the orphanage was close to the *Umschlagplatz*, where the trains to the death camps were ever present.

When I entered the building, it seemed deserted. At first, I was not sure whether I had come to the right place. Only as I climbed the stairs to the second floor did I hear the faint echo of children's voices. A boy appeared in the dim corridor. Frightened, he asked me something and disappeared before I could answer. He soon returned, accompanied by an elderly man, who scrutinized me for a moment or two and questioned me in Polish as to where I had come from and the purpose of my visit.

His penetrating questions disturbed me; at the same time, there was something familiar about my interrogator's voice and Polish diction. It was Grinkraut, an old acquaintance. Prior to the war, he had been a substitute teacher of Polish at the Jewish *folkshul* from which I had graduated. I remembered him as good-natured, modest, forever smiling, with eyes that sparkled behind his glasses. As soon as I mentioned my name, he dropped his reserve and became as friendly as he had been in the old days.

We looked at each other in silence for a few moments. Memories of the school, the class, the ghetto, flashed across our minds. Grinkraut was now employed at this institution, where he lived with the last of the ghetto's surviving orphans, trying to be a parent as well as a teacher to them. I ventured that, under the circumstances, teaching must be very difficult. My comment brought a faint fleeting smile to the aged, haggard face.

"One does one's best under the circumstances," he replied. He showed me the classroom, the hard bunks, the peeling walls. He said nothing about himself and I did not try to question him about his personal life. Throughout our conversation one thought kept running through my mind: How could one go on teaching children so close to the deportation center? Wasn't Grinkraut aware that all his efforts were worthless because sooner or later a German roundup would uproot and destroy everything?

In the meantime Bolek's brother Luzerel appeared. He was untidy and disheveled, but otherwise he was looking quite well.

"How are things over here, Luzerel?" I asked him.

"Much better than things over there," he answered with satisfaction. "Sometimes there isn't enough to eat, but at least I am here with other children."

I handed him the food package I had brought with me and asked him what message I should take to his brother.

"Nothing in particular," he said. "I would love to be with him, but otherwise things are not so bad over here."

After exchanging a few more words with him I saw he was impatient to rejoin his classmates so I said good-bye to him and let him go.

Grinkraut waited for me at the door. "And what will happen when the roundups start again?" I ventured to ask, but I immediately regretted my question. I should not have reminded him of the grim reality. But his answer was quick and to the point: "If there are any, we'll just go together."

I asked him no more questions and we parted.

A few weeks later deportations from the ghetto were resumed. The *Centos* orphan asylum was not spared; nor were Luzerel and his teacher, Grinkraut.

19. JANUARY 18, 1943:
THE FIRST BATTLE

On January 18, 1943, brisk gunfire broke out in the ghetto. The occasional bark of a machine gun had been a common sound in the ghetto all along. But this was different.

Michal, Celek and I hurried toward the ghetto wall to see what was happening. We could not get too close; a reinforced squad of S.S. and Ukrainian guards was keeping the curious at a distance. It seemed that a major deportation was taking place in the ghetto. Whenever the Germans deported a substantial number of Jews, additional guards were placed near the wall. We were unable to make contact with the brush factory. Anxiously, we remained near the wall, trying, through casual talk with the Polish police and civilians, to find out what was happening in the ghetto. The rumors varied: Jews were shooting at Germans; Jews were resisting deportation; dead Germans lay strewn about the streets of the ghetto. But no one knew for certain what was going on behind the ghetto wall. The Poles were restless; people gathered in knots, exchanged whispers, shrugged, then dispersed.

Was it true that Jews are killing Germans? the Poles wondered. Whatever it was, something extraordinary was taking place on the other side of the wall. How would it affect them, the Poles?

At dusk the shooting stopped. We still had no word from our comrades. For two days there was great unrest; on the third day things seemed a little quieter. The Germans reduced the number of guards around the ghetto wall, but the Ukrainian patrols remained. We decided, come what may, to enter the ghetto and make contact with the Fighting Organization.

On the fifth day after the initial outburst of gunfire, Michal succeeded in climbing over the wall. We waited impatiently for his return. When he came back, he had a report of what had been happening in the ghetto.

Several German detachments had entered the ghetto to carry out a large-scale roundup. The freight cars had been lined up at the *Umschlagplatz*. As usual, the Germans and Ukrainians had broken into the houses and workshops to get the Jews. But this time they found only empty rooms. Forewarned of the coming raid, the Jews had gone into hiding.

Nevertheless, after much effort, the Germans succeeded in flushing out a sizeable number of Jews from the "wild ghetto," the area that had been cleared of German factories and which had not been officially approved as living quarters for Jews. As they were taken, under reinforced guard, to the *Umschlagplatz*, some of the deportees had started to shout, "Fellow Jews, run for your lives! Run as fast as you can!"

That was when the shooting began. The mass of deportees fell upon the German troopers tooth and nail, using hands, feet, teeth and elbows. There was shooting, and a pitched battle ensued. The Germans, caught off balance, became confused. By the time they realized the seriousness of the situation, and had increased their fire, practically all of this group of deportees had escaped and found shelter in the nearest buildings. Dead and wounded, Germans as well as Jews, lay in the streets.

The clash had been instigated by a group from the Fighting Organization under the command of Mordecai Anilewicz. It was the first time that the Jews had offered organized resistance against deportation. Still other skirmishes took place at Zamenhof 56, Muranowska 44, Mila 63 and elsewhere, all carried out by Itzhak Zuckerman, Eliezer Geller, and Aryeh Wilner.

Their only weapons were four revolvers and a few hand grenades. The fighters had hidden inside the buildings, waiting for the Germans to come by with the marching Jews. With their few weapons they had actually succeeded in killing a number of Germans and seizing their weapons, eventually retreating to other positions through attics and alleyways.

Schultz's shop had served as another focal point of resistance. A detachment of S.S. troops had begun an extensive "selection" there of

Jews still strong enough for slave labor. Angered by the small number of Jews he had found working, the German commandant had stepped out on the balcony of Nowolipie 44 and exhorted the Jews below to increase their production. Should their output diminish, he warned, he would deport all the Jews from the ghetto and shoot or hang all those who went into hiding.

Suddenly several shots rang out from an entranceway facing the balcony on which the commandant was standing. The German was silenced. As Jews ran every which way for cover, the gunfire intensified. In the melee that followed, Avrom Feiner, the energetic leader of the underground Bund youth movement, whose fighting group had used its only revolver to fire the fatal shot, attempted to wrest a more useful carbine from the hands of a German. He paid for his attempt with his life. But the other members of his group succeeded in escaping.

The Jews barricaded themselves at other points in the ghetto, resisting the enemy with their meager supply of weapons.

On the night of January 17, acid was thrown at a German *Werkschutzmann* at Hallmann's furniture shop. The guards there arrested a young worker, Zandman, who belonged to the Fighting Organization. They found a bottle of acid on him, and were about to turn him over to the Gestapo, when a group of masked men, led by Mordecai Anilewicz and including Gabriel Frishdorf and Boruch Spiegel, close friends of mine who later participated in the ghetto uprising, entered the shop. At gunpoint, they bound the guards and destroyed their records, then left with Zandman, warning the guards not to move for the next fifteen minutes. This bold stroke was carried off cleanly and with dispatch.

Only a few men of the Fighting Organization had taken part in the struggle. Arms for larger-scale resistance were still lacking. Just the same, the Germans, caught unprepared, had been forced to interrupt their deportations. They had received their first blow at the hands of the contemptible Jews. Nevertheless, the Germans succeeded in deporting several thousand Jews from the "Little Ghetto" and from the workshops.

The ghetto was proud of this event. "They panicked," the Jews told each other gleefully, going over the details again and again. Yet it was clear that the Germans would return, that they would relentlessly pursue their objective of making Warsaw *judenrein*.

The Fighting Organization also knew that there was little time left to prepare an open challenge to the latest German attempt to deport all the Jews from the ghetto. Very little could be accomplished with the few revolvers the organization possessed. "Weapons, give us weapons!" was the impassioned plea of the ghetto.

20. THE TURNING POINT

After the January uprising, the Jewish Fighting Organization received from the *Armja Krajowa* (Polish right wing underground army) a shipment of arms: fifty revolvers and fifty grenades. The few Jewish activists on the "Aryan side" were consumed by excitement and spared no effort to obtain more revolvers, grenades, or dynamite. Our one aim was to obtain arms as soon as possible. In the evenings we gathered at Gornoszlonska 3 and dreamed out loud how good it would be if we could manufacture hand grenades ourselves. But we were beset with many difficulties. We had few connections, and there was hardly anyone from whom we could buy arms.

Urgent appeals came continually from the ghetto. One windy Sabbath night, I found Yurek Blones in the apartment of Henryk (Fishgrund) at Senatorska 9. Yurek had just come from the ghetto, where he was a leader of a fighting unit. His dark blond hair was disheveled, his face pale and grim, his clothes torn from the climb over the wall.

He had come on a special mission, he explained. Frantic preparations were being made within the ghetto for the forthcoming struggle. There was a great shortage of weapons; he had come especially to expedite the procurement of arms.

"But we hardly know anyone from whom we could get more arms," I tried to explain.

"That is your problem. We in the ghetto can't help you with that," he retorted. "All I want is to urge you to hurry—or else it may be too late."

Yurek remained on the "Aryan side" for one day. I took him to my apartment at Gornoszlonska 3. As I walked with him I was in constant fear that he might be arrested. He looked so typically Jewish with his dark eyes in a gaunt face. Michal, Celek, and I spent the day with him, discussing the situation in the ghetto.

"We, the Fighting Organization, are now constantly on guard; there could be a roundup any minute. Weapons—that is our greatest need!" Yurek spoke vehemently. He asked about our connections with the Gentiles.

Our report was hardly encouraging. Yurek, usually a good-natured fellow, lost his temper. "Are we actually to be left defenseless?" he shouted. It was hard for him to accept the reality of our tragic plight, and he kept on repeating, his voice breaking, "Tell me, why are they helping us so little?"

What could we say to him, when we ourselves were asking the same questions?

"If only this could be done without outside help," someone muttered under his breath.

Michal listened, hardly participating in our conversation. Now and then he got up, took a few paces around the room, and sat down again.

At dusk I accompanied Yurek back to the ghetto wall, leaving him at the corner of Krasinski Square and Swientojerska Street. I saw him talk to a Polish policeman, then hand him some money; whereupon the policeman turned away and Yurek climbed over the wall and disappeared from my sight. This time it had gone smoothly.

What could we do? Where could we get arms? Time was running out.

The following morning, Michal met me in the cellar on Gornoszlonska Street. He was carrying a chemistry book.

"Hurry up—I want to explain something to you," he said.

He read from the book a passage dealing with the possibilities of mixing potash, hydrochloric acid, cyanide, sugar, and gasoline to manufacture homemade bombs. Chemical formulae filled my head, together with the thought that all this might yield some tangible results.

"It's worth a try," Michal concluded.

"But what about the equipment?" I asked, skeptically.

"We'll try to mix the chemicals in ordinary bottles. They could work like shells or hand grenades. Something just might come of it," he said excitedly.

"Do you really think such bottles will be useful to our people in the ghetto?"

"Do I think so! If we could only succeed!" He sat up until late at night, studying his formulae.

But where would we find the chemicals and where would we work with them? After a few days, we had collected only a small quantity of the necessary ingredients. We did our mixing secretly whenever our Gentile landlords happened to be out.

Once our bottles were ready and the fuses in place, a new problem arose—where could we test our new weapon? After all, there was bound to be a big explosion, and this could not easily be hidden from our neighbors. Michal managed to bribe his new landlord, Stanislaw Dubiel, into permitting him to perform his experiment.

Late that night, Michal tested his weapon in the deserted lime kiln of the factory where Dubiel lived. With a powerful explosion the bottle shattered and the liquid inside burst into a blinding flame. We had scored a success! Michal was delirious with joy. Later on, he admitted that he had performed this same experiment in secret once before, but that it had failed miserably. But now, at last, we had hope of producing homemade bombs.

Mikolai introduced Michal to a Polish underground officer named Julian, who was an expert on explosives. Their first meeting took place at dusk in a church on Fabryczna Street. Michal soon learned the art of manufacturing grenades, bombs, and "Molotov cocktails." Silent but pleased, he would return from the church, loaded with leaflets and formulae, to sit up all night studying the material.

The Fighting Organization authorized us to purchase and process as much material as possible. We were delighted in the new turn our work had taken. We were no longer dependent on unreliable and grudging suppliers. We were actually making the weapons ourselves. However, we had to guard against informers. It would be impossible to manufacture the explosives in quantity on the "Aryan side"; there just was no room for such a project.

Michal, therefore, climbed back over the ghetto wall to organize small "munition plants" throughout the ghetto under the noses of the Germans. Wherever groups of the Fighting Organization were to be found, they were taught how to make grenades and mix "Molotov cocktails."

Our job on the "Aryan side" was to acquire the necessary chemicals and smuggle them into the ghetto for processing. It was difficult to get the gasoline, acid, and potash we needed. In order not to attract attention, we purchased the "merchandise" from suppliers in various parts of the city, and occasionally had to run the risk of transporting the ingredients across Warsaw by horse-cart. If we were discovered, it would mean death. Until they could be smuggled into the ghetto, the bags and boxes of chemicals were hidden under our own beds.

21. AN INFORMER

The greatest peril facing the underground was that of being informed upon. Several of the *melinas* we used were suddenly discovered and raided; we suffered one blow after another. We suspected—no, we were sure—that an informer was amongst us, reporting to the Gestapo and the Polish police. Our suspicion first fell on Stephan Machai, our former landlord. Stephan had suddenly stopped working and had taken to loafing at home for days on end, sporting new and expensive clothing, indulging in costly food and drink. Where had all his new-found wealth come from?

Knowing Stephan's economic status and having observed his mode of life, we were naturally suspicious. But we could find no incriminating evidence against him, and to suppose that the kindly and generous Stephan had betrayed us was almost unthinkable. He knew many of us intimately, allowed us to use his quarters for meetings, and occasionally even to spend the night there. He knew about the hideouts of some Jews as well; we thought of him as almost one of our own. How could he be working for our enemies?

At the time, Anna Wonchalska harbored a thirteen-year-old Jewish girl named Zoshka Ribak. Zoshka was able to move freely about the city; no one suspected her true identity. One day, quite unexpectedly, Stephan visited Anna at her home under the pretext that he had some minor problem to discuss with her. I happened to see Anna later that same day.

What was Stephan up to? Suspicion nagged at me. I urged Anna to send Zoshka away from the house for a few days and to get rid of any articles that might serve as evidence of the girl's having stayed there. Perhaps, I said, my suspicions were unwarranted, but it was best to be careful.

Anna did as I told her. Two days later Gestapo agents raided her house at night and turned the place upside down, looking for incriminating evidence, but they found nothing.

Was that visit from the Gestapo nothing more than coincidence?

One Sunday morning the Dubiels, with whom the Blit sisters had found shelter, received a visit from two Polish police agents. Fortunately, the two girls were out; they had gone to church with old Mrs. Dubiel. The pious woman was in the habit of taking the two children out on Sundays, and church was the most logical place to go.

Only her husband was at home when the police came. He told the agents that while it was true that he had at one time given asylum to Jewish children, they had long since gone elsewhere; moreover, since his son's arrest he had broken off all contact with the Jewish activists. Finally, the old man boldly invited the agents for a drink at a nearby bar. When Mrs. Dubiel and the girls returned from church, the police had gone. Apparently, they had been persuaded that the old man had told them the truth.

Immediately after this incident, we found another home for the children. Stephan had also known where they had been staying, and we were becoming more and more convinced that he indeed was the informer. Still, we had no proof.

Then came the arrest of Michal Klepfisz. Michal now was living in a flat on Panska 48. One evening, while walking near his lodgings, he was arrested by a Gestapo agent.

We knew a police agent who accepted a bribe now and then. Through him we learned where Michal was being detained, and actually managed to communicate with him. But we were unable to obtain his release. Two weeks later our contact with Michal was cut off. We assumed that he had been deported.

Our anxiety increased, I obtained a new identity card as Michalina Wojczek, giving my new address as Przemyslowa 5. It was not a place of my choosing; it simply was the only place available. I lived there together with my landlady and an elderly woman, bent with age, in a dark, dank room. The old crone was a strange undernourished character, who rarely opened her mouth and hardly ever ventured out of doors. She watched the door constantly to make sure it was bolted. A daughter visited her once a week. I suspected the two women were Jewish. The old lady was utterly uncommunicative, disregarding all my efforts to draw her out. Shortly after I came, she moved away, evidently fearing that I would recognize her Jewish identity.

After the old woman had left, I prevailed upon my landlady to allow my friend, Zoshka Kersh, to occupy the tiny corner the old woman had formerly occupied. Zoshka had escaped recently from the ghetto and had found employment with a dressmaker but had no place to sleep. Several days later, Krysia Zlotowska, a young student who had worked with me at Toebbens, also escaped from the ghetto. She, too, was looking for a place to sleep; for a few extra zlotys my landlady allowed her to share my bunk.

Then we acquired yet another tenant in our little room: Michal Klepfisz. Following his arrest, Michal had been taken to the ghetto along with other Jews who, like him, had escaped to the "Aryan sector." On reaching the *Umschlagplatz*, the prisoners had been herded onto the overcrowded freight cars. Michal knew he had nothing to lose; the train was headed for Treblinka. For a long time he tinkered with a metal screen over the small window in the car until, with the help of several others, he finally succeeded in breaking through it. Squeezing through the narrow opening, he tumbled from the speeding train amid a hail of bullets from the Ukrainian guards atop the cars. Fortunately he was not hit, and lay in a ditch at the side of the roadbed until the train was out of sight. Then he struggled to his feet, wiped the blood off his face, tied a piece of his shirt around his scraped knee, and limped all the way back to Warsaw.

Celek and I were in our cellar when the door flew open, and there stood Michal Klepfisz, bruised and bloodied, his feet swollen, but very much alive. For two days he was unable to move, but on the third day he resumed his underground activities. However, he had no place to stay. After much pleading on my part, my landlady agreed to let Michal remain for a few days, provided he slept on the floor. The good woman knew that we were all Jews; yet she and her sons accepted the discomfort and crowding in the small room. We were convinced that Michal's arrest could hardly have come by chance. Someone had betrayed him.

Despite our reverses, we continued our activities, procuring explosives and smuggling them into the ghetto, finding shelters when we could for women and children, and smuggling them out to the "Aryan side." Our rooms were always filled with underground leaflets, notices, and forged documents. We kept most of them in my bed out of sight of our landlady. We lived in constant fear. We had reason to believe that the informer in our midst, whoever he might be, was continuing his work. We changed our addresses and identity cards with utmost secrecy. We avoided Stephan. Every evening we met, our faces reflecting our inner anxiety: What new misfortune had befallen us today?

One cold winter morning I was roused by a loud knocking at the door. I looked at my clock. It was 7 A.M. Everyone was still asleep except for Zoshka, who had already gone to work. Who could it possibly be at this hour? The knocking continued and the landlady opened the door. A harsh voice asked, "Does Vladka Kowalska live here?" I shuddered: this was my code name! Michal and Krysia were still asleep beside me.

"No, there is no one by that name," I heard the landlady answer. "The one who lives here is sleeping over there." Heavy footsteps approached my bed. The covers were pulled from me roughly.

"What's your name?"

I opened sleep-filled eyes. Two men were standing over me—one with a felt hat and black mustache; the other stocky and wearing a cap. I sat up, rubbing my eyes and pretending to be surprised. It was obvious who they were; I would have recognized their polished boots and the revolvers in their hands anywhere.

"I am Michalina Wojczek," I answered calmly.

"Now, don't beat around the bush! We know for sure that Vladka Kowalska lives here," the black mustache snapped at me.

I could feel the blood pounding in my head. They had not recognized me; perhaps they would not remember what I looked like. I was determined not to admit anything.

"Yes, she lives here," I answered firmly, "but she left for work at least half an hour ago."

Would the landlady betray me? All she knew was that I was called Vladka, but she had never heard the name Kowalska.

The agent asked her a few questions. I looked about me. Michal was getting dressed without uttering a word. Krysia kept her eyes fixed on the landlady, waiting for her to speak.

"Yes, twenty minutes ago one of them went off to work," the old woman answered in a quavering voice. I heaved a sigh of relief.

"Get dressed, all of you—and be quick about it!" the stocky plainclothesman shouted. "We know who you are. You're all Jews!"

We dressed in silence. Avoiding the attention of the police, I managed to empty my pockets of all papers and shove them under the pillow where there were still other illegal leaflets in Polish, as well as a forged foreign passport intended for one of our leaders, Bernard Goldstein.

My only hope was that the men would not ransack the room. If they did, heaven knew what awaited us. Those who engaged in illegal activities were often cruelly tortured before they were finally put to death, in efforts to force them to divulge the whereabouts of their comrades. Conflicting ideas flashed through my mind. How could we escape our captors? Could we offer them a bribe? There was nothing to lose by trying.

Michal had already reached the same conclusion. He was talking to the men, arguing that, though they had failed to nab their suspect, Vladka, they would at least benefit financially if they left the rest of us alone. But Michal seemed to be wasting his breath. Again I heard the coarse brutal voice:

"You want us to forget all about this for a bit of cash, eh? All right, then. But first tell us where this Vladka Kowalska is working."

Nobody answered.

"Well," he continued, looking at me, "where is this roommate of yours working?"

"I don't know," I answered.

"So, you won't talk, eh? Well, that's all right with us; we have ways to make you talk."

By now we were all dressed and in our overcoats. It was only when we reached the door that the stocky fellow asked, "How much money do you have?"

Even before we could answer him, they were rummaging through our pockets. If only they would leave the beds alone . . . The landlady was standing near the stove, watching us sorrowfully without uttering a word; the two agents were eagerly counting the money they had found on us. Then the taller of the two suddenly announced:

"Two of you can stay here, but one of you will have to come with us as a hostage until Vladka gives herself up."

We stared at one another for a moment. Then I made a quick decision. "Very well," I said, "I'll go with you."

I moved quickly to the door and flung it open. The point was for me to be out of the house with the agents before they changed their minds. Then at least two of us would still be free.

I walked along Czerniakowska Street with the two agents. I was no longer afraid; in fact, I felt almost no emotion. The sun shone brightly and the day was cool. No one in the street paid any attention to us.

"Listen to me. Just tell us where this Vladka is working, and we'll let you go," one of the agents urged me.

"I don't know where she's working," I answered coolly.

"And what does she do after work?" he persisted.

"She never tells me."

Why should I give them any information? I was their prisoner, no matter what I said or did not say. We went on in silence.

"When the Germans interrogate you, don't tell them we took any money from you. Understand?" the man with the mustache said to me.

I looked at him and pretended amazement, "Why shouldn't I tell them? You're not afraid, are you?"

Neither of the two answered. They stopped and consulted each other. They were whispering so I could not hear what they were saying to each other. Suddenly, one of them turned to me. "Go home," he said. "It is Vladka we want, not you."

I stared at him in disbelief. Was I really free to go?

They turned their backs on me and walked away. So—they too were afraid of the Germans. Looking about me, I recognized Michal and Krysia some distance off. They had been following us, to see where I would be taken. Now they embraced me, overjoyed at my narrow escape.

We gave up our room that day, but we had no other place to go. Old Dubiel allowed us to spend several nights at the lime factory. We were now convinced that all our trouble had been caused by Stephan Machai. He was the only one to know where we lived. We sent him several letters warning him bluntly that unless he stopped working against us, we would settle accounts with him ourselves. Celek even talked to some leaders of the Polish underground about having Machai liquidated. But this proved unnecessary. A short time later we learned that the Germans, having no further use for Stephan, had finished him off themselves.

22. FINAL PREPARATIONS

The early spring of 1943 was spent in final preparations for the ghetto uprising. We now lived under constant pressure in a frenzy of activity. The smuggling across the ghetto wall continued apace, and considerable quantities of explosives were sent to the Jewish Fighting Organization.

At our meetings held in the home of Muszkat, in Zoliborz, a suburb of Warsaw, we frequently discussed possibilities of cooperating with the Polish underground, and we often had the opportunity of meeting Mikolai, who was our liaison with the Polish resistance. The ghetto was pleading with them for revolvers, rifles, and grenades. But the Polish underground was holding back. According to Mikolai, the underground leaders feared that the planned insurrection in the ghetto would spread to the Poles before the time and conditions were propitious. Urgent telegrams were also being sent to London through underground intermediaries. Arthur Zygielbojm, a member of the Polish government-in-exile in London, brought pressure to bear on the Polish underground leaders in Warsaw to help us with arms. All of us sensed the final, decisive moment was at hand.

I visited the ghetto on the eve of the uprising. It was dawn. I went as usual to Parysowski Place, with the sticks of dynamite wrapped in greasy paper to look like a package of butter. The atmosphere near the gates was uneasy. Nevertheless, a small ladder was soon put up against the wall. I clambered up with my package and from the top of the wall looked for Yurek Blones and Yanek Bilak, my ghetto contacts. They were not there. Their absence was proof that there was trouble in the ghetto. I would have to retreat.

Gunfire echoed in the distance, and while people ran helter-skelter for cover, the ladder was suddenly snatched away. I was stranded on the top of the wall, holding onto the bricks with one hand and the package of "butter" with the other. I couldn't jump because then the "butter" would have exploded, and there was no one to help me down. The shooting came closer. There was not a soul in sight; the smugglers on both sides of the wall had disappeared. I was left, helpless, exposed on top of the wall.

More shots. I had no choice but to try and jump. I crouched, the package held tightly against me, ready for the leap, no matter what befell.

"Vladka, Vladka! Hold on!" It was Yurek's voice. There he was, at the wall and he helped me down. German soldiers were racing toward us. We managed to dash into an empty building opposite the wall, and run up the stairs. In the attic, we hid beneath a heap of feathers and bed-sheets. The footsteps and voices behind us grew louder and louder. Our hearts were pounding. Would they find us?

Somehow, the Germans overlooked our corner. We lay there until all the noise died away. Only then did we venture out, carefully brushing the feathers from our clothes before going down to the street.

Moving through the nearly empty streets, we hugged the walls of the houses, now and then slipping inside a doorway to elude the German patrols, which had been reinforced since January 18. Every Jew was challenged for his identity card, every package inspected and many confiscated. We made our way through buildings, ruins and attics until we reached the brush factory. Things were in an uproar there; agitated and perspiring Jews were scurrying about, lugging bundles and sacks.

"What's going on here?" I asked Yurek.

"They have just learned that the brush factory is going to be moved out of the ghetto," he informed me.

"Where to?"

"New labor camps have been set up in Poniatow and Trawniki—both of which are close to Lublin. At least that is what the Germans want us to believe. That's what their posters say. Even the children can be taken along."

"And do people really believe that?"

Before Yurek had a chance to answer, we were stopped by Zlata Lichtenstein, an old friend of my mother's.

"I heard that you're living in the Polish sector now," she began. I nodded in agreement, wondering how she knew.

"You probably know that my daughter, Rushka, had a baby before the deportations began," she continued. "Her husband was deported with the rest of our family. My daughter and I are struggling along with the child. Every day, on my way to work, I take the child along in a shopping basket covered with newspaper so the Germans shouldn't notice. We've been lucky so far, but now the factory is going to be shut down, and . . ."

"And so you have no place to hide, right?" I interrupted her. With the package of explosives in my arms, I was anxious to move on.

"That's our main worry just now. We don't believe the Germans. We don't want even to hear about that Poniatow camp. We have a bunker, together with a couple of other Jews, but they don't want to take in the baby, because it may start crying and give us all away."

Her face was deeply lined with anxiety, hunger and exhaustion. Her breath came in short, wheezing gasps.

"I'd appreciate it very much if you would pass on this letter to a Gentile friend of mine in Praga," she continued after a momentary pause, handing me an envelope which she apparently had prepared in the hope of meeting someone to whom she could entrust it. "Maybe she'll be able to help us."

I promised to do so. Then Yurek and I hurried on.

"Everybody in the ghetto is busy digging bunkers for themselves," Yurek explained, "or else they're partitioning attics and lofts for secret hiding places."

We hurried past knots of Jews intently and excitedly reading the wall posters. Pausing to look at one of the bulletins, I stared in disbelief. It was an open appeal from the Fighting Organization! Yurek grinned happily. It called upon the Jews not to follow the orders of the German industrialists demanding that all Jews report to the deportation depots. The Poniatow and Trawniki labor camps were actually new death-camps. Instead of submitting to deportation, the appeal proclaimed, we were to offer active resistance.

Others reading along with us were engrossed in the message, but now and then looked over their shoulders for signs of trouble. They gathered in small groups, discussing its implications in whispers.

"This appeal was posted this morning—and it is not the first one either," Yurek informed me with gratification in his voice.

"In that case the preparations for the uprising must be common knowledge."

"We no longer need to conceal our activity. All the Jews know what we're doing."

"And what about the Germans?"

"The Germans also understand what's in store for them. That's why they promise us such good conditions in the camps."

Toebbens and Schultz, the German industrialists, had warned the Jews for their own good to disregard the appeals of the Jewish Fighting Organization and not to resist the orders of the German authorities but to submit to deportation.

We were stopped once again, this time by Genya Brillianstein, a nurse, whom I knew from before the war.

She wanted our advice: should she go into hiding or should she enlist in the Fighting Organization?

But instead of waiting for our reply, she bade us a quick farewell and was gone.

"It may interest you to know that her brother, Stasio, recently asked to join our group. He is anxious to join us and take part in the uprising," Yurek told me.

I remembered Stasio quite well; we had spent some time together at a summer camp and had worked together in *Skif*. In the ghetto he had kept aloof from us. But now, at the most critical moment, he wanted to join his old comrades.

At last we found ourselves at the headquarters of the Jewish Fighting Organization. There, among many old friends and acquaintances was Itta Weintraub, who had worked with me at Toebbens' factory. She was aware of my connection with underground activities. She asked me quietly whether I had read the new posters.

I assured her that I had read them. I tried as gracefully as I could to break off the conversation. The smuggled package of "butter" that I was carrying could cause disaster should its contents be disclosed by a suspicious German patrol. I was anxious to get to my destination without further stops.

But she would not let me go. "Perhaps you know where I could get a

Mordechai Anilewicz, commander of
Z.O.B. (Jewish Fighting Organization)

Eng. Michael Klepfish,
organizer of armaments
for the Jewish Fighting
Organization, Z.O.B.

Itzhak Zuckerman
("Antek"),
deputy commander
of Z.O.B.

Marek Edelman,
deputy commander
of Z.O.B.

David Hochberg, commander
of a fighting unit

Zygmunt Friedrich, representative of
the Jewish Fighting Organization on
the "Aryan" side

Arie Wilner ("Yurek"),
first representative of
Z.O.B. on the "Aryan" side

Yurek Blones, commander
of a fighting unit

revolver?" she asked me in a furtive whisper. "My husband has been looking for a revolver for the past few weeks. We've been offered a hiding place on condition that we bring along arms."

So, the Fighting Organization was not alone in seeking arms; unaffiliated Jews, going into hiding, also were arming themselves to resist the Germans.

Indeed, the mood of the ghetto had changed. Jews now would resist deportation, go into hiding, defend themselves—at any cost. The Jews no longer believed the promises of the Germans. The ghetto felt impelled to collaborate with the Fighting Organization. The ghetto Jews wanted to stand fast, to hold their ground. Of course, some still deluded themselves and believed the German promises. The majority, however, would not submit to deportation; they would go into hiding in the hope of surviving the German assault. People even toyed with the idea of attacking the Germans, instead of merely disobeying them. The fact that the ghetto was now practically unanimous in its stand against the Germans was in itself heartening. The Fighting Organization was now the spokesman for the ghetto—the agency toward which the eyes of the majority of the ghetto were directed.

The headquarters of the fighting group at Swientojerska 32 had been expanded. Since my last visit, new bunks had been built in the small room, with new recruits occupying them. The door was constantly in motion; every few minutes another person was called into the corridor for whispered consultations. Couriers, mostly girls of seventeen and eighteen, from *Hashomer Hatzair, Dror,* and the Bund, came and went. In addition to messages, they brought revolvers, grenades, and ammunition concealed in their handbags and baskets.

My friends sat on their bunks, cleaning revolvers. Miriam Shifman, wife of Avrom Feiner, came in. She and I had gone to school together. Now she was active in the Fighting Organization. She opened a package she had brought with her and smilingly held up a German army uniform and several German caps for us to see.

"Where did you get those things?"

"At Roerich's shop," she replied. "They're now turning out German uniforms." A group led by Velvel Rozowski was active at that factory, Miriam explained. Although every worker was searched at the end of the day by the German guards, Miriam was able, from time to time, at great risk, to make off with a German uniform or cap.

"It's bound to come in handy," she grinned, with a trace of grimness. There was much joking and an exchange of sarcastic comments as one after another tried the uniforms on. It was one of the few lighter moments I remember from that time.

My friends were eager to show me the new "munitions factory" they had set up in an adjoining room. As the door opened, my nostrils were assailed by a pungent odor. The room was very dark, the windows tightly curtained. Gradually, I made out a long table and several chairs, all spattered by chemicals.

Two youths of about twenty were at work. One bent over a huge cask, slowly stirring its contents. The other cautiously transferred liquid from the cask to bottles, careful not to spill any of the precious mixture. Thirteen-year-old Lusiek Blones turned from storing the filled flasks and drew me aside to ask about the prospect of getting bottles from the "Aryan side." It was his job to obtain the bottles and he had scoured the ghetto to find them. His task was becoming more and more difficult.

The work continued as I watched. The "Molotov cocktails" were lined up against the wall. Everything was painstakingly weighed and measured—a single slip or oversight, and the entire house could blow up. Every face reflected grim determination. Something close to a feeling of sanctity pervaded the room.

"A couple of nights ago we tested one of our homemade hand grenades," a dark young lad said gleefully. This was Romanowicz. He continued, "You should have heard the bang and seen the flash! The German sentry must have been scared out of his wits." The others smiled.

Abrasha had come in. Marek and Yurek supervised the project, but he was its guiding spirit. His calm and assured bearing inspired everyone else with confidence and his practicality and keen observation made any task seem possible.

Abrasha told me that the Fighting Organization anticipated a roundup at any moment. It was expected that the Germans would try to deport all the Jews from Warsaw. The underground was preparing feverishly for resistance. Special observers, changed every two hours, were ceaselessly on the watch for new developments in the ghetto.

"On your next visit," he concluded, "I will show you a whole row of bunkers. If the struggle should go on for a long period of time, you will know where to find us."

I returned to the "Aryan side." Little did I think that I was leaving the ghetto for the last time.

23. THE GHETTO IN FLAMES

The preparations of the Fighting Organization and its representatives on the "Aryan side" proceeded at full speed. No one knew when the ultimate roundup would take place; it was assumed that the Germans would wait until the end of April, perhaps until May, but who could be sure? The Jewish fighters had to be ready at a moment's notice.

On the morning of April 19, 1943, the eve of Passover, sporadic gunfire erupted in the ghetto. It was not the usual gunfire one heard from the ghetto; this time the bursts were deafening. Powerful detonations made the earth tremble. The ghetto was surrounded by soldiers. Special S.S. detachments, in full battle array, stood opposite the ghetto wall. Machine-gun muzzles protruded from balconies, windows and roofs of the adjacent Aryan homes. German scouts reconnoitered through holes drilled through the bricks of the ghetto wall. The streets alongside were blocked off, patrolled by German police on motorcycles.

The battle had begun.

Although all of us had anticipated the uprising, the actual outbreak caught us by surprise. Spontaneously, a number of activists on the "Aryan side" gathered in the apartment of Samsonowicz, a member of the Central Committee. The group consisted of Bolek (Chaim Ellenbogen), Czeslaw (Benjamin Miedzyrzecki), Stephan (S. Mermelstein), Celek (Yankel Celemenski) and myself. Our assignment was to obtain arms, to break through the German lines, and to cooperate with the Fighting Organization in the ghetto. Mikolai was to reach an accord with the Polish underground in the hope that they would help us implement our plans.

We waited for an answer from the Polish partisan leadership. Things in the ghetto were relatively quiet that morning, but by noon sporadic fire had resumed on both sides of the wall. The Germans had wheeled in artillery along Krasinski, Bonifraterska, and Muranowska Streets and it was keeping up a steady barrage. German planes, gleaming in the sun, swooped low and circled above the ghetto. Muranowska Street was ablaze, thick black smoke billowing from its north side. Every few minutes, the ground shook from an explosion; with every artillery volley, windowpanes shattered and buildings crumbled into rubble.

I looked at Swientojerska Street. Machine guns had been trained at the remains of the brush factory. Evidently, the Germans were encountering strong resistance there; the air was filled with gunfire. I could see familiar buildings, now in ruins, floors collapsed, huge gaping holes, pillars of rising dust.

Suddenly, there was a deafening explosion, louder than anything yet heard.

Tanks rolled along Nalewki Road toward the ghetto wall. Thousands of Poles had gathered in the streets near the wall to watch the struggle. They came from all over Warsaw; never before had the city witnessed so bitter a struggle in its very heart. The Poles found it almost impossible to believe that the Jews were confronting the Germans without outside support.

"They must have some of our officers over there," they insisted. "Our men must have organized the resistance." They were stirred, thrilled, exhilarated. They had never expected the miserable Jews to put up a fight. The steady stream of ambulances carrying dead and injured Germans to their field hospitals gave them satisfaction. "Look at all those casualties," they cried with delight as the ambulances rushed by, sirens screaming.

A broadside of fire from the ghetto sprayed the "Aryan" streets beyond the ghetto wall. The bystanders scattered and the Germans threw themselves flat on the ground. During a lull in the shooting, everyone dashed for cover. Afraid to get too close to the wall, the Germans posted Ukrainian guards there to counter the Jewish guns.

That evening Mikolai briefly summarized the situation for us. On the night of April 19th, he said, he had been awakened by a telephone call from Abrasha Blum in the ghetto.

"Active resistance has begun," Abrasha told him. "All the groups of the Fighting Organization are participating in the struggle. It's all very well organized and disciplined. We are now engaged in a battle near the brush factory. For the time being there have been only a few casualties among our fighters. There are more casualties among the Germans."

That was all: no appeals for help, no wail of despair. Just a simple, terse communique from the battle-front.

A second telephone call came on the night of April 22. "Michal Klepfisz is dead. He fell in the fighting. We are short of ammunition. We need arms." The conversation had been interrupted by the telephone central office. It was the last phone call from Abrasha Blum.

What was there to add? Our dear Michal was no longer among us. I could not even bring myself to think about it.

On April 17, his own birthday, as well as the birthday of his two-year-old daughter, Michal had succeeded in obtaining a revolver. Celek and I had visited him in the morning and examined the weapon. Michal was ecstatic; he caressed the weapon and played with it like a child with a new toy.

"If only I could keep it!" he sighed.

Because it was his birthday, we suggested that Michal give us the revolver, and we would try to smuggle it into the ghetto. Michal insisted that since he had bought the gun himself, he had the right to smuggle it in himself. "Who knows," he said, "perhaps I will teach them a little lesson with this little instrument." We pleaded with him, but to no avail. That very day he took the gun into the ghetto, and he remained there to fight, once the uprising had erupted, rather than return to the "Aryan side." We learned later that Michal had fought in the neighborhood of the brush factory, where he had set up the "munition plants." On the third day of the revolt, Zalman, Marek and Michal had gone out to scout the enemy positions. While crossing from one house to another, they were met by a fusillade of machine-gun fire. Zalman and Marek managed to escape. After the shooting stopped, they recovered Michal's bullet-riddled body.

Our thoughts were constantly with the fighters in the ghetto. All our plans seemed to have come to naught. The Polish underground kept dragging its feet, urging us to be patient, to hold on a little longer, another day. Restless and depressed, we idled about the Polish streets, trying to establish contact with the ghetto.

Cut off from the ghetto, we were aliens on the "Aryan side," all alone. Aryan Warsaw watched the Jewish resistance with amazement and observed its toll of hated Germans with grim pleasure; but it scarcely lifted a finger to help. The ghetto was isolated; we on the "Aryan side" were helpless. Extra guards had been posted around the ghetto, making it all but impenetrable.

On the sixth day, the gunfire subsided; the Germans withdrew their heavy artillery and mounted machine guns instead. Stuka dive bombers continued their deadly rain of incendiary bombs. The muffled detonations of bombs and grenades in the ghetto never stopped. Dense clouds of smoke streaked with red flames rose from all over the ghetto, spiralling upward, obscuring the buildings. The ghetto was on fire.

That day I succeeded in getting past a German outpost on the corner of Nalewki and Dluga after I had persuaded the sentry that I was on my way to see my mother at Swientojerska 21, the house of the Dubiels. Perhaps, from the vantage point of their dwelling just outside the ghetto wall, they might have seen something or heard some news. The streets were filled with soldiers. The entire quarter from Nalewki to Swientojerska had been barred to civilians. Numerous German and Ukrainian guards patrolled the ghetto gates, through which a brisk traffic of military vehicles and ambulances passed. The cars of high-ranking S.S. officers stood parked alongside the wall.

I was stopped and interrogated several times by German sentries. Reaching the house of the Dubiels at last, I found it virtually in ruins, littered with debris and dust, windows shattered, walls riddled with bullets. The elderly Mrs. Dubiel was confused and frightened. Every once in a while her husband let some Germans into what remained of the building to search for Jews. Nellie and Vlodka moved about listlessly with silent, frightened faces, occasionally peeping out of a window at the burning ghetto.

During the German raids, old Dubiel had barely managed to conceal the children. The girls had to be rescued—but how? I tried to get near the window, but Mrs. Dubiel held me back; it was too risky. Her husband had almost been killed the day before. No Pole could show himself at a window. I peered through the window from behind a closet. Swientojerska and Wolowa Streets were deserted, glowing dim red from the fires raging in the distance, outlined by the billowing black clouds of smoke that hung over the ghetto. Two groups of German machine-gunners hunched behind a fence at the intersection of the two streets. Germans and Ukrainians in full battle array were stationed every fifteen feet along the wall. At intervals, Germans armed with machine guns darted past on motorcycles, amid occasional bursts of gunfire.

"The shooting comes from our roof," Dubiel told me. "The Germans mounted a machine gun up there. This has been going on all night. Today it's been a little quieter than usual."

"Could I make contact with the ghetto through this house?" I asked.

"No, the area is crawling with Germans," he told me. "You could never slip past them. Stay here for the night, and you'll see for yourself."

Several squads of Germans were now moving among the houses on Wolowa Street, sprinkling some sort of liquid from cans onto the houses and then retreating.

"They're trying to set the houses on fire," old Dubiel said. "Yesterday they tried the same thing, but it didn't work." As he spoke, I could see Germans throw burning rags on the houses and then hastily withdraw. The building caught fire amid a rain of heavy gunfire. Grenades exploded nearby. The earth shook. The flames spread.

"Look over there," Dubiel pointed. On the balcony of the second floor of the burning house stood a woman, wringing her hands. She disappeared into the building and a moment later returned carrying a child and dragging a featherbed, which she flung to the sidewalk. Obviously, she meant to jump, or perhaps to drop the child, hoping that the featherbed would break the fall. Clutching the child, she started to climb over the railing. Amid a spray of bullets she slumped. The child dropped to the street. The woman's lifeless body remained draped over the railing.

The flames had enveloped the upper floor by now and explosions were occurring with increasing frequency and intensity. Figures appeared in windows, jumped, only to die by gunshot in mid-air or on the ground.

From the third floor, two men fired a few rounds, then retreated.

I turned from the window in horror, unable to watch any more. The room was now filled with the acrid smoke and stench of the burning ghetto. No one spoke.

The Ghetto on flames

The Polish population looks on as the Ghetto burns

The gunfire continued sporadically throughout the night. There were no more screams now. The crackling of dry woodwork, the occasional collapse of a weakened floor were the only sounds heard in the eerie stillness that had settled over Swientojerska and Wolowa while the blazing buildings turned night into day.

All night long I stood at the window in a state of near-shock, the heat scorching my face, the smoke burning my eyes, and watched the flames consume the ghetto. Dawn came quiet and ghastly, revealing the burned-out shells of buildings, the charred, bloodstained bodies of the victims. Suddenly one of these bodies began to move, slowly, painfully, crawling on its belly until it disappeared into the smoking ruins. Others, too, began to show signs of life. But the enemy was also on the alert. There was a spatter of machine-gun fire—and all was lifeless again.

The sun rose higher over the ghetto. There was a knock on the door. Quickly I moved away from the window; Dubiel moved to the door. Two German officers entered.

"Anyone except your family living here?"

"No, I do not harbor any Jews."

The Germans did not even bother to search the place; they went straight to the window and unslung cameras.

"It's a good site for pictures," one remarked, "if it weren't for those damned fires."

For a half hour they continued their picture-taking, laughing and joking about those "Jewish clowns" and their comical contortions.

When they had gone, the old woman begged me to go, too. She was terrified, crossing herself and mumbling prayers. The little girls bade me a silent farewell. Dubiel escorted me through the courtyard, the steps, and the street, all swarming with Germans. Afraid even to look in the direction of the ghetto, I walked quickly away, without a backward glance. Somehow, the ghetto fought on. On the fifth day of the uprising the Coordinating Committee on the "Aryan side" issued an appeal in the name of the ghetto. The message was drafted and written at Zurawia 24. From there I brought the manuscript to a store which served as our "drop," and later brought back a package of printed appeals. Written in Polish and signed by the Fighting Organization, the appeal stressed the heroism of the fighters and the ferocity of the struggle. Every home was a

fortress against the Germans. The insurgents sent their fervent salutations
to all those fighting the Nazis.

"We will avenge the crimes of Dachau, Treblinka and Auschwitz," the
appeal proclaimed. "The struggle for your freedom and ours continues."

On my way back from Zoliborz with the package of printed pam-
phlets, I found Bonifraterska Street impassable because of the acrid
smoke. Waves of intense heat rolled in from the ghetto; tongues of fire
flicked hungrily across the wall at the Aryan homes. Polish firemen had
mounted the roofs of the houses in an attempt to stave off the flames
advancing from the ghetto. A German sentry stood by, halting
pedestrians and searching them thoroughly.

I turned quickly onto Konwiktorska Street where I came upon some 60
Jews—men, women and children—facing the wall, surrounded by guards
with fixed bayonets. The unfortunates, including some very small
children, looked gaunt and wild-eyed. Yet none of them cried. Their fate
was sealed.

Three days later I happened to pass the same way. A crowd of Poles
was impassively staring at a roof nearby.

"Some Jews broke out of the ghetto and hid in the loft of a Polish
house," one of the spectators was telling a newcomer as I came within
earshot. "But the Germans found them and attacked the place. The Jews
returned fire and tried to escape over neighboring roofs. Soon afterwards
a tank drove through, firing broadsides. Now you can see dead Jews lying
along the roof."

The burning had now gone on for two nightmarish weeks. Some areas
had been reduced to smoldering ruins. The gunfire had diminished, but it
had not stopped. The Germans marched into the ghetto every morning
and each evening at dusk they withdrew. They worked only in broad
daylight. The Stukas still circled and swooped overhead, raining incen-
diaries on the ghetto without letup; the explosions could be heard
throughout the city.

At night, however, things were quiet. Poison gas was released into the
water mains and sewers to kill any Jews who might be hiding there. Gentile homes facing the ghetto along Leszno, Przejazd and Swientojerska
were burned to the ground by the Germans. Among the houses that fell
victim to the flames was the house of the Dubiels.

Nevertheless, the revolt continued unabated. Jewish resistance continued. The Germans had succeeded in penetrating only a few outer sections of the ghetto, and had contented themselves with setting the Jewish homes afire.

Before long the admiration and excitement of the Poles over the Jewish uprising was replaced by a gnawing apprehension. "What's next now?" the Poles wondered. "Will the Germans turn on us also?"

With their pitiful assortment of arms and explosive-filled bottles our comrades in the ghetto had dared to challenge the modern, sophisticated weapons of the enemy. We on the "Aryan side" were bursting with admiration for them, but we were consumed also by a sense of guilt at being outside the ghetto, in relative safety, while they were fighting and dying. We should have been there with them, amid the roaring fires and the crashing walls.

We stared into the fiery sky over Warsaw. Why was there no response from the rest of the city? Where was the help our neighbors had promised? And the rest of the world—why was it so silent?

24. STRUGGLE AND DEATH IN THE GHETTO

On the eleventh day of the uprising, Zygmunt and Kazik succeeded in making their way out of the burning ghetto through an underground passageway. I met them at my new quarters at Barokowa 2 after they had reported to Antek (Ytzhak Zuckerman). Their hollow, haunted eyes and emaciated faces reflected an inner toughness, a quality that seemed to me a mystical strength drawn from a holy shared experience, upon which I dared not intrude with my questions. They spoke very little about the ghetto proper but kept saying, "Help! How can the ghetto get aid without delay? No effort must be spared to relieve the few ghetto fighters who are still left. If they don't get help soon, even that handful will perish!"

I considered every contact we had with the Gentiles that could possibly be of use. Nothing seemed practical. The only course that seemed feasible to Zygmunt and Kazik was for a relief force to infiltrate the ghetto by way of the sewer system. Every effort must be made to contact the necessary guides.

Kazik, one of our group, was blond and short-nosed; he looked Polish. From early morning until dusk he was busy making contacts and carrying out missions, returning shortly before curfew to his hiding place. He stayed at my apartment for two days. On the night of the second day, as we watched the flames and shadows of the burning ghetto, Kazik, speaking in whispers, recounted his experiences.

Jewish fighters killed in battle

Captured Jewish fighter

Roundup and deportation

On the second day of the uprising, he had been in a group stationed at Wolowa 6, opposite the entrance to the brush factory, the position which guarded the planted land mine in the ghetto. Suddenly his group caught sight of an approaching detachment of armed Germans. The small group of fighters watched motionlessly as the Germans came closer and closer. Just as the Germans reached the brush factory gates, the group, at a signal from Henach Gutman, their leader, Kazik connected two wires together.

The blast that ensued reverberated through the ghetto. The house in which the fighters were hiding shook, plaster raining from walls and ceilings. A pillar of dust, helmets, wood, glass and human bodies shot into the air. Scores of German dead and injured lay strewn about the street. The mine had exploded at the proper time.

After this, the enemy took greater precautions. The S.S. men hugged the walls as they launched an attack on Wolowa 6. They were routed by a hail of grenades and Molotov cocktails. The successful counterattack and mine explosion were a bitter blow to German self-confidence.

"But that is not the whole story," Kazik pointed out.

On April 19, the ghetto walls had been surrounded by Germans, Ukrainians, Lithuanian and Polish police. The siege, intended for the final *Aussiedlung*, was carried out under cover of darkness. The sentries of the Fighting Organization noted the secret preparations and sent word to their headquarters. The fighting groups were ordered to posts throughout the ghetto: five groups under Marek Edelman in the so-called "brush factory zone," along Franciszkanska and Wolowa Streets; eight groups, under the direction of Eliezer Geller in the manufacturing zone, along Leszno, Nowolipki and Smocza Streets where the German shops were located; and nine groups under Zecharia Artstein in the central ghetto, along Gesia, Zamenhof, Mila, and Nalewki Streets. Headquarters, under the command of Mordecai Anilewicz, were in a bunker at Mila 18. Couriers criss-crossed the ghetto, warning the community of the imminent roundup and exhorting everyone to resist deportation. Under cover of darkness, the Jews took to their prepared hideouts in cellars and bunkers, in lofts and attics, ready for the inevitable.

The next morning, German columns in full battle array came marching through the desolate streets of the ghetto. At the corner of Nalewki and Gesia, they suddenly encountered a hail of bullets, grenades and Molotov cocktails from behind the windows, balconies and gates of Nalewki 33. Bewildered by the unexpected assault, the Germans beat a hasty retreat, only to return shortly with reinforcements, machine guns blazing. The Germans set up a barricade to ward off the bullets and Molotov cocktails. Nevertheless, the fierce defense of the Jewish fighters prevailed and, after heavy losses, the Germans were forced to retreat a second time. The defenders suffered no casualties. After setting fire to a Germans arms cache in the same building, the Jewish fighters shifted to a new position.

A German column advancing along Zamenhof Street showed greater caution. Nevertheless, it drew raking fire from three resistance groups located in Mila 28 and Zamenhof 29 and 50. The Jewish counterattack was so intense that the panic-stricken Germans themselves ducked behind doorways and scurried into deserted houses. The Jewish fighters aimed their Molotov cocktails with deadly precision. Scores of Germans were killed. The Germans began to retreat, only to be cut off by the group at Zamenhof 29. Two tanks came to the support of the harried Germans. A well-aimed Molotov cocktail put one out of commission; the other turned back. The survivors of the German column retreated under a hail of bullets, leaving many dead and wounded. Once again the insurgents had been victorious. Their enthusiasm was tremendous. It was the first time they had seen so many casualties, the first time they had triumphed over a detachment of the invincible *Wehrmacht*.

That same day, a last-ditch fight took place on Muranowska Square, where a combat group organized by the Revisionist Zionists, an underground organization in the ghetto, rather well armed, fought independently of the Fighting Organization. They repulsed several enemy attacks and for two days kept the Muranow district completely clear of Germans.

The Nazis made several cautious attempts to invade the nests of the Jewish fighters, only to be routed each time. Afraid to penetrate deeper into the ghetto, the Germans changed their strategy. Their aim now was the total destruction of the ghetto. From outside the walls they rained heavy artillery shells on the ghetto while their aircraft dropped incendiary bombs on pockets of resistance. Entire streets were set afire. Giant tongues of flame and billows of smoke rose from the battleground. The conflagration devoured more and more territory, along with the Jews living there. There was no water to fight the fires; the Germans had cut off the supply of water and electricity. Bloodcurdling screams came from the burning houses. The artillery fire was deafening. During the day the insurgents retired to their bunkers (where numbers of noncombatant ghetto residents also sought refuge) and continued the fight from there.

At night, small groups of Jews went on stealthy forays among the smoldering ruins, mounting sneak attacks on enemy positions. In such operations, the first side to open fire was the victor. Melech Perelman, who had fought in the central ghetto under Leib Gruzalc, headed one such nocturnal mission. Suddenly this group ran into some Germans. The fight lasted only a few minutes. The Germans fled, but two of the fighters paid with their lives, and Perelman was critically wounded in the stomach. Bleeding profusely, he struggled back to his group's bunker. Wounded, he could not be accommodated in the bunker and was sheltered in an adjacent house. He pleaded to be put out of his misery, but none of his friends had the heart to do it. When he saw the Germans approaching, the wounded leader urged his comrades to take his weapons and retreat to the bunker. He was no longer of any use as a fighter, he said, but his revolver might still come in handy. His friends agreed to his request and left him in the house. The Germans, fearing to enter the house, set it afire from the outside. Melech Perelman died in the flames.

The bunker housing the brush factory group as well as many other Jews was located at Swientojerska 30. The initial German assault on the bunker was repulsed. However, the Germans soon returned, aiming a barrage of machine-gun fire into the main entrance to the bunker. Some Jews attempted to flee through side exits, but the fighters stayed at their posts. The escaping Jews came staggering back, clutching their throats. The Germans had been using poison gas! The bunker was being suffocated. The barrage of bullets made any attempt to leave by the entrance suicidal.

At the command of Marek Edelman, the resistance fighters leaped out of a side exit and attacked the Germans. A fierce fight ensued in the small open space. The resistance fighters, few in numbers and short of arms, made every bullet count. When Stasio Brilliantstein fell, Yurek crawled over to him and taking his gun, continued firing. The Germans finally fell back, unaware that the fighters had expended all their ammunition. This encounter had given the few remaining Jews time to escape.

Another bunker, at Mila 29, was suddenly surrounded by Germans, who ordered all Jews to come out. Not one of the defenders yielded. A German grenade opened a hole in the bunker wall, and the firing began. Laib Gruzalc called on his comrades to defy the enemy openly. Then he himself leaped through the hole, and was shot on the spot. The enemy intensified its barrage. There was a side exit from the bunker, but to make escape through it possible, the German assault would have to be halted, at least temporarily.

David Hochberg, nineteen-year-old leader of a fighting group of the Mila-Zamenhof defense, handed his revolver to Berel Tanskroit, his best friend, and with his own body, shielded the breach while the Germans attacked ferociously. He was hit and died instantly. By the time David's body could be removed, his comrades had managed their escape from the bunker.

The resistance of the Warsaw Jews was not restricted to the central ghetto. Zygmunt Igla, one of the few insurgents who survived the uprising, fought in the area of Schultz's workshop and later gave me the following account. By burning the ghetto, the Germans had intended to punish the Jews, and to make them abandon the workshops and submit to deportation. As a matter of fact, the German industrialists had announced publicly that Jews would be permitted to move about freely until a certain date, after which they were to pack their belongings and report to the shops for deportation to the labor camps. Only a few frightened Jews fell for this ruse.

While on a mission for the Fighting Organization, Meir Schwartz and Henryk Kleinweiss had fallen into the hands of the Germans and had been sent to the *Umschlagplatz*. There they stopped Apollion, the proprietor of the plant, and informed him that some relatives of theirs who were then hiding had decided to join the deportees. Apollion consulted the Germans, who agreed to the proposition. Under guard of two S.S. men, the two fighters proceeded to the "hideout." En route, they ducked into a dark alley and, before the guards had a chance to think, several bullets found their mark—and there were two less Germans to kill. The insurgents took the S.S. arms and made their way to their fellow combatants. The time when Jews had submitted to deportation without protest was past.

A dozen groups of the Fighting Organization participated in these battles. The group headed by Heniek Kawa fought at Leszno 74, that of Eliezer Geller at Leszno 76, that of Nowodworski at Nowolipie 67. Velvel Rozowski's group fought at 8-10 Smocza, and Shloima Winogrom's at Nowolipki 40. There were engagements also at other points.

All groups maintained constant contact with each other. The couriers often made their rounds under a hail of bullets to deliver instructions and to keep posted on developments in the various units. Meir Schwartz, Lilith and Tobcia Dawidowicz and others distinguished themselves on such missions.

German attacks on hideouts were met by barrages of homemade grenades, bombs and Molotov cocktails. During one fierce battle, a group under Eliezer Geller was completely surrounded. To avoid capture, the Jewish fighters retreated up the stairs until they could go no higher. As a last resort, the defenders began to climb down a rope from the attic. Some escaped. Shimek Heller, unfortunately, was killed when the rope snapped and he was hit by a German bullet.

At one point, the Germans had surrounded Winogrom's and Rozowski's units in the attic of Nowolipki 43. The defenders lobbed hand grenades down on the Germans, who retreated, only to return later with heavy reinforcements, fighting their way to the top of the stairs leading to the attic. The only available exit for the group was a secret opening leading to another house. It was impassable, however, because it was covered by an enemy machine gun firing from the building directly opposite. Gabriel Frishdorf crept over to a small window, hid behind a mattress, aimed his revolver, and silenced the machine gun. The group escaped in time.

When the Germans began setting fire to entire blocks of dwellings, the resistance fighters followed suit by putting German warehouses and granaries to the torch.

On April 29, a group of about 40 Jewish fighters under Eliezer Geller made their way through a secret tunnel to the "Aryan side." There, with the cooperation of the watchman at Ogrodowa 27, a friend of the ghetto fighter Stephan Grajek, they made their way to a hiding place from which they were driven by truck to the Lomianki Forest outside Warsaw by several members of the *P.P.R.*(*Polska Partja Robotnicza*—Polish Communist Party).

Three weeks after the start of the revolt, the bunker of the garbage collectors at Mila 18, headquarters of the Fighting Organization, under the command of Mordecai Anilewicz, sent emissaries to try to contact the outside. They returned frustrated. There was no escape, no prospect of help from any quarter. They could only wait now for the inevitable end.

On May 8, the Germans surrounded the bunker and ordered everyone out. The insurgents clung to their posts, prepared to resist to the death. The Germans, afraid to descend into the bunker, hurled gas, bombs and grenades from a safe distance. The insurgents responded with gunfire. But they were soon felled by the gas. None would submit to being taken alive. Aryeh Wilner was the first to call for suicide. One by one, the other defenders followed him, turning their weapons upon themselves. Somehow, two escaped through a side exit. They were among the very few whose fortitude and idealism inspired the ghetto Jews to challenge and resist the enemy—and who had survived. Most of the members of the Fighting Organization, together with thousands upon thousands of fellow Jews, gave their lives in the struggle.

In the final agonizing days of the heroic struggle of resistance, all those who had perished in the hideouts and bunkers, all those who had fallen in the unequal fight, were united by a unanimous will to resist, to fight deportation, and to die with dignity. Exactly how many of them died no one will ever know.

S.S. General Stroop, commander of the forces that had destroyed the Warsaw ghetto, reported to his superiors that the uprising was liquidated on May 16, 1943. This is not true. Even after the death of the commanding officers of the Fighting Organization, and even after an additional 50 fighters had escaped to the "Aryan side" by way of the sewers, groups under Zechariah Artstein and Yosef Farber, together with other ghetto Jews, continued the struggle. Isolated gunfire in the ghetto continued for many weeks more.

The Warsaw ghetto uprising ended only after the last Jewish insurgent in the ghetto had perished.

On the fifth day of the ghetto uprising, Mordecai Anilewicz sent a note to his representative on the "Aryan side." The text of this communique best reflects the magnificent pride, the rare exaltation, with which the ghetto insurgents faced their struggle and their death:

April 23, 1943

"Dear Itzhak:

I don't know what to write to you. Let's leave out personal matters this time. I must tell you how my comrades and I feel. Something has happened beyond our wildest dreams; the Germans had to flee from the ghetto twice. One of our units held out for forty minutes, another for over six hours. The mine we laid in the area of the brushmakers' shop went off. . . .

All the workshops in the ghetto and outside are closed, except for Werterfassung, Trans-Avia and Daring. There are many fires in the ghetto. Yesterday the hospital was burning. Schmerling has reappeared. Lichtenbaum was saved from the *Umschlag*. Not many people have been taken out of the ghetto. The situation in the shops is different. I have no details. By day we sit in our hiding places.

I cannot describe to you the conditions under which Jews are living. Only exceptional individuals will survive. The rest will die, sooner or later. Their fate is sealed. In all the bunkers where our comrades are hiding it is already impossible to light a candle for lack of air.

As of this evening we are switching to partisan methods of action. Three units are going out tonight, to patrol the area and acquire ammunition.

You should know that pistols are of no use. We hardly use them. What we need is hand grenades, rifles, machine guns and explosives.

Only one man from the fighting units is missing thus far—Yehiel. This, too, is a victory. I don't know what else to write to you. I can imagine that you have many questions, but let this be enough for you this time.

Keep well. Perhaps we'll see each other again. What's most important; the dream of my life has become a reality. I have lived to see Jewish defense in the ghetto in all its greatness and splendor."

Mordecai

25. GHETTO FIGHTERS ON THE "ARYAN SIDE"

Life on the "Aryan side" was now hell on earth. Our ranks were diminished daily as our hideouts were betrayed. The very ground seemed to scorch our feet.

Most tragic was the fate of the surviving ghetto fighters. Approximately seventy of them succeeded in reaching the "Aryan side" by way of the sewers. They were taken from there in broad daylight through the "Aryan side" of the city in covered trucks under guard of a few armed underground workers. They hid in the Lomianki Forest, near Warsaw, awaiting help. This forest consisted of low, thick pine saplings. The Polish peasants in the vicinity, afraid to be caught harboring Jews, threatened to report them to the Germans if they did not leave. There was the constant danger that a German patrol might surround the survivors in the forest and kill them all.

We searched frantically for hideouts and explored again every possible contact with Polish partisan groups. We could find very few lodgings in Gentile households now. Our isolation seemed complete. Just as during the ghetto uprising, we felt powerless, impotent to do anything to save the lives of the few who had survived the terrible agony of the ghetto struggle.

The Polish underground had been awed by the heroic Jewish resistance. Illegal Polish publications praised Jewish courage and composed hymns to Jewish strength and fortitude. But that was the extent of the response. Almost no practical assistance was ever extended; not during the ghastly hours of the final struggle of the Jews and certainly not now. Instead we encountered the typical Polish indifference to the sufferings of the Jews and their extermination.

Days passed. The city of Warsaw gave shelter to thousands of Polish underground freedom fighters, but was unable to provide asylum for some 70 survivors of the ghetto uprising hidden in the forest.

On May 13, three days after the insurgents had emerged from the sewers, Zygmunt, Bolek and I met on Starynkiewicz Street with Bolek Nosowski, leader of the Polish Socialist partisan group to discuss the possibility of incorporating some of the partisans in the Lomianki Forest into a Polish Socialist partisan detachment. Bolek and Nosowski traveled to the town of Ryki, near Demblin, to get a first-hand view of the situation. Bolek returned with a negative answer; it would be impossible to maintain a Jewish partisan group there, he claimed. The Polish partisans found refuge among the peasants, who were unable—and unwilling—to shelter Jews.

Antek sought contacts through the Armja Ludowa, the underground of the left wing parties, which had helped rescue the last insurgents from the ghetto. Any hiding place offered by Gentiles which might prove safer than the woods was eagerly welcomed.

In the town of Pludy, near Warsaw, a Gentile peasant, who at the time was sheltering a family named Wasserman, agreed to take in four more Jews. Yurek, Lusiek, and Gutta Blones, together with Faigele Goldstein had been hiding in the forest. Zygmunt picked them up in a truck which he had purchased for this purpose with money from the Coordinating Committee on the "Aryan side." After an uneventful journey, the group arrived in Pludy. The truck stopped near a grove, not far from the Gentile's hut. Zygmunt left his friends and went to inform the landlord of their arrival. But at the door he found himself surrounded by the police. He was searched, the revolver was found on his person and he was taken into custody.

The other four waited with rising anxiety for Zygmunt's return. Dusk set in. It had been a sultry day, and everyone was very thirsty, especially Yurek, who was ill and feverish. Finally, his need overcoming his good sense, he approached the nearest hut to plead for water. There was no one in sight. He tapped cautiously on the door. The knock was answered by the peasant with whom the bargain had been struck, but he denied all knowledge of any Zygmunt. Nevertheless, he said, he was willing to shelter Yurek and his friends for a few days, but they would have to come after dark to avoid being seen by the neighbors. After dark the four ghetto fighters crept to the peasant's hut and were locked up in a small room, where, exhausted, they fell asleep, only to be taken a few hours later by a contingent of Polish police, who overpowered them after a bitter struggle.

The next day, the captives were bound, handcuffed, and carted through Pludy and the neighboring villages, with placards proclaiming:

"They will be shot. They are Jewish bandits. That's how all
Jews will be taken care of. Those who help such people will
be dealt with in the same way."

The very next day, the four ghetto fighters were shot.

I was numbed by shock and the sense of loss, incapable of accepting the fact that these friends were gone. They had been classmates, friends, associates. Together, we had endured terror, sorrows and agony in the ghetto. They had been my collaborators in hazardous missions. With them I had planned and plotted. Together we had evaded and outwitted our German oppressors, succored and saved other Jews. It was impossible that I should become reconciled to their deaths. The pain of loss was so great it made mourning meaningless. The tragedy lay upon my consciousness like a smothering blanket, choking my emotions.

They still live in my memory, as they were in their brief brave lives:

I see Zygmunt, standing tall, with lively blue eyes, always restless. He had been impatient to buy that truck with which to rescue the insurgents. The price was 75,000 zlotys, an exorbitant sum, but he was not to be deterred. And he had pressed his search for an honest and competent driver. "They must be rescued as quickly as possible," he said over and over. He had known that he was risking his life to save his comrades, and now he had paid with it—and in vain!

Yurek Blones, young and tousle-haired: I had known him since my school years. He had always volunteered for the most tedious tasks and had carried out the most dangerous missions with zeal and efficiency. Yurek had, as usual, escorted me to the ghetto wall at the end of my last visit to the ghetto. "If we found you a hideout on the 'Aryan side,' would you go there?" I had asked him, on the spur of the moment.

He was astonished. "How can you even ask such a question? My place is here. I must stay here and teach them a lesson!"

His role in the struggle had been heroic, his fearlessness and presence of mind repeatedly winning the commendation of the ghetto command.

Luszek, Yurek's thirteen-year-old brother: he, too, distinguished himself in the ghetto battles and had been rewarded with a revolver.

Gutta, their sister, a beautiful girl, had been like a mother to them. She had cared for the brush factory fighting group with zealous devotion and, during the days of the uprising, had stood side by side with her brothers.

Faigele Goldstein, eighteen, was vivacious, stunning, sprightly, always witty. During one of my visits in the ghetto she had accompanied me to her hiding place on Mila Street. Consumed with curiosity about the life on the "Aryan side," she had once remarked, "If only I could get there, that is where one can really live!" She never realized that Jews were dying there also.

I learned later that the Gentile owner of the ill-fated hideout in which this brave group had been captured had betrayed the hiding place to the police. I heard this story from a Pole, Tadek Niewiarowski, who resided at Stolarska 6. This Gentile had worked with Tadek in an ammunition plant, and had related the details of the affair to him. He even complained that the Polish police had cheated him by not sharing with him the money they had confiscated from the Jews. And this was the same man who had once sheltered a little Jewish girl named Krysia—who survived only because his wife had taken her to another hut to hide her from a searching party. How could such a man be capable of so heinous a crime?

Another victim was Velvel Rozowski. He and Marek Edelman shared a temporary hideout which Marysia (Bronka Feinmesser) had found. Two blackmailers threatened to report them to the Gestapo unless they paid a substantial bribe. Velvel went to Fishgrund to see about raising the money and returned to his hideout after curfew. A railroad official recognized him as a Jew and he was taken into custody.

A Polish policeman brought us a letter from Velvel—his last call for help. He was killed before we had a chance to do anything for him.

Tragedy was our constant companion. In a cellophane factory in the suburb of Praga, on November 11, eight ghetto fighters were hidden in a loft crammed with crates and boxes of ammunition and explosives. While one of them was trying to heat a spoonful of ointment for one of the girls who had been wounded, a lighted match fell to the floor, igniting some combustible material which triggered an explosion. The crates detonated one another, and within minutes the entire loft was ablaze.

Eliezer Geller, Tosia Altman, and Meir Schwartz escaped from the inferno by breaking through the ceiling and climbing out onto the roof. With their bare hands, which blistered on contact with the scorching ceiling, they succeeded in making an opening through which the three climbed out. Tosia's dress caught fire; unable to stand, she fell on the roof, helpless. People came running to put out the fire.

"There are Jews there!" voices shouted above the confusion. "Jews are burning!"

The presence of the three miserable Jews, threatened by immolation in the spreading flames, seemed to strike more fear into the Poles than the fire itself.

Someone set off a fire alarm, but no one thought of helping the unfortunates stranded on the burning roof. Eliezer succeeded in scrambling to the ground and, thanks to his Aryan features, was soon lost in the crowd. Meir Schwartz dashed into a nearby house and pleaded with the Gentile occupant for asylum. The woman hid him in a clothes closet. The firemen were followed by S.S. men who combed the area. The Gentile woman was in mortal fear that the Jewish stranger might be found in her clothes closet, but the Germans did not search her apartment. She hurried back after the search and opened the closet. Meir Schwartz toppled out, lifeless; he had suffered a fatal heart attack.

Eventually, the Germans came upon the charred body of Tosia Altman, and rounded up most of the fugitive ghetto fighters. Only Eliezer Geller survived.

The succession of misfortunes crushed our spirits, further depressed as other harrowing reports reached us. Zygmunt Igla was one of a group of survivors still hiding in the forest. As a member of the Fighting Organization, he had fought in the area of Schultz's shop and had performed outstanding services all through the uprising. I first met him at Grzybowska 29, Tadek Niewiarowski's hideout. Igla was a tall young man of twenty-three, with dark eyes and a snub nose, hardly a Jewish face. He was in Warsaw on a special mission from the forest to secure money and arms for his group of partisans and to try to find hideouts for several girl partisans.

In the dim cubbyhole of Grzybowska 29, we spoke of mutual acquaintances and the survivors of the ghetto uprising, about life in the forest and his earlier missions.

"The situation in the woods is quite hopeless," Igla told me. No hideouts had yet been found for his group still in the Lomianki Forest. Tadek, Kazik and Krzaczek of the *P.P.R.* (Polish Labor Party), as well as "Little Stephan," a Gentile, were trying to get cars. After a week in Lomianki, they had been ordered to move to the Wyszkow Forest, where they were to meet with a group of Polish partisans who had agreed to take in some Jewish comrades.

The other ghetto survivors, together with a ghetto team of *pinkertowcy* (undertakers) and gravediggers, formed four partisan groups, one of which was under Igla's leadership. The partisans soon found themselves in unfamiliar territory. Without directives or experience, and lacking effective arms, the Jewish partisans encountered endless hostility from the surrounding Gentiles. Because of their Semitic features, it was difficult for them to procure food from the peasants. It was even more difficult for them to find a safe spot in the forest. The Germans hunted them mercilessly. Deserted by all, without contacts, bereft of leadership and threatened by the treachery of the Polish underground, the Jewish partisans were in constant danger. Some had left, hoping to find other hiding places. Most of them had perished.

One group, comprising Israel Romanowicz, Szymek Shental, David Nowodworski, Henryk Kleinweiss, Rivka Saperstein and Dorka Dembinska, had decided to make their way to Hungary. Before leaving Lomianki, they had stopped at the home of a friendly Gentile for directions. On their way they were seen by a German soldier who reported their whereabouts to the German police. The six ghetto rebels put up a fierce fight, but all of them were killed.

Distressed and shaken, the surviving Jewish partisans had decided to send an emissary to the city in hopes of reestablishing communications with our underground. The mission had been entrusted to Igla, because he looked the most Aryan. Clad in rags, without any documents, and armed with only a revolver, he had finally made his way to Warsaw.

He had come directly to my living quarters at Barokowa 2, only to find the door locked. By some miracle, none of the other tenants noticed him. He made contact through another address, conferred with Mikolai and Antek, told them under what conditions his group was living in the woods, and then returned to his comrades with money and clothing.

In time, Igla became a regular courier for the Coordinating Committee. He was killed together with Gutta Kawenoki, Yaakov Feigenblatt and others resisting the Gestapo raid after their hideout was betrayed.

26. ABRASHA BLUM

When the fighting in the ghetto had ended, the ghetto had been reduced to desolate, smoldering ruins. The Germans were busy destroying the deserted bunkers. The Warsaw ghetto was gone. We, the small group of survivors hiding out in the "Aryan sector," felt bereft. The ghetto had been the soul of our entire struggle, the motive for all our efforts. We had lived only for the ghetto. We had drawn strength and unity from one searing need—to take vengeance.

All that was gone now. What was there left to live for? The smell of the burning ghetto still lingered over the city. The streets of Warsaw were teeming with S.S. and Gestapo patrols, and with jeeps bearing armed Germans. Searches and arrests were the order of the day, even in Polish homes. Huge posters, warning of the "Jewish peril," ordered the arrest on sight of any Jew, warning that Poles who extended aid or shelter to a Jew would be shot. As an object lesson of sorts, the Germans set fire to a house on Kazimierz Square, killing the entire Gentile family living there because they had given shelter to Jews. The Poles were frightened. "The Germans are capable of anything," they said apprehensively over and over again.

Spontaneously, defense committees arose to safeguard Polish homes from "misfortune," a euphemism for Jews. These Polish committees constituted the greatest obstacle to our "illegal" relief efforts. These committees were constantly on the lookout for strangers and reported all new faces to the police.

As a result, it was impossible at first to find suitable living quarters for

163

Abrasha Blum. At the time I was staying in a small room on the fourth floor of Barokowa 2. Stephan Niewiarowski, my Polish landlord, was aware of my identity and occasionally cooperated with us. It was here that Abrasha finally found temporary asylum.

Abrasha directed the activities of the Bund during those critical years. He was the creator and moving spirit behind the Bund partisan groups, in which he, himself, participated. Together with the last surviving fighting groups, he had escaped to the "Aryan side" through the sewers and hid for several days in the Kampinowskie Forest. There he had been befriended by a Gentile who had helped him get to Warsaw. Because of his Jewish appearance he could not move freely in the open. He had to avoid being seen and had trouble finding lodging. I considered it my joy and privilege to have such an important guest in my house, even if only for a short while.

Abrasha had changed very little. His face was emaciated and his lips chapped, but he had remained reserved and serene as ever. He showed no sign of his harrowing experiences in the blazing ghetto. He worked tirelessly, reading, writing, talking at length with the members of the Coordinating Committee who called upon him: Mikolai, Antek, Henryk and others. Every Jew, young or old, whom we assisted, every person whom we contacted, commanded his interest and concern. Yet he spoke very little about himself and others.

I first heard Abrasha discuss the ghetto revolt on the day news reached us that Zygmunt, Yurek, Lusiek, Gutta, and Feigele Goldstein were murdered. He spoke of the heroic conduct of the ghetto fighters, exclaiming again and again, "We did not even realize what kind of people we had fighting on the other side!" His words were filled with love and pride.

Abrasha remained in the room for days on end. I had to be out of doors most of the time. When I returned home at night, I informed him of the day's events. He listened attentively, commenting on items of significance. If some new undertaking were suggested to him, he would ask first, "What do you think of it?" Only then would he offer his own opinion.

Abrasha's tone in speaking of even the most dangerous undertakings was serene and confident. "It's worth trying—perhaps it will succeed," he usually said. The "perhaps" was uttered with such confidence and

Aufruf

An die Einwohner des jüdischen Wohnbezirks.

Gemäss Anordnung der Behörden vom 22 Juli 1942 werden alle Personen. welche nicht in Anstalten und Unternehmen tätig sind, unbedingt umgesiedelt.

Die Zwangsaussiedlung wird ununterbrochen weitergeführt. ch fordere erneut die der Aussiedlung unterliegende Bevölkerung auf. sich freiwillig auf dem Umschlagplatz zu melden und verängere auf weitere 3 Tage, d. h. den 2., 3. und 4. August 1942 lie Ausgabe von 3 kg. Brot und 1 kg. Marmeade an jede sich freiwillig meldende Person.

Freiwillig zur Abreise erscheinende Familien werden icht getrennt.

Sammelpunkt für Freiwillige: Dzika 3 – Stawki 27.

Der Leiter des Ordnungsdienstes

Warschau, den 1. August 1942

The Nazis deceived their victims as to their final destination by giving them the impression they were to be transferred to other places of work. Increased food rations were distributed as a decoy to the starving populace. A poster put up during the summer 1942 period of mass deportations from the Warsaw ghetto promises transfer volunteers 6 lbs. of bread and 2 lbs. of jam.

The historian
Dr. Emmanuel Ringelblum

Leon Feiner ("Mikolaj"), a leader of
the "Bund" and the Coordinating
Committee on the "Aryan" side

Abrasha Blum, a leader of the
"Bund" and a member of the
Coordinating Committee

assurance that any misgivings we might have had vanished. On hearing of the success of one of us or of an escape from a dangerous situation, his long face lighted up with a bright, open smile.

His thoughts were preoccupied with the insurgents still hidden in the woods, but he allowed himself only the minimal emotional outlet of saying sadly from time to time, "I miss them."

Within a week of Abrasha's arrival, his wife Luba, found living quarters for him. He never got a chance to use them. Two days before he was to move, I returned home in the evening to find five men near the door of my room: the concierge, three other Poles and one uniformed German. My first thought was that someone had reported me to the authorities.

"Your keys—and hurry, we've waited long enough!" the German demanded. He grabbed my handbag, took out my keys and opened the door. I was pushed into the room and ordered to stand near the window. There was no sign of Abrasha, but the intruders did not give in. Clutching revolvers, the two Poles searched under the bed, under the table and all through the room. When they opened the closet they gave loud grunts of satisfaction, "There's the Jew!" and dragged out Abrasha.

Abrasha was pale, but outwardly calm. He was searched; then both of us were questioned. Abrasha explained that he had come to see the landlord, but had found only me—he referred to me as "the girl," implying that we were complete strangers. "The girl," he said, had had to go to the store, and, fearing to leave him alone, had locked him in.

Admiring the quick wit that had contrived this fiction and the composure with which it was recounted, I fought to keep my own head as the questioners turned on me. I repeated what Abrasha had said. No, I did not know him. There was nothing more I could add.

The uniformed German was becoming impatient. He did not like my answers; he pounded the table with his fist and brandished his revolver. He ordered us to stand up against the wall with our hands up—"No, not together," he roared. He aimed his revolver and began to count. I watched him, and prepared myself for death.

Then suddenly, he lowered the gun, ordering one of the Poles to keep an eye on us, while he ransacked my clothes and bedding. My friend, Krysia Zlotowska, had left a sack of her belongings with me; he rummaged through them, dumping the cash and valuables on the table. He and his friends were so engrossed in their search that they hardly spoke to us. His task finished, the uniformed German stepped out into the corridor and summoned the concierge. Pointing his revolver at us, he said to the concierge, "These people are Jews. We're leaving; in about five minutes, we'll be back with a car to pick them up. Keep an eye on them."

He stuffed all the valuables and cash into his pockets and ordered his companions and the concierge to follow him. Abrasha and I were left alone in the room. I could hear the key being turned to lock the door. The sounds of footsteps died away. Quickly I lit the gas oven that was in the room.

"What are you going to do?" asked Abrasha.

"Burn all our papers," I whispered.

We worked together, destroying every bit of incriminating evidence. When we were finished, I was utterly drained of feeling, overcome by apathy, indifferent to my surroundings, neither thinking nor caring about what might lie ahead. I sat on the edge of the bed and stared blindly into space.

Abrasha put his hand on my shoulder. "Don't despair," he said, in his soft, gentle voice.

We talked of death, while we awaited our executioners. We spoke without emotion about the various forms of murder to which the Germans resorted.

Time passed. No one came for us. Could they have forgotten about us? Dusk set in; I switched on the light. Everything was quiet outside the door; the curfew had begun. Whenever we heard an automobile pass, I shuddered. But not one stopped at our gate.

"Why not break out of here?" Abrasha finally suggested. He went to the door and tried to open it. It was locked. All attempts to force it open were fruitless. We opened a window to gauge the distance to the roof; it was too high for us to reach. We were caged. One possibility remained: to lower ourselves by rope from the fourth floor. Bedsheets tied together would have to substitute for a rope.

We tied the sheets together and tested the knots. Would they hold? "Let's try, anyhow," said Abrasha.

Then we fastened one end of the makeshift line to the radiator near the window. Abrasha insisted that I should go first. I was younger, had Aryan looks, and my services were needed for the cause. No, I said. He was more important than me. He had a wife and children, and he was the leader of our work. He finally agreed to go first.

We waited until all the other tenants had gone to bed. As the house quieted down, Abrasha took off his shoes and tied them around his neck. We put out the light, lowered our improvised rope slowly. After a moment's pause, Abrasha leaned out of the window and disappeared into the darkness. I listened with bated breath. Suddenly there was a sickening crash and a loud groan. The sheets had snapped; Abrasha had fallen to the ground.

I sank back on my bed. I was sure that Abrasha was done for. The entire building came awake. I could hear the neighbors shouting and pummeling my door, but I was only semi-conscious. I was unable to move.

When I returned to my senses, the room was swarming with angry people who were bombarding me with questions. They were afraid that their house would be burned because of me. Three Polish policemen entered, ordering everybody else out of the room and proceeded to interrogate me alone. I was still confused, and my answers were incoherent. I tried to repeat the account I had given to the German officer who had searched the house. The Polish police ransacked the room again, now and then slipping something into their pockets, but I was indifferent to all that. My only thought was that the end was near. My only question was: What had happened to Abrasha? Was he still alive?

A policeman brought Abrasha into the room. I shuddered. He looked horrible. His face was livid and swollen on one side, his head bloody, his hands bruised, and his mouth bleeding. He was barely able to walk. I appealed to the police to let him lie down. They allowed him to do so but continued to torture him with their questions. Abrasha was weak and incoherent.

I do not know how long the questioning went on. At last, the police sent us out of the room. Abrasha did his best to walk, grimacing with pain. When I asked him in a whisper how he was feeling, he was unable to utter a word.

Dawn was breaking; the streets were deserted. The police took us to the precinct house on Danilowiczewska Street. Abrasha slumped into the only empty chair in the waiting room. A few moments later, however, he was escorted out of the room while I was taken to the office.

Mechanically I repeated my story. After the interrogation, a policeman escorted me through a long, dark corridor, one side of which was lined with even darker cells. I peered through the gratings of each cell searching for Abrasha. I caught a glimpse of him just before I was hustled into a cold and dreary cell near the cell which held him. For the first time in my life I was behind bars. I was dimly aware of a small electric bulb imparting an eerie light to a bare white-washed room and of a heavy iron door being shut. I was too exhausted to be frightened. My head was throbbing and my legs felt unsteady. Chilled to the bone, I sat down on a stone bench and dozed off.

I was awakened by the screeching of the door on its hinges. A woman was shoved into my cell. I could not distinguish her face in the darkness; all I could hear was her wrangling with the guard. Evidently, she was a prostitute or a thief. I pretended to be asleep. I was starting to think more clearly. I had to find some means of informing our comrades of our misfortune. Abrasha's wife and some others were due at our lodgings in the morning. How could they be warned? Could I persuade the prison guard to transmit a message for me? I still had 60 zlotys in my pocket. Polish police could be obliging in such matters, if the price was right.

My cellmate was fast asleep. I tiptoed to the iron door, hoping to talk to the guard. One could never tell.

The guard accepted my money, gave me a sheet of paper and a pencil for writing my message and urged me to be quick about it. He even handed me a cup of coffee.

I pleaded with him to let me see Abrasha. He hesitated, but finally complied, opening the door to Abrasha's cell, then turning away to keep an eye on the central grating.

Abrasha was dozing. I wakened him and, handing him the coffee, told him about the message I wanted to transmit. After a moment's silence he managed to say between gasps for breath, "Remember, don't write any of the addresses of our comrades. The police can't be trusted." Then he added, barely audibly, "Stick to the story that you are a Gentile. Perhaps it will help you . . ."

Those were Abrasha's last words to me. The guard returned, and I had to go back to my own cell.

At 8 A.M. I was summoned for another interrogation. Afterwards, the investigator informed me that "the Jew," meaning Abrasha, would be taken to *Aleje Szucha* at 3 P.M. and that a half-hour later, I, the supposed Gentile, would follow.

Aleje Szucha was the headquarters of the Gestapo. To be sent there was to be sent to one's death. I thought I had become reconciled to the thought of death during the last few hours; but the actual verdict was a shock. Later, back in my cell, I could think of nothing else. My macabre thoughts were interrupted by the guard. He asked whether I had a Polish passport, or a *Kennkarte*, the identity card issued to Aryans. No, I had neither. Why not? Because I had not had a chance to pick it up as yet.

"At which office did you apply for your papers?" he persisted.

I mentioned an office. What difference did it make?

The only way for a Jew to obtain a genuine *Kennkarte* as opposed to a forged document was to buy one from the family of a deceased Gentile. I had no papers made out in my new name, Michalina Markowska. I had always used forged documents with fictitious names and dates. But I thought that all this no longer mattered. I was already doomed.

Again the questions: Who was that Jew? Who were my other contacts? Where was the landlord? I was exhausted and unnerved by those questions. Finally, I was again left alone. For an hour or more I stood leaning against the massive iron door, listening for the slightest sound. No one came for me. Time passed. Surely it was afternoon. The time for our removal to the dreaded Gestapo headquarters must be at hand.

I heard the door of an adjacent cell being unlocked. Someone was being taken out—Abrasha, most likely. I glanced hastily through the grating but saw nothing. Soon it would be my turn. But still no one came for me. There was no sign of the policeman to whom I had given the message. The guard claimed total ignorance. The night passed without sleep.

The next morning, I was informed that I was to report at Gestapo headquarters at 11 A.M. My anxiety grew even more acute, but again, no one came to pick me up. Why were they keeping me here?

At 5 that afternoon, I was taken from my cell. My Gentile landlord was at the door. What was he doing here? Had he also been arrested? His smile allayed my fears. Everything was all right, he said. The police had been bribed. My note had been delivered to the proper address—to Anna Wonchalska, our Gentile confidante, my "adopted" mother, at Krzyzanowski 44. She had immediately informed my friends, who in turn had succeeded in bribing the chief of the precinct with 10,000 zlotys. I was freed within half an hour.

Not so Abrasha. Help had come too late for him; he had already been taken to the Gestapo, never to return.

Abrasha had been the very soul of every aspect of Bund activity—the public soup kitchens, the supervision of illegal cultural activity, the publication of illegal literature, and finally, the leadership of the uprising in the Warsaw ghetto. Abrasha's indefatigable efforts, his humanity, his indomitable optimism and his sincere concern for his fellow man had gained him recognition not only in the Bund, but throughout the ghetto.

Even in the face of death, when he was lying in his prison cell bleeding and in excruciating pain, Abrasha's concern had been for the safety of others. About his own fate, his own suffering, he had said not a word.

27. IN THE COUNTRYSIDE

After I was freed, Mikolai advised me to leave Warsaw for a time. We could not learn who had betrayed Abrasha and me. I had lost my lodgings on Barowkowa Street and I had to change my name again. "Michalina Markowska" was now not only subject to endless harassment by the Polish police, but a prime subject for exploitation by blackmailers.

Unable to find shelter in Warsaw, I looked for lodgings outside the city. Mrs. Dubiel, who had hidden the Blit twins in her house, was planning to spend her summer vacation with her sister-in-law in a village near Siedlce. She agreed to take one of the twins with her and found a home for the other with another Gentile woman. After extended negotiations, she also agreed to take me with her, passing me off as her husband's cousin.

Mrs. Dubiel's sister-in-law lived in a small house on the edge of a dense forest. In the village I had to register with the *Soltys*, the district leader. This created a new problem, because I had no documents. As a last resort I used my old name, Vladislawa Kowalska, under which I had already been shadowed by the secret police.

Endless days of idleness followed. I spent most of my enforced leisure time in the woods. Here I did not have to be tense and uneasy. I did not have to pretend to the trees that I was a Gentile; I had time to daydream and wonder. Why was I here? Why did I yearn so much for the alien world of Warsaw? Would it not have been better for me to have been deported with my family? At least I would have shared their final agonizing hours . . . .

171

My mind filled with memories, visions—of my parents, my sister, my brother, my friends, my relatives, my comrades. In my imagination, I returned to the turbulent world I had known before. I heard their loud voices, my mother puttering about the kitchen. I saw her wrinkled, emaciated face, her keen brown eyes, the swollen blotches left by hunger. She seemed to be smiling. Yes, she could be at ease now—I was no longer starving, and now I could get enough bread for her too. The swelling on her face would soon vanish, if only she could have stayed with me a while longer. But her face receded and harsh reality returned to engulf me with its full force.

My mother was gone—and with her the street, the house, my brother, my sister. Only the gnawing grief lingered. I was alone in the woods, not far from where Mrs. Dubiel was staying with her family, back in a "normal" peaceful Polish world. Back among the freedom and wildness of nature. Precisely here, I felt more intensely than ever the naked truth of what had befallen us.

Sundays were a particularly excruciating ordeal for me. Early in the morning, together with all the young Gentile women of the village, I hurried off to church, carrying my shoes in my hands, like all the other peasant women, and a Bible under my arm. During the murmured prayers, my imagination would carry me back to a world now gone from me. . . . I saw my father standing with his prayer shawl draped over his head. He had died in the ghetto, of pneumonia. There was my mother, weeping as she pronounced the benediction over the Sabbath candles. What would my parents have thought of their daughter chanting Roman Catholic hymns and kissing the priest's hand, whispering Christian prayers! Now and then I became so lost in thought that Mrs. Dubiel had to nudge me as a reminder of who and what I was supposed to be.

Afterwards, I joined the others around the fire station and watched the villagers dancing and having a good time. The solemnity of the morning service and the gaiety of the Sunday afternoon only served to deepen my depression.

I pleaded with my friends to rescue me from my isolation, arguing that the police had most likely forgotten about me. But only after five more weeks in the country was I able at last to return to Warsaw.

Shortly before my return, while still in the country, I was awakened at daybreak by a gentle scraping at the door. At first I thought it was our dog, who had been let out for the night, but listening more closely, I caught a subdued, cautious knocking.

Who could it be at this early hour, when all the villagers were still fast asleep? I heard the landlady open the door and go into the kitchen with someone else. Could it be a partisan? The hut stood at the edge of the forest, and the landlady had mentioned that forest rangers occasionally dropped in.

I could hear whispered talk from the kitchen. I slipped into a robe and tiptoed there. In the dim light I could make out three figures: my landlady, her daughter, and a barefoot stranger. The landlady motioned to me to sit down by her side and then said to the stranger in a friendly tone, "Well, Berko, what was it like afterwards?"

My heart began to pound. The stranger was a Jew! He stared at me in fear.

"You can talk, don't be afraid," the landlady's daughter said to him. "She's one of us."

The stranger sighed deeply, then went on with the story I had evidently interrupted.

"Marcin's boys used to bring me a little bread and a few potatoes every other day or so to my children in that hut on the hill. The forest ranger knew about the children and also about me, but he kept quiet," the stranger was saying. He spoke a fairly good Polish. "But when the *Soltys* found out, he ordered the little ones to leave right away. They left while I was away, and I don't know where they went. Marcin's boys don't know, either. I have asked the Poles in the neighboring villages, but no one seems to know. Or perhaps they don't want to tell me the truth?"

The stranger's voice broke; he buried his face in his hands. I looked at his bowed figure, his tattered clothes, his grimy, scratched hands, and the beggar's sack dangling over his shoulders. I yearned to reveal to this sorrowing fellow Jew how deeply I felt with him, but I had to maintain a detached air, without showing the least sign of kinship, posing as a total stranger, lest suspicion be aroused and all of us be endangered.

Nellie, the Blit twin whom Mrs. Dubiel had brought with her from the city, came in and sat down beside me. The landlady sent her daughter outside as a lookout. Then she handed the stranger a slice of black bread and a mug of cold milk. How I would have liked to be alone with him for a few moments, to shake his hand, to tell him that Nellie and I were

Jewish also. But I dared not stir. The landlady was puttering about in the kitchen, telling Berko the latest local news. It seemed that Berko knew everyone in the village. One farmer had lost a cow, another's barn had burned down, and the son of a third had been deported to Germany for forced labor.

Of what interest could all these stories possibly be to this Jew? He was absorbed in the fate of his two children whom he had left in the woods and who were no longer there. But he did not interrupt his hostess. He sipped his milk slowly, put the slice of bread in his sack and nodded in silence.

As he was about to leave, the woman handed him a few onions. He bowed his disheveled head and, holding out his hand, mumbled, "Thank you. Thank you ever so much."

"You'd better go now, Berko. Day is breaking," Mrs. Dubiel's sister-in-law said.

Picking up his knotted stick, which he had left at the gate, the stooped figure trudged off into the woods. Nellie and I followed him with our eyes until he disappeared among the trees.

"That's one of the Jews of our village," the landlady informed me. "You're not to tell anyone of his visit here. The poor fellow doesn't know that his two children are already dead and gone. The Germans shot them long ago. Poor soul!" she concluded with a sigh.

28. A NEW TRAP

While I was still in the country, a number of visas became available for Jews hiding in Warsaw. The visas came by way of Switzerland, Palestine and South American countries. The Jews for whom those visas originally had been issued were no longer alive, but the Gestapo authorities agreed, in return for cash awards, to give them to other Jews, who then would assume the names written on the documents. Jews acquiring such visas were immediately classified as aliens and transported to a special detention camp in France, where aliens and prisoners of war were kept until they could be exchanged for Germans held in Allied countries.

The glad tidings about the visas spread among the Jews in the city like wildfire. At a time when the Germans had devastated the Warsaw ghetto, when special S.S. troops were assigned to the task of ferreting out and killing Jews, when any Gentile harboring a Jew was doomed, when Polish homes were set on fire and hideouts were reported to the police—at such a time of terror against Jews, the Gestapo suddenly instituted a center for the new Jewish emigration.

Wherever one went, and whomever one encountered, Gentile or Jew, this new emigration was the preeminent topic of conversation. Just imagine—Jews, whom the Nazis had been exterminating until now, were suddenly granted the right to live! The Gestapo was according the status of alien to Jews!

On the other hand, it might really mean freedom. Some Jews were skeptical. Perhaps this was just another German trap. On the "Aryan side" death lurked everywhere for the Jew; sooner or later he was bound to be trapped there. But in this instance, the Germans had to deal with foreign consulates and with the free outside world. Abroad, the Germans would have to account for the visas.

Moreover, if this were a new swindle, why did the Germans demand the payment of so many thousands of zlotys for each visa? If they were trying to entrap Jews, they could snare many more by offering the visas gratis!

True, the Germans were not to be trusted; but how could one neglect such an opportunity for reaching the civilized world? Indeed, the visa transformed an outlawed Jew into a citizen who was respected and protected.

Thus the Jews rationalized, throwing their lot in with this risky venture.

The new hope for liberation seemed to be confirmed by letters which arrived from the first of the evacuees. This group of Jews had indeed arrived in Vittel, a city in France, just as the Germans had promised. Conditions at the camp were good, and Jews were treated with the courtesy the Germans accorded the other citizens.

The fact that David Guzik, who had been an executive with the Polish branch of the American Jewish Joint Distribution Committee before the war, had taken part in the feverish emigration 'undertaking,' served more than anything else to raise the hopes of the Jews.

Wealthy Jews began to abandon their best hideouts and children were being retrieved from shelters at churches and orphanages so as to be ready to leave for France at a moment's notice. Anyone who could get his name placed on to the emigration register considered himself as good as saved. Jews sold their last trinkets—rings, gold chains, diamonds—to raise the money needed for the coveted passports.

The offices at which these visas were issued were located in the Hotel Royal, on Chmielna Street, later the Hotel Polski, Dluga 29. Crowds were waiting there for this transfer to France. Some thirty Jews had been sent from the Poniatow camp near Lublin. I, too, was anxious to appraise the situation for myself.

Unauthorized persons were not supposed to enter the hotel, but the Gestapo was not too strict and admitted everybody. Immediately upon entering the office one was struck by the 'voyage departure' atmosphere. The courtyard was teeming with chattering Jews. Frenzied men and women kept dashing inside to see whether the office was already open for business. Others hurried up the stairs or hauled bundles and luggage to their living quarters in the hotel building. Still others called their friends aside and conversed in whispers.

"Did you talk to them?"

"Well, how much do they want?"

"What kind of passport will you get?"

One day Palestine immigration certificates were available at a reasonable price, while the price of South American visas was high; the next day, the values were reversed. The prices fluctuated with the demand. The restlessness seemed haunted by fear. Amidst the feverish preparations for departure, faces reflected inner misgivings: were they being duped?

Before the evacuees left for the detention camp in France, the Germans addressed them, explaining courteously that once they reached their destination they would have to be patient for a while until exchanges for German prisoners of war could be arranged. The Germans apologized for the hardships and inconveniences of the journey.

"There's a war on, you see," they said. "You have to make allowances for us; we Germans can't get everything we want, either."

These speeches caused some perplexity; never before had the Jews heard Germans apologize or even explain. Some Jews were not only perplexed but dubious; some sought out Guzik for his counsel. Guzik commanded the respect and trust of the Jewish community. His word was the decisive factor. After all, he had sent his own family abroad! If he had such confidence in this process it had to be reliable. Why, he was even able to maintain direct contact with friends overseas! How else could one account for his retaining a position of prominence?

The Gestapo, moreover, did everything it could to emphasize the privileged status of the Jews at the Hotel Polski. There were known cases of arrested Jews being released upon their showing that they were registered there.

Two incidents caused a great stir at that time. Jews were forbidden to leave the hotel, but some occasionally ventured out despite the prohibition. One woman who had obtained a visa was picked up by police while she was out for a walk—a normal occurrence in itself. The woman's friends promptly lodged a complaint with the Gestapo officers in the

Hotel Polski. Using as their "intermediaries" Skosowski, whom the Fighting Organization had at one time beaten up in the ghetto as a Gestapo agent, and Zurawin, another Gestapo collaborator, these friends protested against the "illegal" treatment accorded to the woman, who was now officially an "alien." The woman was set free within hours.

The other incident involved a Jew registered at the Hotel Polski who sought to retrieve some belongings from a Gentile friend to whom he had entrusted them. The Gentile now refused to return the articles. This was an occurrence so commonplace that to challenge it was almost absurd. But, in this case, the Jew insisted to the Hotel Polski "intermediates" that, as an alien, he was privileged to take his belongings with him. Two Germans were dispatched to help him reclaim his property.

While such instances helped to enhance the credibility of the new passports, doubts increased during the month of June. By that time, passports could be obtained for a pittance, or even for the mere asking. All applications were approved almost routinely. Uncertainty began to gnaw at us. Somehow, it all went too smoothly. Could not the entire operation be some kind of trap, after all?

I heard such questions from friends and acquaintances to whom I gave modest aid from our relief funds before they left.

Ziman had misgivings. My friend of long standing, he had a very good hiding place at Grzybowska 29, and had placed his five-year-old daughter with a Gentile woman. He was at the Hotel Polski, waiting for his turn to emigrate, having already attended to the formalities. He voiced his doubts:

"I have settled all the details, but I'm not sure whether I'm doing the right thing. You're actually putting your life in their hands!"

Indeed, a number of our leaders had begun to feel the same way. Yet they could not be absolutely certain. They cautioned against trusting the Germans, and sent out inquiries through underground channels. But they could not definitely denounce the operation. Isolated as we were from the world outside Warsaw, we had no means of proving that the passports were really a German ruse to coax Jews out of hiding. How could we assume the responsibility of urging fellow Jews to stay where they were likely to be liquidated, instead of taking the chance offered them to escape?

Eliezer Geller reasoned along similar lines. I met him at the hotel, his scorched hands still bandaged from the fire at the cellophane factory. "All I want is to get out of Poland; afterwards, I'll be on my own," he told me earnestly. Eliezer was waiting his turn together with Israel Kanal, another group leader in the ghetto uprising, and survivor who had recently returned after staying with a partisan unit in the Wyszkow woods. Even before the uprising he had gained fame by shooting Szerinski, the notorious Jewish police chief.

After all the wavering and questioning, the majority decided to go, despite the risks.

Only when the last transport of Jews was ready to leave did the duplicity of the Germans become fully apparent. As usual when Jews were being assembled for the journey, the hotel was surrounded by German armed guards, and all exits closed. Several military vehicles were in readiness. The circumstances stirred disquieting recollections. Amid growing uneasiness, someone whispered that he had overheard Gestapo officials say something about being "rounded up." And, when the order was indeed given for all Jews present in the Hotel Polski to board the vehicles, there was an eruption of clamor and tumult. *All* Jews were to go? Heretofore, only those registered had been selected! Among those present were many whose documents had not yet been processed or who were waiting for their families to join them.

Running to the office for an explanation, the horrified Jews found it swarming with police. Some Jews refused to get into the vehicles, contending that they would join the next group. But protests proved futile. The Germans searched thoroughly. They left no one behind—not even Guzik.

Among the very few who escaped was my future husband, Benjamin Miedzyrzecki. He hid in an attic and was not detected. Some four hundred Jews were deported to the Pawiak prison.

Within a few hours it became known in Warsaw that half of the Jews with passports had been shot by the Germans in the prison courtyard; the others were deported to the Bergen-Belsen death-camp. Only a few escaped through bribery, among them, David Guzik.

Those of us remaining on the "Aryan side" were both heartbroken and enraged. The Germans had played craftily on the Jews' last vestige of hope for survival. Jews who had miraculously escaped death in the ghetto had now been duped into surrendering themselves to their torturers and executioners under the lure of a legalistic procedure promising final release from the inferno.

Of the more than 3,000 victims taken out of the city as emigrants, it turned out that only 40 or so held genuine foreign passports, which were honored. Only they escaped this final roundup. After the war, I learned more about this tragic episode. The Germans at first respected foreign passports and treated the Jews who possessed them in a fairly decent manner. Jewish organizations abroad made every effort to obtain fictitious passports from Latin American countries for Jews living in the Nazi-occupied countries. And there were even negotiations, carried out with Nazi officials for the release of a certain number of Jews against a corresponding number of German prisoners of war held by the Allied powers. But, tragically, only a handful of Jews were saved by all these efforts. The rest found themselves saddled with forged papers which the Germans refused to honor, and ultimately met the same end as so many of their brethren who had elected not to take the chance.

29. JEWISH RELIEF WORK
ON THE "ARYAN SIDE"

The Jewish Coordinating Committee that came into being in the Warsaw ghetto on October 20, 1942, for the purpose of working on the "Aryan side" in conjunction with the Polish underground, and subsequently, helping the Jewish Fighting Organization in the ghetto, included representation from almost all Jewish political factions. The presidium consisted of Abrasha Blum and Menachem Kirshenbaum, who represented the General Zionists, and Itzhak Zuckerman, who represented the Labor Zionist *Hehalutz*. At the same time, the leadership of the newly-created Jewish Fighting Organization was set up with Mordecai Anilewicz of *Hashomer Hatzair* as commander-in-chief.

Prior to the ghetto uprising, practically all efforts and energy were directed toward arming the Fighting Organization. After the uprising had been crushed, the few surviving Jewish leaders dedicated themselves to helping the survivors of the revolt.

The Coordinating Committee members who had escaped to the "Aryan side" maintained contacts abroad. They sent out reports, letters and appeals for aid through the Polish government-in-exile in London. Funds eventually began to reach us through the same underground channels, first mainly from the Jewish Labor Committee in the United States, subsequently from other Jewish organizations and, to some extent, from the Polish government-in-exile as well. The money reached the Coordinating Committee in American dollars, which were exchanged for zlotys on the black market.

In addition to the Coordinating Committee, there were other relief organizations, such as the Jewish National Committee, the Bund and the Relief Council for Jews, which had been organized by the Polish underground movement. Representatives of the various Jewish political factions participated in the Coordinating Committee, whose representatives were active on the Polish Relief Council for Jews.

The primary objectives of the Jewish Coordinating Committee were to Supply material aid for Jews hidden in the "Aryan sector"; to provide Jews with necessary documents; to find hiding places for Jews; to provide aid for children; to establish contacts with inmates of slave labor camps, with Jewish partisans, and with friends abroad; and to keep in constant touch with the Polish underground.

For all these extensive activities, the Coordinating Committee had the services of only a small staff. Most of the varied tasks were carried out, under the most arduous conditions, by devoted volunteers.

News of our relief project spread quietly by word of mouth among the Jews on the "Aryan side." The Coordinating Committee worked cautiously, fearing betrayal. But calls for help mounted daily.

In Warsaw and nearby areas, we ministered to some 12,000 persons. Among them were Jews from various other cities and towns, such as Piotrkow, Cracow, Lvov and Siedlce. In Warsaw it was easier to go into hiding than it was in smaller localities. It was easier to make contact with clandestine Jewish relief organizations.

Very few lower-class Jews managed to escape to the "Aryan side." They had no money to pay the professional smugglers, nor did they know any Gentiles, and their Polish was usually too faulty for them to pass as Gentiles. Most of the surviving Jews had belonged to the liberal professions before the war and had been successful doctors, lawyers, engineers, teachers and civil servants. Some Jews had smuggled money into the "Aryan sector" in the hope that this reserve would tide them over. They even made plans for the future, placing their trust in Gentile friends with whom they had kept in touch. In most cases, their plans were eventually thwarted and their money vanished, together with their confidence in their Polish neighbors. The assimilated Jewish intelligentsia, the erstwhile merchants and social figures, were transformed into distressed, bewildered paupers.

Very few Jewish children survived, although the Coordinating Committee paid special attention to their welfare, paying for their upkeep and care. We searched them out with determination and perseverance, asking every friendly Pole whether he knew of any Jewish children.

It was impossible to determine the precise number of refugees in hiding. It was rumored that some thirty or forty thousand Jews were living in the Warsaw area. But we were not in contact with them nor were we aware of all of them nor could the Coordinating Committee provide every Jewish applicant with the help he needed. Often, in order to provide a certain minimum for every applicant, the small monthly allowance had to be reduced below the usual 500-1000 zlotys at a time when at least 2,000 zlotys were needed for bare subsistence.

Every applicant for assistance was required to submit a written application to the Coordinating Committee, on the basis of which the committee determined the amount of assistance he would receive. The entire project depended on honesty, good faith and mutual trust. I myself processed scores of applications for assistance, mostly short, scribbled notes indicating abject despair.

"I am the only survivor of our entire family . . ."

"I had a wife, children, a family—they are all gone . . ."

"I escaped from one of the death camps . . ."

"I jumped from a speeding deportation train . . ."

The kinds of assistance requested were as varied as the stories the applicants had to tell. One Dr. Goldman of Piotrkow had survived together with his son. An oral surgeon, he needed instruments. "It is not my wish to impose on your good will," he wrote. "In return for your help, I would be glad to work for you."

There was Blumenthal, an engineer from Lvov whom I met through Wolanska, a Gentile woman. He had survived through his own efforts. After managing to locate his brother's two children, he had found a hideout for them with a Gentile family. He was not asking anything for himself—he would get by somehow, he insisted—but the two little orphans were in dire need of help; there was no money to pay for their upkeep.

Mietek Rozenfarb, of Warsaw, had escaped from Treblinka. He had lost his wife and two children. Thanks to his skill as a tailor, he had succeeded in finding employment and a hiding place by toiling from dawn to dusk for his Gentile exploiter. All he wanted was forged Polish documents. "These papers are a matter of life and death for me," he wrote.

Irena, of Siedlce, was hiding out in a loft. "My hideout is in danger," she wrote. "Try to find another place for me—don't let me die. I am all alone in the world. . . ."

Hundreds of such messages reached the Coordinating Committee, every phrase a world of woe, echoing one single agonizing appeal, "Help us to go on! We want to live!"

Often, when I went to meet a Jewish friend, he or she would be accompanied by some stranger, a man or woman. The newcomer would usually identify himself and, with fear in his eyes, stammer out the purpose of his coming. Usually, he had learned from friends about the assistance being offered to Jews, and usually he was in dire need. Only the Coordinating Committee could save him.

The supplicants were cautious, suspicious and afraid—above all, afraid. Jews on the "Aryan side" were not only wary of the German and Polish police but, in general, of everyone they had not already learned to trust. They avoided new personal contacts. After their experiences of secrecy, danger, blackmail, hunger and deprivation, who could blame them for being reluctant to expose their Jewish identity to some unknown courier, to actually reveal their hiding places and divulge their true circumstances? Yet we had to know, so that the necessary visits could be made at least once or twice a month to supply them with funds and documents, and to find new hideouts for them.

For these visits we enlisted the help of a few reputable Jews who could move about freely in public because they looked and acted like Aryans. I had occasion to work with several such devoted couriers, to whom I would give substantial sums of money to be distributed among the needy. It was our job to keep in close touch with the Coordinating Committee and to see to it that the allotted funds reached their proper destination.

Krysia Mucznik of Warsaw was the most active and diligent of these aides. Beautiful, slender, blonde, about twenty-two years old, she shared her living quarters with her ailing mother, whom she often had to lock in, to hurry off on some errand with which she had been entrusted.

Helenka of Piotrkow, a seamstress, also young and pretty, was another aide. She carried on the relief work among her own townspeople. Both girls survived.

Another was Yurek Igra.

We were able to help many people, but we also met with failure and tragedy. Zoshka Kersh, a woman of good Aryan appearance, had survived the ghetto and was working for a Gentile woman as a seamstress. Her only wish was to rescue her brother—her only remaining relative—who was in the Skarzysko labor camp. She wrote that he could be rescued if funds were made available. Zoshka's request was granted. When her brother was due to arrive in Warsaw, she went to spend the night at the home of the woman smuggler who had undertaken the rescue. Celek also happened to be spending a few nights at the same address. The two awaited the return of the woman smuggler with deep anxiety. Extricating a Jew from a labor camp and transporting him to Warsaw by train was a highly hazardous exploit. Finally, after midnight, the escaped camp inmate and his liberator arrived. It is impossible for me to describe the joy of the sister and brother, reunited after each had thought the other long dead.

Suddenly, there was a knock on the door and the sound of angry German voices outside. In a panic, the landlady opened the door. The Gestapo guards were in search of a suspect who had moved out long ago. Instead they found three other Jews, Zoshka, her brother and Celek. Celek, thanks to his presence of mind and the document he carried, succeeded once again in eluding the Germans, but Zoshka and her brother were immediately removed to the Pawiak prison, where they were put to death.

30. CLANDESTINE LODGINGS

As our activities expanded, the need for living quarters grew. Couriers were constantly on the lookout for lodgings. First priority in housing was accorded to those who were Jewish in appearance. We gathered for conferences and general conversation in such meeting places as the homes of certain co-workers of Aryan appearance for whom receiving guests seemed a normal social function.

At Senatorska 9, Henryk Fishgrund occupied a small room on the third floor. Representatives of the Bund had held their special sessions there even before the Warsaw Ghetto uprising. It was there that I met Abrasha Blum and Berek Shneidmill, a representative of the Central Committee in the ghetto and a leader of a fighting group during the ghetto uprising, along with other underground leaders such as Samsonowicz, Muszkat, and Leon Feiner. This hideout was also visited by other couriers to pick up money, forged documents and "illegal" literature obtained from the Polish underground for distribution among Jews who lived in hiding or who were trying to pass as Gentiles.

Now and then, for the sake of caution, we arranged to meet elsewhere. For a time I made contact with Mikolai in Muszkat's house, dropping in every other day to report on progress and to receive further instructions. But the Gentile landlady became suspicious of the comings and goings, and I had to curtail my visits. Moreover, the constant traveling by trolley to the suburb of Zoliborz was dangerous because the trolleys were constantly raided by police.

Thereafter, meetings with Mikolai were held at Zurawia 24, where

Samsonowicz lived with Wasowska, a Gentile. The landlady, a courageous woman who herself had participated in the underground movement, knowingly allowed us to hold our conferences in her home.
Eventually she even collaborated with the Jewish relief organizations.
Her house served as the central meeting place for the various leading per-
sonalities of the Polish and Jewish underground movements. For this
reason, access to it was restricted. Only a limited number of couriers
could drop in at specified times—and only on matters of urgency. Some
of our illegal documents were hidden under the floorboards, and a camouflaged niche served as a safe for some of the money which reached us
by various means from London and elsewhere.

Zurawia 24 served our purposes until after the uprising in "Aryan"
Warsaw, about a year after the ghetto revolt. Thereafter we used an
apartment at Leszno 18.

This house had been converted into a hideout for Tzivia Lubetkin,
Antek, and Marek Edelman, the surviving members of the military command of the ghetto's Fighting Organization. It also served as a coordinating center for other surviving ghetto fighters, Jewish partisan
groups, and the fighting organizations active in various concentration
camps throughout Poland. Later the house was used by Bernard Goldstein and Rivka Rosenstein. Couriers also met there occasionally.

A most important meeting place, especially for our couriers in the early
period of our work on the "Aryan side," was the house at Miodowa 24.
Inka Schweiger, a young fair-haired, blue-eyed doctor, and Bronka
Feinmesser (Marysia), both of whom looked like good Aryan types, had
rented this one-room dwelling following the uprising with money supplied by the Coordinating Committee. This was the rendezvous for all
our co-workers, mostly young girls with Aryan features, who spoke
Polish fluently, knew how to act like Poles, and did not arouse suspicion
among the Gentiles.

The bond forged among all members of the resistance forces in the
ghetto during the days of the *Aussiedlung* remained strong even after
these people had escaped to the "Aryan side." This was true particularly
of the couriers, who carried on the day-to-day relief assignments of the
underground. Very few of those who visited the Miodowa Street hideout
had known one another before the war. They had come from different
social strata and belonged to diverse political groups. Nevertheless,

together they formed a close-knit group, almost a family, each looking after the other.

The couriers were in constant danger of detection and lived under continuous tension, only seldom relieved by a few hours of respite. Between assignments we relaxed when we could at Inka's and Marysia's at Miodowa 24. There we reported, chatted, or shared an occasional meal. Whoever could move about freely in public, or had come out of his hideout for a few hours, would visit the small room on Miodowa Street to relax and spend some time at the nerve center of our activity. In the warm atmosphere of camaraderie we felt much more secure and at ease than even in the best hideout, despite the fact that it was impossible to hide even a scrap of paper in the crowded room.

If one of us failed to appear there for a time, everyone was worried, because we were always carrying money, forged documents, or illegal leaflets for distribution. We never knew when any of us might fail to elude the German patrols, *lapanki* (roundups on the Polish streets), or the Polish blackmailers.

There was one especially tragic period, when many of our people were arrested, when Igla and Zoshka Kersh had come to grief, together with Little Yuzik (who had indirectly caused the death of several persons). Despondency pervaded the room on Miodowa Street. The unspoken question, "Whose turn is next?" haunted us. Our faces showed what we did not dare say openly: our constant awareness that death was a constant prospect.

There were also cheerful moments, periods when we forgot ourselves and blocked out the reality of the entire nightmare. There were small birthday celebrations, arranged according to Polish custom, to cover up our frequent gatherings. Quite often, in the course of our conversation, a word dropped inadvertently would trigger pent-up emotion, and someone would give way to tears. No explanations were needed; we understood one another.

In this room I met Tzivia Lubetkin, Antek, Kazik, Fishgrund, Mikolai, Celemenski, Irka, Marysia, Zoshka Moszkowicz, Ala Margolis, Krysia, Halina (Perele Ellenbogen) and many other couriers and activists. Somehow, this clandestine center weathered the storm; somehow, the Gentile neighbors failed to perceive the Jewish comings and goings. This underground center was to be our haven until our departure from Warsaw.

Finally, there was the dwelling of David Klin, who had been a Bund activist before the war, and had been a supervisor of food supplies for Jewish self-help in the days of the ghetto. Klin's place was on the fourth floor and belonged to a Gentile official in the municipal gas works. Two small nailheads protruding unobtrusively near the doorbell were, in fact, electrical contact points; if one placed a coin across them a bell inside the apartment was activated. In this way a caller could signal that he was one of our comrades.

Klin had contacts for securing arms. He also owned a radio, so that one could always learn the latest news from the battlefronts—not only from German sources, but directly from abroad. The first time Klin adjusted the earphones for me and I heard the Polish radio *Swit* broadcast from London I trembled with joy. There seemed to be another world—a world without Germans! I listened with bated breath to the fifteen-minute Polish broadcast, calling upon the Polish population to endure, not to despair, not to capitulate or lose hope, that the time of liberation was drawing near . . . I glanced at the others, who were also listening; they were moved to tears, and so was I. I waited to hear something about us, the Jews. Could the broadcast close with no mention of the Jews, the most tragic of all Hitler's victims? It could, and it did. There was a Polish soldier's song—that was the end of the broadcast.

I was overwhelmed by a strange mixture of emotions. The broadcast meant that we were not alone, that we had allies in the fierce struggle against our common enemy, against the Germans! But why had they not so much as mentioned us, the surviving Jews who were continuing the struggle? After all, we were still there! True, there were only a few of us left but still . . . .

31. POLISH FRIENDS

It must be stressed that not all the Poles with whom we dealt were treacherous blackmailers or calculating mercenaries. Most of the Gentiles did, indeed, demand cash for any service rendered. But there were also those who were kindhearted and sympathetic to our sufferings. Some even risked their lives to rescue Jews. Without the cooperation of this handful of friendly Gentiles, the Jewish underground on the "Aryan side" would not have been able to accomplish much. At crucial moments and at times of great peril, these friends enabled us to carry out our missions.

Wanda Wnorowska was one of the first Gentiles with whom I had any contact after I left the ghetto. The widow of a Polish officer, she was in her forties and belonged to the so-called "better" Polish society. She operated a dressmaker's shop where I found employment almost as soon as I crossed to the "Aryan side." Not only was I assured of a job and warm quarters during the winter, but I also had an important front for my underground activities.

When I was called upon to devote all my time to underground work and had to give up my job as a seamstress, Wanda gladly accepted in my place friends of mine who had just succeeded in getting out of the ghetto. She welcomed them all warmly and paid them relatively good wages. Wanda made friends with her new employees, took an interest in their difficulties, and endeavored not only to give them advice but also to help them through her contacts with other Gentiles. Gradually she became one of our confidantes.

Before long, Wanda's home at Wspolna 39 became a secret meeting place for Jews, especially for those who came from Piotrkow and were passing as Gentiles. Generous and kind, she opened her heart as wide as her door to the frantic, despairing Jews who sought her help and counsel. Whatever the problem, be it living quarters, documents, or anything else, Wanda usually knew the right contact to solve it. She would take me aside to discuss "her" poor Jews, insisting that more help must somehow be obtained for "her" people.

I managed to transfer considerable sums of money to her from funds of the underground organization, and she in turn distributed these funds in accordance with our instructions. She never asked anything for herself, and was offended when we offered her money to ease her own strained circumstances.

"You are in worse straits than I am," she said with dignity, declining our offer.

Another compassionate Polish woman who ran great risks for Jews hiding from the Nazis was Juliana Larisz, who before the war had worked for the Zilberbergs, a Jewish family in Praga. When the *Aussiedlung* began, the kindhearted Juliana, responding to the pleas of her Jewish friends, began cautiously to smuggle them out of the ghetto. With her help, 21 of them escaped. Some were hidden in her own house at Brzeska 7; eight were with a friend at Targowa 38. Iza Blochowicz, a three-year-old Jewish girl, was sent to a friendly Polish family in Radzymin, while one Jewish woman with Aryan features was put up elsewhere.

Juliana operated a prosperous meat supply business, with most of the profits providing food, clothes and books for the Jews in hiding. This splendid woman was constantly preoccupied with Jewish affairs, running from one secret hiding place to another seeking to lighten the burdens of the unfortunates. She helped them observe the Jewish holidays and even lent a hand in baking the *matzot* for Passover.

To divert the attention of her neighbors from the huge baskets of food she sent to the hidden Jews, Juliana invited her Polish and German customers in for snacks. Through the thin walls of their hideout, the Jews eavesdropped on the German and Polish conversations, often hearing venomous anti-Semitic remarks.

For some months, everything went smoothly. Then, early one morning, the German police knocked on Juliana's door. The Jews in hiding managed to conceal themselves in time and nothing suspicious could be found. Juliana quietly and calmly answered all the questions of the Germans, but they persisted; they demanded to be taken to the house of her friend on Targowa Street. On some pretext, Juliana managed to slip away from the guards and telephoned her friend. Thus, when the German police arrived there, they found no one at home. Later, Juliana learned that her own employees, suspicious of her activities, had trailed her to the hideouts and reported her to the Gestapo. Undismayed, she continued her work of mercy until the end of the war, sheltering refugees until new hiding places could be found for them.

I used to make the rounds of Juliana's hideouts, supplying the Jews there with forged documents. Of these Jews, seventeen survived: three Blochowiczs, three Ziffermans, four Zilberbergs, four Miedzyreckis, and three Goldsteins.

Pero, a middle-aged Gentile clerk in a Polish hotel on Marszalkowska Street, was another friend. He had become our ally through a Jewish woman named Mala Piotrkowska and her thirteen-year-old daughter, Bronka. Compelled to leave her hideout in broad daylight, Mrs. Piotrkowska, who looked Jewish, wandered about with her daughter in search of lodging for the night. Eventually a band of Gentile hoodlums recognized the unfortunate woman as a Jewess. They tried to snatch her pocketbook, pursuing her with shouts of, "*Zhydowa! Zhydowa!*"

Mrs. Piotrkowska ran straight into the arms of the Polish police, who took her and her daughter to the German authorities. Mala had obtained forged Aryan documents for herself and Bronka and decided to carry on the deceit, although she had little confidence in her prospects. Interrogated about their origins, and about their knowledge of Christian prayers and customs, the daughter gave acceptable replies but the mother fumbled. Both were kept in jail overnight. They were told that unless they could produce a Pole who would vouch that he had known them before the war and that they were real Christians they would be executed.

Pero was the only Polish friend they knew who might be willing to give them such testimony. It was evening. There was no telephone in Pero's home, so they had to pray that he could still be reached at the hotel where he was working. Even so, would he risk his life perjuring himself on their behalf? In any case, he was their only hope.

Pero came to the Gestapo headquarters the next morning, swore that he had known the Piotrkowskas for quite some time before the war, and that they were Christians. When the Germans warned him that perjury was punishable by death, Pero assured them in flawless German that he would never run such a risk, and asserted once again that the Piotrkowskas were good Christians. Convinced at last, their captors released Mala and her daughter and apologized to them for the inconvenience to which they had been put. Should *Frau* Piotrkowska ever be molested or questioned in the future, she had only to report the incident to the Gestapo to be cleared!

Though his own home was under surveillance, Pero allowed the Piotrkowskas to stay with him. Later, we persuaded him to give shelter to still other Jews. All the Jews who found asylum with Pero survived. He himself died as a Polish officer in the general Warsaw uprising of 1944.

Helena Sciborowska of Krochmalna 36 was another dedicated worker for the underground. A small, dark-skinned widow with children of her own, she neglected her own household while she was busy helping Jews. Though her house had been raided because informers had reported her to the authorities, she still occasionally sheltered some desperate Jews there or tried to persuade her Gentile friends to accommodate Jews, often overcoming resistance by cajolery and persuasion. Each time, she hurried to our secret meetings to tell us joyfully of her latest success.

She lived in poverty but whatever money she accepted for her efforts she immediately spent on the Jews under her care or for the sheltering of Jews with other people. She sold her jewelry and donated the proceeds to needy Jews. Many Jews owe their survival to the efforts of this dedicated little woman whose kindness and compassion were pure and selfless.

Unfortunately, there were very few like her. Had there been more Gentiles among the Poles, with hearts and consciences such as hers, many more Jews might have survived.

32. "JEWISH ARYANS"

The common denominator of Jewish life on the "Aryan side" was fear! Fear of the Germans, fear of the Poles, fear of the blackmailers, fear of losing one's hideout, fear of being left penniless. Fear was a constant companion not only of those who, because of their typically Jewish appearance, had to keep out of sight in Gentile lodgings but also of those of us who had the "Aryan" features—fair hair, blue eyes and snub nose—which meant the chance to move about the streets.

The so-called "Aryans" had to blend with their surroundings, adopt Polish customs, habits, and mannerisms, celebrate Christian religious holidays and, of course, go to church. They had to watch their every movement, lest it betray nervousness or unfamiliarity with the routine and weigh their every word, lest it betray a Jewish accent.

Nevertheless, there were always trivial but telltale signs that could not be controlled, and these could betray one's identity. For example, lack of known relatives or reluctance to cultivate friendships with Gentiles aroused mistrust. The eyes were a special danger sign. A careworn face might be transformed by a smile; an accent could be controlled, church customs and prayers could be learned, but the eyes . . . How could one hide the mute melancholy, the haunted look of fear?

"Your eyes give you away," our Gentile friends would tell us. "Make them look livelier, merrier. You won't attract so much attention then." But our eyes kept constantly watching, searching the shadows ahead, glancing quickly behind, seeing our own misfortune and foreseeing even worse to come. Haunted by fear of betrayal, our eyes betrayed us; and this knowledge only increased our fear.

Jews with Aryan features were forever asking their Polish friends and themselves, "How is it that everybody seems to know we're Jews? Don't I look completely Aryan?"

Appearance could, indeed, be faultless, the face authentic, the deportment utterly correct, the speech one hundred per cent Gentile—but we were recognized as Jews. Apparently there was something innately Jewish about us which the Polish eye, particularly the discerning eye of a Polish policeman and, above all, the trained eye of the *szmalcownik* could detect at a glance. The Jews who thought that their Aryan looks allowed them to walk about freely in public were those most often victimized by the ubiquitous blackmailers. Wherever they went, curious and piercing eyes seemed always turning in their direction.

The strain of eluding the *szmalcownik*, the constant changing of names and addresses, the incessant fear of exposure drained the last drop of vitality brought by these latter-day Marranos from the ghetto. The life of almost every Jewish survivor was a harrowing saga.

Benjamin Miedzyrzecki

Picture taken from his first "Aryan" identity card as Czeslaw Pankiewicz in Warsaw, 1942. In the upper right corner is the remnant of the official German stamp.

33. YUREK IGRA

One day, our devoted Gentile friend Helena Sciborowska appeared at our customary meeting place and asked me to come along with her to a small cafe on Chlodna Street where, she said, someone was waiting to see me—someone presumably Jewish and in need of help. It was, she said, a young man who insisted on meeting one of us and who had been introduced to her by a Jewish acquaintance, to whom she transferred financial aid from our funds.

"There he is," Helena whispered when we reached the cafe, indicating with her eyes a gaunt young man with fair hair and an emaciated face, clutching a cup of coffee and staring toward the entrance. When he saw us, he got up from his chair. He said that his name was Yurek Igra. After a few words of introduction Helena left us alone. The stranger launched almost at once upon an account of his adventures.

He had escaped from the Kielce labor camp and had made his way to Warsaw. Though he had very little money, he had managed to buy a forged passport in order to find a job in some workshop, as well as a place to sleep. He wrote letters to himself and mailed them in outlying districts of the city, or traveled to a neighboring village and mailed a food package to his lodgings in the city. He did this in order to give his landlady the impression that he had Polish relatives and friends. Time went on; he was treated kindly, earned his living and passed as a Gentile.

But then his employer hired some new workers. A whispering campaign began, and suspicious remarks were made in his presence. Eventually a friendly worker informed him that a rumor about him was going around in the shop; it was said that he was Jewish. Suspicious characters began to shadow him. He was forced to give up his job and look for new living quarters. But the blackmailers caught up with him. They took from him what they could, and did not cease tormenting him even after they had stripped him of his pitiful savings.

After much trouble Yurek finally managed to find new lodgings in another section of the city. He changed his name and claimed to be a mechanic. Afraid to seek work in another factory, he left his house each morning with his lunch in a paper bag, ostensibly for work, but actually to roam the streets until five o'clock and then trudge home.

But the street offered scant refuge. The Germans conducted frequent checks, during which one was likely to be arrested or taken for forced labor in Germany. He had already had several narrow escapes. The cafes were little better than the streets; even if one stayed clear of the shady characters who frequented them, the sad fact was that he had no money even to pay for coffee. He had sold all his belongings and allowed himself only one meal a day. With no prospect of help from anywhere, he would have been lost if a friend had not put him in touch with Helena and me.

Only a short time before we met, he had spotted the blackmailers who had held him up in the street.

"If they ever got their hands on me," he told us dejectedly, "I would surely be done for."

Within a few days, having submitted the required application and brief biographical sketch to the Coordinating Committee, Yurek began receiving assistance. He soon regained his composure, but for a long time remained fear-ridden, looking about him as he walked, darting into doorways to escape the *szmalcownicy*, of whom he was in terror.

Several months later, Yurek became a part of our underground group, helping me to contact other concealed Jews and provide them with better *melinas* (hiding places).

34. MARIE

One of the most desirable jobs for a Jew in hiding on the "Aryan side" was that of housemaid. It provided living quarters and food, together with a good "cover." Such positions with Polish or German families were much sought after.

Marie Zilberberg, of Aryan appearance and with a fine command of Polish, was a good housekeeper. Seeking a place of refuge as well as a chance to earn a few zlotys, she answered an advertisement in the newspaper: a small motherless German family was looking for a maid with good references. Germans were not so adept as Poles at detecting Jewish traits, she told herself. As reference, she gave the name of a friendly Gentile woman who had agreed to attest to her honesty and diligence. To her great joy, she was hired—no minor accomplishment, a job and living quarters and with a German family, at that!

Alert to possible detection and exposure by other servants in the household, she kept to herself and went out only on rare occasions. She did her work efficiently and earned the trust and approval of her employers. There seemed no reason to suppose that her origins were known or suspected.

One morning, while she was cleaning and dusting, the only daughter of the family entered the room and after observing her briefly asked, without any preliminaries: "Marie, tell me something about the Warsaw Ghetto."

Marie broke into a cold sweat. What could have impelled the little girl to ask about the ghetto? Had she, by some chance, discovered her identity? Stammering in her anxiety, she said she knew nothing about the ghetto and declared that, as a devout Catholic, she had never had anything to do with Jews. The child smiled, and turned away without comment. Marie remained uneasy, puzzled by the youngster's questions. Could someone have put her up to it? For the next few days she worked in a state bordering on panic, not daring to ask for an explanation.

But the explanation came as unexpectedly as the question. One day the daughter pointed to a framed photograph on the sideboard and told her it was that of her mother. "She's Jewish, you know," the girl explained. Her father was a German Christian. When the ghetto had been set up, he had sent his wife there immediately and ordered the daughter never to mention her mother again. That was the last time she had seen her mother; she never dared to question her father. But her curiosity had been pricked by her father's sternness in forbidding her to speak of it, and she hoped that Marie might be able to give her some of the information she sought.

A few days later, the Gestapo paid a visit to the household. Marie and the other staff as well as the members of the family were interrogated. Afterwards the little girl confided to the maid that the Gestapo was still looking for her mother.

"They don't believe my father," she said. "They think she's hidden somewhere in the house."

From that time on, Marie lived in constant fear that her German employer would report her to the police. If he could act so heartlessly toward his own wife, he would certainly not spare a servant. To make matters worse, she could not quit her job. Her employer needed her and would not let her go. Her anxiety became obsessive; she was sure she would unwittingly betray herself, or that, forced to remain in that house, she would lose her mind.

Finally, yielding to her tearful entreaties, I supplied her with new forged documents. Marie left her relatively safe sanctuary as a servant to return to the infinitely greater hazard of surviving without visible means of support.

Luck, initiative, and the proper connections were necessary for a Jew passing as an Aryan who wished to establish contact with the Jewish Coordinating Committee. Many never succeeded. Many lonely, desperate, Aryan-looking men and women, finding themselves trapped in the Polish world, resorted to the last alternative—registration for employment in Germany.

Many people from towns and villages all over Nazi-held Poland had volunteered for such employment. In far-off Germany, there was less risk of being detected. To Germans, foreigners were foreigners and all that mattered was the extent to which they could be exploited. The Polish volunteers were put to work on the farms, or in factories. Usually they were assigned the most menial, exhausting and dangerous tasks.

35. YUZIK THE NEWSBOY

Yuzik was a twelve-year-old boy from Piotrkow. He was first pointed out to me by one of my Jewish friends to whom I brought subsistence funds. Scrawny and persuasively "Aryan," Yuzik sold newspapers at the corner of Krolewska and Krakowskie Streets. His suit, shabby and torn in places, his cap wrinkled and lopsided, his shoes, too big for him, worn flat at the heels: this little news vendor attracted nobody's attention. I myself would not have believed that he was Jewish. Nothing about him—neither his appearance, nor his cocky demeanor, nor the way he touted his wares distinguished him from the other newsboys.

He had been expecting me. I bought a paper and quietly introduced myself as coming from the Coordinating Committee. Glancing quickly around at the other boys, he asked me to turn into a side street where, within a few minutes he told me his life story. He spoke like an adult, soberly, briefly, and to the point.

He had been living in a hideout with his mother, father, and younger brother. He had happened to be away when the Germans staged a raid and took his family. A friend of his father's looked after him for a while. Together they rolled cigarettes. which they sold to the street vendors. But he could not remain with this friend for very long. Their lodgings came under suspicion and both of them had to flee. Now the youngster was on his own. He had been a guttersnipe, begging a few pennies and sleeping out-of-doors, until a kindly Gentile woman had taken an interest in him, unaware of his Jewish identity. Yuzik had told her that his father had been rounded up by the Germans for forced labor, and that he was now all alone. The lady believed him, financed his newspaper venture, and allowed him to live with her. Nevertheless, he had received the traditional hazing from the other newsboys who beat him up, took his papers and drove him away from all the corners, shouting, "*Moszek!*" after him. "*Moszek! Moszek!* (Moe! Moe!)."

The child did not know whether one of the boys had identified him as a Jew, or whether this was simply their way of hazing all the new boys. However, he did not give up, nor did he tell anything of this to his benefactress, lest she order him out. Eventually, the other newsboys got used to him and left him alone. He turned over all his proceeds to his landlady, who washed his shirts, prepared his food, and looked after him in general. All that he dreaded now was the approaching winter. His earnings were not enough to buy him an overcoat and a pair of shoes, and without these, he would not be able to work in the winter time. What would his hostess do then? Would she continue to keep him?

I asked him whether he would prefer to live in a hideout, where we would take care of his needs. Yuzik said he did not; he was afraid of hideouts. He did not want to be alone, dreading the least noise; he did not want to die like his parents. He said he was better off in the open, where he was free and could run for cover in case of danger. He was now where he wanted to be—out in the street. All he needed was clothes.

He was the only Jew I met in Warsaw during that time who was not afraid.

After the war, when I was at the Displaced Persons Camp Feldafing in West Germany, I learned that the boy had survived and was living somewhere in the American zone in Austria.

36. JEWS IN HIDING

The worst lot was that of the Jews who had typically Jewish features and had to go into hiding. They were completely at the mercy of their Gentile landlords, to whom they paid exorbitant rents. In dark, dreary cubbyholes, unable to go out for any reason, to do anything for themselves, they remained cooped up day after day, fear and anxiety their constant companions, despondency eating away their spirits. They were afraid to complain or to show any dissatisfaction lest their host evict them from their hideout. This would have been a sentence of death.

Not all of the hideouts were accessible to us. Some landlords barred any strangers, including our couriers, from dwellings where "their" Jews were lodging. It took considerable time and effort to persuade a Gentile landlord of this sort to let us enter his house.

But to the Jews in hiding, such visits were rays of hope. At the sight of one of our couriers, those tired, pale, haunted faces would come alive; their eyes would gleam and tears of relief would trickle down their pallid, hollow cheeks. The world had not forgotten them after all! Hope and faith were renewed as they asked anxious questions about family, friends and life on the outside. To some, these visits were all they lived for. The courier was one of the few people they could trust, one of the few whom they did not have to fear.

If a courier was delayed, or did not show up at all, their apprehension knew no bounds. Had anything happened? they would wonder. Had anyone, or perhaps even they themselves, been betrayed?

Often, life in a hideout turned the Jew into a bundle of nerves and fears, less a person than a hunted animal.

Mrs. Mermelstein and her son Stefan and Clara Hechtman and her sixteen-year-old daughter Gutka had a hiding place at Radzyminska 53, with a Gentile family. The landlord occupied one small room and a kitchen in an old wooden house. The Jews were lodged in a smaller room. The door to that room was always locked. The four Jews cramped together, listening fearfully, congealed by terror each time there was a knock on the door. They felt especially apprehensive when their landlady entertained guests for hours in the adjacent kitchen while the Jews crouched in a corner holding their breaths, to catch the least sound. If one of the guests were to enter their locked room. . . .

When their pitiful savings gave out, they subsisted on one meal a day. The landlady threatened to put them out. When I visited them for the first time they looked horrible, barely able to stand. The landlady had already told them to get out, and they did not know where they could go next. For a large amount of money, the woman allowed them to remain a while longer.

But a new misfortune befell them: Clara Hechtman became ill. At first she became melancholy; then she began to have recurrent seizures of insanity, screaming in Yiddish and flailing about with her arms. Doctors prescribed medication, but all to no avail. We tried to pacify her with tranquilizers, but her condition continued to deteriorate. The hiding place turned into a hell. The other Jews were terrified that her screams would betray their presence, and the landlady became ever more insistent that they must move out.

We could find no other refuge for Clara. To remove her to a hospital would mean discovery—and death.

One day—at the request of all the occupants of the house—the landlady's son poisoned Clara Hechtman. She was buried beneath the clay floor of the room where the Jews were hidden. But the others could no longer bear to live there. Her daughter Gutka was inconsolable and all three seemed to be succumbing to the same insanity that had doomed their late companion. In the end, we rented a house at Orla 6, and paid the landlady to move there along with her tenants.

Clara Falk and her ten-year-old son Adash lodged with a Mrs. Riba, a Gentile, in Miedzeszyn, a summer resort near Warsaw. As a child I had stayed a few times at the Medem Sanatorium there. I remembered it as a place filled with laughter and song. But ever since the Germans had murdered the Jewish children at this sanatorium, a deathlike silence prevailed there. The sanatorium itself stood desolate and deserted.

I approached a cottage surrounded by a well-kept garden filled with trees and flowers. What an excellent hiding place! I thought to myself. I was received by an elderly Polish woman and her dog. Mrs. Riba—it was indeed she—greeted me and told me that I would have to wait; they were loading potatoes next door and the vehicle blocked the access to the hiding place. In the meantime I engaged the old lady in conversation. She complained about the low rent she was receiving from her tenants—only 1,500 zlotys a month. Of late, she said, the situation had worsened; her Jewish tenants could hardly afford to pay her that much. They subsisted on the proceeds from their clothes, which their landlady sold for them. Finally, she asked me to take the Jews and move them elsewhere. I told her that before taking any action, I would have to speak to the Jews themselves.

She led me to a wooden shed, opened the door and asked me to go in. The tiny room was so cluttered with lumber and old pieces of furniture that I could hardly turn around. I strained my eyes in the semi-darkness but saw no one. The landlady pointed to a corner, littered with debris and branches, from which a hand protruded, barely visible. Then I heard a faint, "Good morning!" The same hand began to scrape away the debris. I opened the door a little wider to get more light.

Clara and Adash lay crouched side by side on the bare earthen floor. Pinned under the debris, they could hardly move. They were skin and bones, their faces haggard, their lips chapped, their eyes bulging, their hair disheveled and matted with chaff. They looked like spectres; they no longer seemed human.

They begged me to close the door. The daylight, they said, hurt their eyes. They ate, slept, and spent their waking hours in that crouching position; there was no space for them to stand upright or to lie down full length.

Twice a day the landlady brought them some scraps to eat. She would not allow them to go outside. They had not washed during the past few months. On rare occasions, when Clara's limbs became numb, she risked venturing outside at night for a few moments. Her right arm felt lifeless, but it gave her excruciating pains.

"I think I will never be able to walk again," Adash said from under the rubble, his eyes dull and lifeless.

His mother's eyes filled with tears. She herself could endure anything, but what about her son? Lying on the earthen floor, he had caught a severe cold and had run a high fever for several days. She did not know what to worry about more, his coughing, which could betray their hiding place, or his fever, which could kill him.

"Didn't Mrs. Riba offer any help?" I asked.

"No. She was afraid even to offer him a bed," Clara replied.

The unfortunate woman urged me to be discreet in dealing with the landlady, for she could order them out at any moment, as she had already done once, when she had been frightened by a false alarm. At that time Clara and her son had been forced to spend two days in the nearby woods before Mrs. Riba could be persuaded to take them back again.

"Please," Clara seized my arm as I started to leave, her hand trembling, "do not forget us!"

We found them a hideaway in Warsaw, where we looked after them. Clara Falk and her son survived the war.

One day, on a public thoroughfare, I was accosted by a tall man who asked, "Are you by any chance the Vladka who distributes money to the Jews?"

Taken aback for a moment—had I been betrayed again?—I tried to move on; but the stranger followed me. "You need not be afraid of me," he explained. "I'm Jewish myself. My bunker is in a bombed-out building not far from here, at the corner of Miodowa and Krakowskie Streets. I am living in those ruins together with four other Jews who managed to escape the ghetto."

Their group of ten men had been reduced to five, the others having been caught by the Germans. They had no funds whatsoever to rent living quarters and had been haunting those ruins for months.

"Only one of us can leave once in a while. We subsist on the pennies I can beg from kindhearted Poles. Sometimes, when we're really hungry, we sneak out of the ruins to go through the garbage on the sidewalk."

On several occasions, he had stumbled upon persons near the ruins, who seemed to be meeting some others, from whom they received some object, and then disappeared. His companions had urged him to risk talking to one of the recipients; perhaps the secret might prove of benefit to them. For a fortnight he had tried to find someone to enlighten him—and finally he had succeeded. One recipient gave him the name of Inka Schweiger, who had advised him to seek me out. "Have you any idea what your assistance means to us?" he concluded.

I nodded. The tattered garments, the pale, emaciated face, and the constant nervous glancing around to see if anyone was watching—all these confirmed his words. He was indeed a Jew, who needed our help.

Thereafter, he and his comrades in hiding received regular support from our Coordinating Committee.

Two Jews were in hiding at Napoleon Street 3—a huge house occupied by German officers and high-ranking officials. An elderly Polish maid who worked in one of the apartments had been identified as the contact through which I was to reach them. She first denied having any contact with Jews and ordered me to leave, but after I had mentioned several names, and answered some of her questions, she left the room for a few moments, then returned and asked me to follow her. Inside a tiny room adjoining the kitchen I found, seated around a small table, Jadzia Rosenberg, a beautiful young woman, formerly a nurse in the Jewish hospital, and her husband, a physician. Both of them were Jewish in appearance.

They had had to leave a previous hideout when their Gentile landlord was arrested. In desperation, they had appealed to Jadzia's old nursemaid, now a servant with the German occupants of the very same apartment where Jadzia had lived before the war. Contriving to get past the concierge, who had known Jadzia as a girl, they implored the former nursemaid to save them, knowing that discovery could mean death for all three. "You see, we didn't want to die!" the man observed, as if by apology.

The gracious and kindhearted woman had sheltered them in the tiny room in which she herself slept. They had thought of it only as a temporary refuge, but the days had dragged into months and they had despaired of ever finding another place.

All three were distraught. The owners of the apartment were two S.S. officers and two German officials, who occasionally came into the tiny room to talk to the servant. During such visits, the Jewish couple hid in the old lady's clothes closet. They lived in constant dread. They showed me their hiding place. I could not understand how anyone could remain there for any length of time.

At that moment, we heard footsteps and the couple darted into the closet, while the elderly woman resumed her kitchen chores. I remained alone in the tiny room. What if they found me? After all, I was supposed to be a Gentile!

I could catch snatches of conversation from the kitchen, but my main concern was with the man and woman in the closet. As the footsteps receded, the couple emerged.

"They will catch up with us sooner or later," Jadzia commented. But her chief concern was about the elderly nursemaid, who was risking so much to give them shelter. She had grown nervous and haggard. They feared she would break down.

"Tell us, is it worthwhile to go through all this?" Jadzia and her husband asked me.

"Indeed it is," I answered. "This will not last forever," but could I guarantee that they would survive in that clothes closet of theirs? I promised to provide them with financial aid and to get a forged Polish passport for the doctor. I was generous with words of consolation. But all this did not raise their hopes. What mattered was to find some other place, to get out of there as soon as possible.

But where else could they go?

37. THE BETTER HIDEOUTS

By contrast, life was almost relaxed in the "normal" *melinas*—those hideouts in which one could somehow carry on as a human being and retain one's identity and sanity.

Despite the incessant fear of being discovered and daily harassments from the landlords, Jews were busy working, studying, creating in their hideaways. One of the largest of these, which came to grief, was the *melina* situated in Grojecka Street.

A group of Jews had—for a substantial consideration—persuaded a Polish gardener to build a bunker on the site where he was working. For a while I was the distributor of funds and other assistance for the Jews who lived in that bunker, and had to make all the arrangements at the landlord's residence at Grojecka 83, where I also met some of the others living in the underground shelter. The landlord did not permit me access to the bunker itself; he was extremely cautious and barred all strangers.

The bunker was underground; its walls and ceiling were made of wooden planks, with wooden bunks for sleeping. Access was by a camouflaged door under the glass of the hothouse. The bunker housed men, women, and children—about 30 persons in all. During the day, the *melina* was oppressively hot. Only at night could the camouflaged door be raised to let in a little air. And yet people performed creative work under these conditions. Dr. Emmanuel Ringelblum, the eminent Jewish historian, and Mr. Melman, a Jewish teacher from the Medem School in Lodz, were living in that hideout and writing about Jewish history and Yiddish literature. It was from this bunker that the now-historic report of Jewish cultural activities in the ghetto was issued. And somehow, the scholars in this bunker were able to obtain research material from abroad.

We all assumed that the well-camouflaged *melina* would outlast the Germans. The landlord employed only his family in servicing the hideout. To provide food for so many people without arousing the suspicion of his neighbors, he opened a grocery store. Everything went smoothly. Even when a child was born in the bunker, no outsider was aware of it.

One day the rumor spread that the Germans had discovered a bunker which had served over 30 Jews. The landlord had had a fight with his mistress who knew about the hideout, and she took revenge by betraying the *melina* to the Germans. All the Jewish occupants were killed.

Smaller hideaways were more fortunate. With the help of a Gentile woman named Sciborowska, I found a suitable place in a house at Ogrodowa 55, whose owner—a Mrs. Dankewicz—occupied an apartment of two rooms and a bathroom. A double wall was built into the bathroom, so that the removal of several tiles gave access to the concealed space. Helena Shefner, a former teacher, wife of the well-known journalist, B. Shefner, and Chevka Hodess, a nurse (daughter of the journalist L. Hodess) and her husband, Lutek Svedosh, occupied a small room adjoining the bathroom. They tried to make their room look uninhabited, and at any knock on the door would hide in the bathroom.

The three of them spent their time in studies. Helena Shefner taught French to Chevka and her husband, Polish to the landlady's little daughter. She also studied English on her own. Among other things, I used to bring them books and newspapers. Helena Shefner insisted on giving me lessons in Russian when I visited. No time was wasted in that hideout.

Stefan Mermelstein, who, with his mother, had lived together with Clara Hechtman when Clara became insane at Radzyminska 53, recovered from that shocking experience after being moved to a new hideout on Orla Street. Like many other hiding places, this one contained a map of the Russian-German battlefront. Stefan marked the changing positions of the armies with pins. His intense interest in the progress of the war was shared by nearly all the Jews in hiding, since their very lives depended on the outcome. Stefan had yet another engrossing interest—music. He was a graduate of the Lodz Conservatory of Music. In his hideout he had begun to compose, his only musical instrument a tuning fork. We provided him with musical books and paper for musical notation. Stefan showed me his compositions and sometimes softly sang or whistled his latest waltzes and mazurkas. Though I was no expert on music, I was impressed by his talent.

Unfortunately, Stefan's musical recitals came to an abrupt halt. His mother fell ill and lost the use of her swollen legs. The landlady finally agreed to allow a doctor to visit the hideout. We had just then set up our own medical unit, consisting of a few Jewish and Polish physicians humane enough to treat Jews in hiding and to supply them with medicine. Dr. Anna Margolis of Lodz was one of the most courageous and selfless of these physicians. Dressed in a nurse's uniform and carrying a physician's handbag she made rounds of the most remote hideouts. I guided her to the shelter on Orla Street.

Mrs. Mermelstein was given medicine for treatment of her coronary insufficiency. She was also given an extra allowance for a special diet to make up for vitamin and mineral deficiencies. When his mother recovered, Stefan showed me a copybook filled with newly written short stories. "My mind is not suited for music, so I have turned to writing," he explained. After the war, he began to compose music again.

Benjamin Miedzyrzecki, my closest friend on the "Aryan side" whom I later married, together with his parents and eleven-year-old sister, lived with Kartaszew, a watchman at Grochowska 307, on the grounds of the Russian Orthodox cemetery of Praga.

The family shelter was a kitchen so tiny that one of its occupants has to step outside to admit a visitor. The kitchen was part of a small hut within the cemetery. It could be approached only by first gaining access to the grounds through the gate, which Kartaszew opened to those he recognized through a small gate-house window.

Benjamin alone of the family had Aryan features, allowing him to walk freely about Warsaw to obtain various things for his parents and to lend a hand in our relief work. Kartaszew engaged him as his assistant, and agreed to shelter his parents and sister. Benjamin helped him bury corpses, tend cemetery lots, and build closets and bins. Thus, though he was in hiding, Benjamin could work openly as a gravedigger, gardener, and builder.

In return, Kartaszew allowed the Miedzyrzeckis to observe the religious rules of Judaism to some extent in their hideout. Benjamin's father smuggled out his prayer shawl, phylacteries and prayer book from the ghetto and observed the traditional rituals and prayers, while the mother lit the Sabbath candles every Friday evening. The Gentile landlady had given the family two pots for their own use; with these they did their best to observe the laws of Kashrut, the separation of milk and meat utensils.

On Friday evenings, in that crowded kitchen, the tiny table was spread with a cloth and two candles glowed on an overturned plate. The table was bare of food and the blackout covering over the single small window reflected the haunting fear of the occupants; but an air of Sabbath eve festivity pervaded the cramped space, reminding me of my childhood home.

How different things had been then! The faces of the family circle had reflected serenity and joy; the table, laden with the Sabbath feast, exuded a spirit of peace. My mother's blessing over the Sabbath candles, my father's benediction, my little brother's chanting . . . the memory brought a lump into my throat.

The strong faith of the Miedzyrzeckis helped them bear their agony during those terrible times. Even little Genia, their daughter, used to pray before going to bed.

But the good *melinas* also had their share of anxiety and fear. They too were haunted by death.

38. LIFE GOES ON

During the latter part of 1943 I spent a considerable period of time in a small room in a Gentile household, posing as a smuggler. My frequent night-long absences served to support the credibility of that pose. My documents were half genuine and half forged. I was registered, but for a time lacked a valid *Kennkarte*, and dreaded every German inspection. Finally, I managed to obtain a genuine *Kennkarte* from the German Municipal Bureau in the name of Stanislawa Wonchalska—the long-dead daughter of Anna Wonchalska, our faithful Gentile co-worker. Anna had arranged with her priest not to report her daughter's death, and assured me that if I would be detained as a Jewess, she would intercede on my behalf. At the same time, she told me the names of grandmothers, aunts and cousins. I was now a full-fledged Aryan with two generations of Gentile forebears.

In this manner a number of Jews acquired the names and birth certificates of deceased Poles, with which they obtained authentic Polish identification cards. Such documents afforded substantial protection, but they were not wholly dependable, for the Germans, if suspicious, could check documents against municipal and church records. Any discrepancies could mean trouble, even with authentic papers.

About the time I obtained my *Kennkarte*, I also acquired new living quarters. Bronka, a Jewish woman from Piotrkow, who was passing as Aryan, was planning to escape to Hungary, and she offered me her residence for a small price. What luck! To have a place all my own, without having to stay with strangers, and at a reasonable price! It was like winning the lottery!

Many Jews hiding on the "Aryan side" were trying to reach Hungary. Although Hungary was then under a Fascist regime over which the Germans had great influence, the Hungarians themselves had not been exterminating Jews—so far. Jews were still able to move about freely in the cities and engage in business.

Bronka introduced me to the person who was to smuggle her into Hungary, Riba, a major Gentile wholesaler in the smuggling of tea, coffee, and people. Riba's fee for smuggling Jews into Hungary was 200 dollars a head. According to him, a clandestine committee in Hungary was helping the Jewish newcomers settle there legally. I immediately informed Mikolai and Antek, who conferred with Riba and, after studying the escape route, began to consider sending some people to Hungary.

Meanwhile, I moved into my new quarters, at Twarda 36, near Panska Street, close to the ghetto wall. From my fourth-floor flat (a tiny room and a tinier kitchen) I could see a section of the charred ghetto, where Polish laborers were salvaging usable bricks from the burned-out buildings. Day by day the Little Ghetto became empty space, as signs of the Jewish life that had gone on there were obliterated.

On the wall of my new room, opposite the door, was a full-length mirror concealing a secret entrance to a windowless cubbyhole which, in turn, had a camouflaged opening in the ceiling, through which one could climb onto a loft. Bronka's husband had hidden there in times of danger.

This tiny room served as occasional hideout for Benjamin Miedzyrzecki. Moving about the city and giving a helping hand to the work of the Coordinating Committee, with his fair hair and blue eyes concealing his Jewish identity, he found it necessary from time to time to take refuge from discerning glances that suggested that he might have been found out.

I had scarcely moved into my new home when I wanted to leave. The place was drab; the atmosphere desolate. I felt stifled. Had it not been for Benjamin I would have left immediately. With his exceptional skill in constructing hideouts, he managed to transform the dingy flat into both a comfortable place to live and an excellent *melina*. He even created secret hiding places for the valuables and forged documents—a valise with a double bottom, a ladle with a hollow handle, and even an additional niche beneath a window sill. His words of comfort dispelled my despair more than once. During those terrible times I often turned to him for support. It was only thanks to him that I did not break down.

Nevertheless, the neighbors were hardly aware of Benjamin's existence. Tadek Niewiarowski, a Gentile friend, served as a "cover" for my apartment and acted as my landlord. It seemed we had found asylum at last . . .

But, within a few weeks, that illusion evaporated. One day the janitress informed me that the secret police had been questioning her about the whereabouts of Bronka.

"That meek lamb took us all in," she exclaimed angrily. "She's a Jewess!" Then, looking at me closely, as if to catch my reaction, she added accusingly,

"And what's more, I'd like to know how *you* got her apartment."

I insisted that I knew nothing about any former tenant. An agent had arranged everything for me.

"Is that so?" she said sarcastically. "Are you aware that the tenants on your floor have complained to me about you? They say that you're getting visits from suspicious Jewish-looking types."

The conversation left me quite shaken. It seemed that Bronka had left just in time. What was I to do now? To move out suddenly would merely augment suspicion and further jeopardize my hard-earned status as an Aryan. I had no choice but to stay on in the apartment for the time being and try to allay my neighbors' doubts.

I arranged for my friends to curtail their visits and for Anna Wonchalska to come frequently, representing herself as my mother. I tried to observe all the Christian festivals and, on occasion, would even have a woman neighbor in for tea. I borrowed a phonograph and played it often to create a cheerful atmosphere, which the Poles did not associate with Jews on the run.

Despite all this, I was accosted by one of my neighbors in a state of great agitation one day as I returned home with terrifying news.

"They say that the Polish police or the Gestapo are set to raid the place," she whispered. "They say there are Jews hiding on the fourth floor."

As the initial shock of this report wore off, I began to think: Why should she be fearful? I had been wondering about her for some time. She seemed to be avoiding her neighbors, and her behavior was shy and diffident. Now, it occurred to me that she might be Jewish and that perhaps she harbored the same thought about me. Why else would she single me out to tell such news? I decided to say nothing to her of this.

Instead, I asked her where she had heard the rumors about my odd visitors. She said she had heard them from a Gentile friend, and that she had deemed it advisable to pass the news on to me. I thanked her, unlocked my door, and replied curtly, "It doesn't concern me—I have nothing to fear."

"Neither have I," my neighbor replied, a bit too sharply, I thought.

Our place was not raided, and though we passed one another occasionally, we rarely spoke. Several months later, during the uprising in Warsaw, she confessed to me that she was Jewish. All that time she had been sheltering her husband, the son of Topas, a well-known Warsaw shoe dealer. She had assumed that I, too, was Jewish, but had cautiously maintained aloofness.

"That way we could fool the others better," she told me, proud of her astuteness.

The dreariness and anxiety of our lives were relieved occasionally by moments of cheer. Those members of the Bund and *Zukunft* who were free to move about on the "Aryan side" gathered on special occasions such as the first of May or, as happened in the autumn of 1943, for a symbolic celebration of the anniversary of the founding of the Bund. At a time when the very foundations of our lives had been destroyed, this small gathering was no more than a remembrance of the yesteryears of the pulsating Jewish labor movement in which we had been reared. It comforted us somewhat to recall it.

There were nine of us who sat together at Miodowa 24 one night around a table decorated with flowers, the curtain drawn. For some time we faced each other wordlessly. Only after Celek spoke of the reason for our gathering did our spirits rise a bit. Little by little, almost in whispers, we recalled the days when such celebrations had been held in vast halls before huge audiences of workers with songs, music, speeches and fluttering flags. Now, all that remained was pain and the bitter realization that the world had calmly accepted the inhumanity in which we lived.

Nevertheless, we sent greetings to all those in the world who struggle for freedom, primarily to our brothers in the concentration camps, the forests and the bunkers. These greetings were filled with the faith and hope that we, the remnant, will in the end live to see the defeat of our bestial foe. Will avenge the crimes that have been committed against us, and we will continue steadfastly to participate in the struggle for a righteous and just world. . . .

In an inspired solemn mood, we all dispersed.

During those months I often called on my "mother," Anna Wonchalska. Anna, a widow, was living with her sister, Maria Sawicka. Both were devoted co-workers of ours and were connected with the Polish Socialist underground organization. Maria was distributing "illegal" Polish publications. Together they also sheltered two Jewish girls, Zoshka Ribak, thirteen years old, and later, Kazik Rathajzer's seven-year-old sister.

Their apartment was frequented by quite a few "Aryan" Jews. There I met Basia Berman, the wife of Dr. Berman (who was active in relief work), Antek, Kazik and others.

The two Polish sisters were very close to their Jewish friends, and they were especially kind to me. Between Anna and me there was, indeed, a deeply shared affection, apart from our common interests. Seeking to cheer me up, Anna persuaded me to give a party at her apartment on the anniversary of my supposed patron saint, St. Stanislaw. She urged me to invite my Jewish friends and even promised to attend to all the preparations.

I was deeply moved by her offer. Ordinarily, to have had any kind of gathering whatsoever, we would have had to make the rounds of any number of Gentile homes before we could find one that would allow a small group of "Aryan" Jews to assemble. But, out of sheer kindness, Anna volunteered such a risky undertaking in her own house.

Even knowing how dangerous it was, I could not resist the temptation. My need to be with my own friends, not to feel so terribly alone, to see familiar faces together, drop pretense for a while, was overwhelming. On the afternoon of May 8, some twenty of us gathered in the home of Anna Wonchalska. It was the first time that so many Jews had come together for a reason other than underground work.

For a while, we were unable to enter into a festive mood. We were all too tense and constrained to make the transition to relaxation, to accept the fact that there was no one present against whom we must guard, that we could be ourselves. Little by little, though, the tension subsided, we began to talk, we became animated, some of the guests even began to sing. Yet none of us could quite hide the sadness behind our smiles. The laughter was strained. Even the gayest, those who laughed most, fell silent for a few moments, lost in their thoughts.

"All your merry-making seems an act—it lacks joy," Anna told me.

I understood her very well. For a while I was grateful that so many friends had come. I, too, sensed the melancholy that gnawed at all of us. "The more joy, the more sadness," someone remarked.

I had composed a letter to my friends overseas, in which I told of our arduous life, our struggle, our strong will to survive, and of the anguish that each of us had endured. I read this aloud to the assembled guests who, I felt, shared my feelings.

This letter was never sent. It was hard to tell the extent to which it reflected the frame of mind of my guests. Following the reading, they remained silent for a long while, after which they took to quietly humming old Jewish melodies—we were afraid to sing the Yiddish words for fear the neighbors might hear. Some began to whisper Yiddish sentences, others to tell of their experiences. For a while, we were our real selves again.

Those were memorable hours, bringing touches of warmth and joy into our struggling lives.

39. JEWISH PARTISANS

A small group of escaped ghetto insurgents had organized themselves in the Wyszkow Forests as partisans. In time, we established a regular communication with them. Every other week, a peasant woman delivered a letter to Anna Wonchalska from the partisans, and carried back money, clothing and messages; she then returned to her home near the forest hideout of the partisans. There, under cover of darkness, they collected the deliveries, learned whatever the woman knew of the happenings in the village nearby, and gave her money to buy food for them. The elderly woman was their confidante, who alerted them upon learning of an imminent German raid.

Together with Celek, Marja Sawicka and Vladek Wojciechowski, I once visited the Jewish partisans in the forest. We arrived in Tluszcz at eight in the morning and with Celek, who had been there once before, as our guide, we passed quickly through the town and continued along a broad highway at the edge of the forest. The sun glinted through the trees; a spring breeze rustled the leaves. As we walked, we were on the constant lookout for the partisan who was to meet us. The silhouette of a man appeared in the distance.

The figure signalled to us to continue, which we did until we reached a crossroad. There we waited for further directions but our guide was nowhere to be seen.

"Good morning!" We turned to see the broad, smiling face of Janek Bilak—who before the ghetto uprising, had received the explosives we smuggled into the ghetto. I had not seen him in over a year. Tall, sunburned, wearing black top boots and green trousers, with a carbine slung over his shoulder, he was the very image of a partisan fighter.

He urged us on, into the woods where we would not be observed. Following him, we penetrated the dense undergrowth. The air was fresh with the smell of pines, birds chirped; a squirrel darted past. The ground was dappled with sunlight, its rays playing hide and seek with us, dazzling us one moment, gone the next. So much brightness and freshness, so many colors! This was a totally different world!

"Don't make so much noise when you walk," Bilak cautioned us.

We tried stepping as carefully as possible; but boughs and branches snapped as they cracked beneath our tread. Bilak moved lightly and almost soundlessly, already an accomplished woodsman.

"One could easily get lost here," one of us remarked after a while. Bilak reassured us with a smile, "Don't worry; if you live in the woods long enough, you gain a sense of direction. I can find my way around here even at night." He stopped short and gave a bird-call, repeating it several times. A similar call echoed from some distance off.

Within a few minutes, the branches separated and two men emerged. One of them, short, with black hair and dark eyes, was known as "Black Janek." The other, somewhat taller, with dark blond hair, blue eyes, and a round, sunburnt face, was Maciek.

"Is the way clear?" asked Bilak.

"Yes, we can go on."

We continued now along a wide forest path. Suddenly we were startled by a voice hailing us from a distance. Looking, we saw a man clearly signalling us to halt. The partisans did not recognize him and we all darted into the dense forest, his voice continuing to call out.

"I'm going to check," Bilak decided. Drawing his revolver and motioning to Janek and Maciek to remain with us, he strode off toward the beckoning stranger.

In a few minutes, he was back. The man was a Jew, one of three who had escaped from a concentration camp and was hiding some distance away. They had neither food nor arms. They had been prowling the woods for several days in the hope of joining a group of partisans. Taking us for partisans the man asked permission to join us.

"Will you let them join us now?" one of us asked Bilak.

The sisters Anna Wachalska and Marysia Sawicka
were awarded the title "Righteous Gentiles"

Jakub Kartashew who helped
save the Miedzyrzecki family

The children of Kotlar and Meltzer
were sustained by the underground
organization until the end of the war

Janek Bilak and Jakubek Putermilch, fighters of the Warsaw
Ghetto in the woods with the partisans

"No, not now. We'll meet them this afternoon and talk things over," Bilak replied.

We walked on through the woods. Gradually, the growth became thinner and the ground grew softer, and, after a while, swampy. The partisans took off their shoes and socks and we followed suit. Hopping from hassock to hassock, now and again sinking knee-deep in mud, we traversed the swamp and emerged upon firmer ground.

"The swamps are our allies," one of the partisans said. "It is harder for the Germans to reach us."

At last we came upon the first partisan outpost: a Jewish sentry with a rifle. We bade him good morning, and he let us pass. Within a few minutes we came to the edge of a small meadow, an island in a sea of trees. This was the stronghold of the partisans. A group of Jews came forward to welcome us warmly. City had met forest; an exchange of the latest news ensued.

The partisans were sunburned and disheveled, and clad in odds and ends of old clothing. Some wore jackets without shirts; others, shirts without jackets. Not one of the men was fully dressed. Most wore leather belts; some were armed with revolvers, others with carbines. The three women in the group differed little in appearance or armaments from the men.

They all bombarded us with questions about the progress of the war, the state of affairs in the city, our mutual friends—a torrent no one tried to halt.

I received an especially hearty greeting from Gabriel Frishdorf and his wife Hannah, two of my former classmates. We had grown up in the *Skif* and later in the *Zukunft*. Both had belonged to the Fighting Organization and had participated in the ghetto revolt. Gabriel's face still reflected the same determined calm for which he was known in the ghetto, where he had distinguished himself by his heroism.

Once, during a roundup, the German *Werkschutz* at the Hallmann shop had captured three members of the Fighting Organization. At night a group of the Fighting Organization from the Roerich workshop, led by Frishdorf, had attacked the German headquarters, disarmed the guards and freed the three prisoners. Every mission he had carried out had shown the same planning and attention to detail and the same valor and heroism. The partisans in the woods had come to admire and respect him.

There were fifteen in the partisan group, including two physicians, a fugitive from Treblinka, and several Jews from small towns, as well as the insurgents from the Warsaw Ghetto. Originally, it had been much larger, but it had been reduced by the intermittent German patrols.

We were shown to a shanty of woven branches and leaves standing solitary amidst the trees. Inside were some planks, an ax, a hammer, and a few other tools. "This is where we store food against the rains," one of our guides explained.

In another nearby hut was the kitchen, a dugout containing the crudest of fireplaces, with a hole in the roof for the smoke to escape. Next to this structure was a water hole, a square pit filled with water, yellow with sediment.

"Is this all your housekeeping?" I asked in astonishment.

"We purposely keep our comforts to a minimum, so that in case of trouble we can destroy everything quickly without leaving traces," was the reply.

"And where do you sleep?"

"Here, on the ground."

"And when it rains?"

"Then we get drenched to the bone and wait for the sun to dry us."

Our conversation was interrupted; it was time to eat. We sat on the ground in a circle, in the center of which a steaming pot of soup was set down. Bowls were supplied. The partisans drew spoons from their boots and pitched in with gusto.

"Don't assume, you city folk, that we never have anything but soup," one of the partisans said solemnly. "Most of the time we thrive on a varied diet. One day we eat; the next day we don't."

The cheerfulness of the talk and the natural beauty of the surroundings were entirely at odds with the perilous lives of these men and women. Death lurked behind every tree. The meadow was constantly guarded, with sentries changing every few hours. The partisans were ready to fend off the Germans no matter when they came, in broad daylight or pitch darkness. On several occasions it had been necessary to change their encampment, but whenever things were quiet, they always returned to the meadow. Here they were on familiar ground, had contacts with friendly peasants in the neighborhood as well as with the forest rangers, and also their liaison to the Polish underground.

However, those relations had deteriorated of late. A wild Polish-Ukrainian partisan detachment had appeared in the neighboring woods, plundering the houses and raping the women of the villages. As a result, the peasants lumped all the partisans together as common criminals. Thus their attitude towards the Jewish partisans also changed, and this made the lot of the Jewish fighters even worse than it had been before.

The partisans had spent the previous winter here. As soon as the cold weather had set in, they had put up several clay huts in which they slept and stored their belongings. These huts offered shelter, warmth and protection from frostbite. But the Germans had suddenly swooped down upon them, killing twelve of their comrades. The rest fled. There was no place to find shelter from the bitter cold. They could not wash or change their clothes; everything froze immediately. Lice became a veritable plague. The fighters flitted through the woods like shadows among the trees, searching for whatever scant protection the trees could offer from the cutting winds. The winter had seemed endless to them.

But the worst of their plagues were the German raids. They knew no season and were completely unpredictable. If they were warned in time, the partisans could usually escape to another position. But if their little encampment were to be surprised and surrounded, they would be in dire peril. To join battle with a superior force could only mean death. The only alternative was to break out of the German trap and escape once again.

Between encounters with the Germans, the group carried out various acts of sabotage: setting fire to occupied estates, cutting telephone lines, raiding German outposts and, in general, harassing the enemy wherever possible.

Now it was our turn to report on the state of affairs in the city. We gave a brief account of our activities, our difficulties, our accomplishments and our failures.

"You're not to be envied; neither are we, for that matter," one of the partisans observed grimly.

The sun was setting now, and the air grew chillier. Our conversation gradually trailed off, and we all became pensive. Then someone started to hum a tune, and the others broke into a sad song:

I miss my little home town,
How I miss my home,
Where life was always quiet
And free from grief and war . . .

Here we sat in a God-forsaken corner of swamp, huddled on the ground, with no shelter against the elements. Old, familiar songs, images of warmth and light—how long had it been since those dear dimly-remembered days? How far had we come from home?

When it had become dark enough, the partisans prepared for sleep. Each chose a piece of ground for himself, found some covering, and lay down on the bare earth fully dressed. They only loosened their shoes. They were soon sound asleep, their weapons at their sides. I lay there on the ground, unable to fall asleep. The rustling of the leaves, the croaking of the frogs, and the occasional twitter of a bird assailed my ears like wild screeching. How would the guard be able to recognize strange footsteps amid such a noisy tumult? But the sentry seemed calm and confident as he paced regularly in front of the camp, and this eased my fears somewhat. The ears of the partisans were probably better attuned to the sounds of the forest than were mine.

Dawn broke at last. We, the visitors, had to hurry. But before we were ready, everyone was on his feet. As we took leave of one another, our warm handclasps spoke silently. "Who knows if we will ever meet again?" Together with Black Janek, we set out for the city.

A few days later I learned that Gabriel Frishdorf had been killed in a German raid. How could this have happened? We had only had a reunion in the woods, and now he was no longer among the living.

I could still see his tall figure, his handsome face, his eyes mirroring deep concern. He radiated calm and fortitude, and nothing escaped his clever eye. He knew almost all there was to be known about life in the woods, and his advice and decisions were usually considered authoritative. He had talked to me about the conduct of comrades and the minor incidents and bickerings that occasionally took place.

"We need not worry too much about all these things," he had remarked. "They are the result of this wretched life. Let us only survive, and everything will straighten out by itself."

He had always tried to see the overall picture, to cut through to the root of any quarrel. He was never petty, but always concerned about the other's thoughts, feelings, and actions, even at the most trying moments.

The news from the Wyszkow woods grew continually more discouraging. The German raids had intensified, completely disrupting the life of the local partisans. Many of them had died, especially at the hands of the Polish-Ukrainian partisan group who apparently found killing Jews a more agreeable and satisfying exercise than joining them in the struggle against the common enemy. Thereafter, the Coordinating Committee tried to place as many Jewish partisans as possible in *melinas* in the city. Nevertheless, some members of that group lingered on in the forest until the time of liberation.

40. FORGED DOCUMENTS AND NEW HIDEOUTS

As the war dragged on and German reverses on the battlefields multiplied, the ferocity of the terror in Aryan Warsaw mounted. The Germans arbitrarily broke into Polish dwellings, ransacked them and deported thousands of Poles to Germany for forced labor or to Pawiak prison for liquidation. The reign of terror threw the entire Polish population into a panic. Even worse was the dread among the Jews hiding in Gentile homes.

Every Pole was required to carry his identification documents and his employment card and to be ready to produce either or both on demand, for inspection. We went to great lengths to provide Jews with forgeries of these all-important documents. In the event of an unexpected raid—or if Jews had to abandon their *melinas*—they would at least have some identity cards.

In this respect the underground Polish Relief Council helped us a great deal. This council maintained its own clandestine presses and employed reliable workers. All that was required for the forged documents was a photograph of the person to whom it was issued. All other information—name, date, place of birth, trade or profession—could be fictitious. But photographs of Jews in hiding were not easily had. Risking a visit to a photographer was hazardous; on the other hand, only a photographer who could be trusted to keep a secret could be brought to a hideout.

I found such a photographer by pure chance one day in a studio at the corner of Zelazna and Zlota Streets. It seemed to me that one of the photographers there was Jewish. I made some inquiries about her, and my assumption proved correct; she was a convert. For an extra fee she went along with me to the hideouts and took photographs, which she later retouched and finished herself. She proved most reliable.

We collected the photographs and recorded the necessary information to pass on to an activist who maintained contact with the secret presses. One such contact was Pan Julian, a Jew who occupied a small room in a house at Mokotowska 31. Twice a week, at specified hours, I brought him a packet of photographs and documents. I often saw other familiar faces in the hallway leading to Pan Julian's room. While we did not exchange so much as a word in that crowded hallway, we were all well aware of our reason for being there, for this was the place where one brought the raw data and picked up the finished document.

Our conversations with Pan Julian were concise and businesslike. On one document the birthplace had to be changed; another required a small seal; the validation date on one employment card had to be extended, or some other detail had to be produced. Without a word Pan Julian would reach under the tiled oven in his room, check to see if the packet was mine, and then hand it to me. I would take the packet, conceal it on my person, and be on my way. The exchange took perhaps two minutes.

Carrying such documents on one's person was extremely dangerous. One could be stopped and searched at any moment. On more than one occasion couriers had to jump off trolley cars and seek safety, even to the extent of knocking on the doors of complete strangers. Despite all this we did our utmost to keep our appointments at Mokotowska 31.

Then, one day, the landlady refused to let me into the house. Pan Julian had been arrested, she said. The secret police had visited her several times. Our visits to Mokotowska Street ceased. We never heard from Pan Julian again. In time, a new address was found where documents could be processed.

One evening I helped a fugitive Jew named Zam move from Krochmalna Street to a hideout on Brudnowska Street. We waited until nightfall so that the darkness would hide Zam's Jewish face. Approaching our destination along a dimly-lit street, we heard suddenly from out of the darkness:

"Your documents!"

It was a German patrol. Zam and I shuddered. Zam had a forged

Kennkarte and a Jewish face; my documents were far from foolproof. Nevertheless, we produced them quietly, and one of the Germans examined them under a flashlight, then shone the flashlights on our faces. He let us go on.

"If the Germans could recognize Jews only by appearance and documents," Zam noted delightedly after they had left, "I would be able to move about freely."

And he was right. Our documents were indeed usually good enough for the superficial street checks. Hundreds of Jews were saved by these forged documents.

The next most vital relief project at that time was the creation of hideouts in Gentile homes, where persecuted Jews might find asylum in the event of a surprise German raid or if curious neighbors—or *szmalcownicy*—became suspicious.

At Pruzna 14, the tailor Rogozinski, a Gentile, provided shelter for two Jews, Notke and Mietek, who were working for him. Over a period of two weeks, Jablonski, the Gentile janitor of their building, surreptitiously carried bricks, sand, and lime into the house. He, with the landlord and the Jews constructed a cubbyhole connected with the hallway. Everything had been done so skillfully that even when the Gestapo made a thorough search, after apparently having been informed, the hideout could not be discovered. Both Jews survived.

Yurek Igra built a small hideout for a woman named Franka Zlotowska, who had found shelter at the home of a Gentile at Krochmalna 36. In a small toilet, Yurek put up a wooden partition with a camouflaged door. The partition was painted and hung with some old brushes.

Dankewicz, a Gentile living in Pruszkow, had a remarkable hideout in which a Jewish woman named Zucker survived the war. The hiding place was actually a large tile stove. It was hollow and could be entered from the top, which looked like a metal flue. Despite frequent searches, the police never discovered the hiding place.

After Clara Hechtman's death, her daughter Gutka and the two Mermelsteins had been moved to Orla 6. As the German terror intensified, Mrs. Gruzel, the landlady, pleaded with me to get the Jews out of her home. But there still was no other place for the three Jews to go. We offered to pay Mrs. Gruzel a higher monthly rent but to no avail. She feared for her life if the Jews were ever found on her premises. As a last resort, we decided to fashion a new hideout in the house, to build a false wall in their tiny room, behind which the Jews could hide in time of danger. At first the landlady protested, arguing that if we brought in building materials it would arouse the suspicion of her neighbors. Besides, she had only recently painted the house and was reluctant to ruin one of her rooms. But we argued and pleaded and cajoled until she finally yielded.

Benjamin Miedzyrzecki was commissioned to carry out this task, the Coordinating Committee allotting special funds for the project. Together with me and the landlady's son, Benjamin cautiously assembled the necessary building materials. The work began that evening. The door was locked, the windows curtained, and we tried to make as little noise as possible. Benjamin used a special drill that perforated the walls and planks, so as to avoid hammering.

Still, we were not able to work without making noise. Sometimes our hearts seemed to pound more loudly than the hammer. The landlady paced the floor, biting her nails, occasionally giving vent to tears. Why were these people taking such advantage of her? she sobbed. The rest of us were scarcely less tense and apprehensive. The room was cluttered with boards, planks, tools, and hardware. The wall stood naked and unfinished. Any outsider peeping into the room would not take long to surmise the purpose of all this construction. We worked in constant fear of discovery, but did our best to maintain an outward calm. "Everything will be all right," we reassured our landlady.

We worked for twenty-four hours without let-up. The most difficult part was the entrance, just large enough to crawl through. The fit had to be perfect, so as not to arouse suspicion. At last this, too, was completed.

That evening the tiny room was tidied up and the walls painted. The new hideout was ready.

Within two weeks, a German official was attacked in an adjoining house on Orla Street. Shortly thereafter German troopers surrounded the area in search of the assailants. As usual, all the landlords and tenants were ordered out of the houses. The Germans searched all the dwellings, including Gruzel's. They used flashlights in the tiny room with the false wall, but they failed to find the hideout and the three Jews concealed there.

41. THE CZESTOCHOWA GHETTO FIGHTERS

The German hunt for Jews was no less thorough outside of Warsaw than within the city. Relatively few Jews achieved the miracle of surviving by taking refuge in bunkers, forests, or among the peasants. We did our utmost to reach the few who were still in hiding. Late in the summer of 1943, Leon Feiner Mikolai asked me to undertake a mission on behalf of the Coordinating Committee, without a travel permit. It was very hazardous to travel without a German permit, for the Germans regularly stopped trains and inspected the passengers, arresting those who lacked proper identification.

I was briefed on the purpose of my journey by Antek (Ytzhak Zukerman). In Koniecpol, in the district of Kielce, a small group of insurgents from the Czestochowa ghetto had found shelter among some peasants. For a while this group had been in contact with Warsaw, but all communications had lately become impossible because of the frequent controls on the trains. The isolated Jews were in desperate circumstances, and it was vital that they should have some money. Antek described the exact location of the *melina*; I was given some money and a letter, and I set out.

The train was filled with smugglers, the passengers boisterously discussing the price of lard and the slim profits gained from transporting commodities from one city to another and cursing the German train officials who pilfered the food parcels. In my own disguise as a smuggler, I carried a big bag of "merchandise" under my arm; the money and the letter were hidden under my belt. The journey was without major incident until Czestochowa, where I was to transfer to a train to Kielce. A rigorous search of passengers' baggage was conducted there by the Germans on the station platform.

While I considered how to evade this inspection, which would almost certainly penetrate my primitive disguise, a voice whispered almost in my ear, "Come with me." One of my traveling companions, an elderly Gentile woman likewise bound for Kielce, climbed out of the other side of the train. I followed with my bag of "merchandise," and together we scurried across the tracks and clambered into an empty freight car standing on a siding.

"Don't worry; we can wait here until the inspection is over," she said, stretching out on the floor of the car. Judging from the voices I could hear in the other supposedly empty cars, my benefactress was not the only smuggler with this idea.

Four hours later we boarded a Kielce-bound train together. A German official and the Polish conductor moved down the aisle, checking travel permits. So I was trapped after all. I decided to take my grandmotherly fellow smuggler into my confidence.

"Try to buy them off," she advised. "Even if that doesn't work, you needn't worry. They'll just put you off at the next station, examine you, and let you go. The German guards are tougher, though."

Until the inspectors reached me, I remained in a state of fear. What if the bribe were to be rejected and I was subjected to a body search at the next station? My money and the letter would be found and I would become another victim of the German dragnet. But there was no alternative. Luckily, my bribe was accepted without any questions.

Fifteen hours after leaving Warsaw, I left the train at Zelislawice and, parting quickly from the group of smugglers, set off alone along the main highway. Following Antek's directions, I soon caught sight of a charred chimney and, rising from a fenced-off patch of land, a wooden skeleton of a hut under construction, the ground around it strewn with planks, bricks and other building materials. To the right was a huge wooden barn and, close to it, a small shed that served as a primitive kitchen. I climbed over the fence.

A dog began to bark, and a woman's voice called out, "Who's there?" An elderly peasant woman came running from behind the barn.

"Whom are you looking for?" she asked suspiciously.

"I want to buy some butter from you," I said loudly. When she had come a bit closer I told her in a whisper whom it was that I had really come to see.

The old woman seemed bewildered. She had no idea what I was talking about, nor had she any butter for sale, and she would thank me to be on my way. Now it was I who was bewildered. This had to be the right place! All the landmarks were just as I had been told. I persisted, remarking for the first time that I had brought some money for the Jews who were hiding. She studied me closely for a long moment, then asked me to wait. She hobbled away and disappeared behind the barn; emerging a few minutes later, she motioned me to enter.

As soon as I had stepped in, she bolted the door. The place was dark and cluttered with straw. There was a great stir in the hayloft. I looked up and caught sight of some heads emerging from the piles of straw.

"Really?" I heard voices raised in astonishment. "Somebody from Warsaw to see us?"

"Yes, from Warsaw," I replied.

A ladder was lowered and I climbed up to a small loft, the roof too low to allow me to stand upright. A dozen young men were lying among the straw; wisps of it were sticking to their clothes and hair.

One of the young men introduced himself as Kuba, the group's spokesman.

"We've been waiting for you for so long!" he said.

"So you haven't forgotten about us after all," exclaimed one of the two girls in the group.

"We had almost given up hope of anyone coming to us," said a third voice.

"You see," came still another voice, this time directed to the peasant woman, "you should have trusted us."

"That is Chaim, our manager," Kuba told me.

"And what might you be the manager of in this straw?" I asked the voice.

"You needn't laugh," said Kuba. "Chaim is our liaison with the peasants. They know him very well and will deal only with him."

Someone picked up my smuggler's sack. I was asked how I had fared during my journey, whether I had encountered any difficulties, about the progress of the war, and about the city.

"Can we call you by your first name?" someone broke in.

"Of course," I replied. The atmosphere became less tense. Before long, it seemed like a reunion of old friends. Kuba urged everyone to sit down. Otherwise, there might not be time for all of us to burrow into the straw, if unwanted visitors showed up. They had seen me coming, through cracks in the barn wall, their vantage points, but could not believe that I had come to visit them.

We got down to the business of my visit. There were 23 Jews in the village; of these, 13 were holed up in the barn, and the rest lodged in two other *melinas*. For several weeks they had been entirely penniless and their landlady had been threatening to put them out. Now they were living on credit and half-starved. At 30 zlotys a day per person, they had run up a debt of 10,000 zlotys. Day and night they wallowed in the dirty straw; some of them were covered with festering sores. They needed medication, clothing and blankets.

Chaim was in close touch with a Communist peasant in the village who was sheltering his cousin. This peasant was anxious to organize a partisan group but lacked the necessary arms. (Later on I met this peasant in Warsaw and put him in touch with Antek.) The Jewish underground was on the verge of delegating one of their group to Warsaw, but had no contact there. Kuba asked me for an address just for correspondence purposes, since they were helpless and cut off from the rest of the world.

"If we lose contact with Warsaw, that'll be the end of us!" Kuba said with finality.

They also asked me to have a talk with their landlady, who, they said, had a high regard for people from Warsaw, and assure her that their credit was good. The group was now in high spirits; after all, they were going to receive badly-needed funds. I heard accounts of how some of the group, disguised as peasants, had eluded the Germans and escaped from the ghetto in Czestochowa.

Most of the Jews in hiding were Zionists, mostly of the Labor orientation. They implored me to tell them news of their comrades among the Zionists whom I knew, and about the course of the war. I told them that the latest news from the front was good; the Germans were being soundly beaten at last, the Polish underground was killing Germans, and people in Warsaw were of the opinion that the war was drawing to a close. They listened intently.

"That means that we may live to see the end of the war," someone remarked.

"Yes, indeed!" I agreed enthusiastically.

My optimism was partly feigned, but I, too, wanted so much to believe! I told them about the uprising in the Warsaw Ghetto. They seemed to take physical sustenance from learning what was going on. They grew animated, analyzing, expressing opinions, interpreting.

We talked until late that night. I gave them the address of Marja Barkowska as a contact in Warsaw, collected the photographs of those who needed forged documents, and also took two letters: one addressed to Tzivia Lubetkin and Antek, and the other to the Coordinating Committee.

"Don't forget about us!" they pleaded as I climbed down the ladder. I left the barn feeling as though I was leaving my own family.

After this first visit I traveled to Zelislawice every few weeks, bringing money, clothes, and medication for the hidden group. Train travel became progressively more hazardous. But, despite all difficulties, our contacts were maintained.

42. THE KONIECPOL WOODS

In the autumn of 1943 our relief work was jeopardized by delays in the arrival of funds from abroad. For several weeks, Jews in *melinas* were driven to despair by sheer deprivation. Urgent appeals from Zelislawice had to go unfulfilled. Finally, I received a substantial sum from our sources and made another trip.

The Gestapo had recently seized a number of travelers lacking necessary credentials; so, when the Polish conductor on the train bound for Kielce warned us that German guards were waiting at the next station, nearly all the passengers without a moment's hesitation scurried off the train, now stopped, and scattered. We were twenty-seven kilometers from Kielce and my appointment was in six hours.

Most of the other smugglers had taken off their shoes and were walking in the same direction as me. Following them, I removed my shoes, tied them together by the laces, slung them over my shoulders and joined the others over paths, fields and fences toward Zelislawice.

It was dark when I arrived at the barn, exhausted, grimy, with scratched and sore feet. The first person I saw was the landlady; she was wringing her hands in despair. My heart began to pound; something terrible must have happened! The old woman wiped the tears from her face and swore by Jesus and the Blessed Virgin that she was innocent. Bewildered, I implored her to tell me what had happened.

It seemed that the barn had aroused the suspicions of her neighbors, who had spread the rumor that the old woman was harboring Jews. Meanwhile, her tenants had run out of money, and she had ordered them out. Some had managed to find shelter with another peasant; the rest had taken to the woods.

The peasant woman paused for a moment, dabbed at her eyes again calling in the Mother of God to bear witness to her innocence.

"Well, get to the end of the story," I demanded.

She resumed her tale of woe. Several days before, Polish partisans had come upon a hut sheltering four Jews, two young men and two girls. The Poles had decided that the Jews were Communists and had beaten them mercilessly and driven them from the hut. All this had happened in broad daylight; the news spread throughout the village; the Polish police captured three of the Jews—two girls and one man—and after parading them through the village in a wagon all day long had executed them at nightfall. The three were among the group of thirteen that I had met on my first visit to the loft. There were two girls and the group's spokesman, Kuba. The other young man had somehow escaped.

I was stunned—I had come too late. I could scarcely speak, but forced myself to ask the old woman where the remaining Jews might be found. She thought that a peasant named Romanow might know. He had a hut at the edge of the forest and was giving aid to the partisans—and possibly to Jews as well.

It was nightfall by the time I arrived at Romanow's. A tall man led me into a well-lit kitchen, asking politely what had brought me there. Two small children were playing on the earthern floor. A young woman was preparing a meal. This, apparently, was only a family, with no outsiders.

"Could I have a word with you in private?" I asked.

Without a word Romanow opened the door into an adjoining room. He invited me to enter and to sit down. I frankly told him the purpose of my visit. Could he possibly tell me whether and where any Jews were hiding in the vicinity? After some hesitation he cleared his throat and asked me which Jews I had in mind. I named those I knew.

"Yes, that checks!" he said. From time to time, he went on, some Jews had been coming to him from the woods under cover of darkness, to beg for food. He would give each one a bowl of soup and a slice of black bread. They had visited him a number of times; he even knew some of them by name. Though he could not tell me definitely where they were, he would let me stay overnight in his hut if I wished. Perhaps one of the Jews in hiding would appear during the night.

He seemed trustworthy. I accepted his invitation. He questioned me in great detail about Warsaw and about news from the battlefront. In due time everyone went to bed. Things quieted down in the hut, but I could not sleep; my hearing had become oversensitive. Even the sighing of the wind put me on edge, and the rustling of the trees was transformed into the sound of furtive footsteps.

Soon, however, imagination turned into reality. There was a scraping at the windowpane, followed by a low but distinct tapping against the glass. I held my breath; the tapping was repeated. The next sounds were those of Romanow clambering out of bed and asking who his caller was.

"Quiet! Quiet! It's us!" came the reply.

"Ah! They're here, Miss." Romanow stepped back inside the hut and nudged me. He lit a candle, went to the door and began a whispered conversation with someone. I was consumed with curiosity. Was the stranger some Jewish fugitive I knew? The small group came out of the doorway and into the light. They were indeed two of the partisans I knew—Staszek and Little Jacubek. We exchanged joyous greetings. The two would not let me get a word in edge-wise; they were anxious to get back to the woods to inform the others of my arrival. "You can't imagine what your coming here means to us!" Jacubek said as he clasped my hand. Then, without waiting for me to reply, he dashed out of the hut.

Staszek remained. In the candlelight I could clearly see his haggard face and shining eyes. "There's a lot of talk about," he began in a quavering voice. "A lot has happened here since you were here last. Some of those you knew are no longer alive."

Romanow suggested that we go into the kitchen where we would be able to talk freely.

"If it weren't for Romanow all of us would probably have starved to death," said Staszek as soon as we were alone. When money had still been available, several Jewish fighters had gone into the woods and, with the help of a certain Pole, formed a partisan unit. The Jews soon adapted to outdoor life, subsisting on whatever bread and potatoes they could get from the estates of wealthy landowners. From time to time they undertook a "job"—blowing up a German factory, killing a German sentry, and so on. The populace was aware of the Jewish partisan group and supported them.

Recently, a brigade of Polish partisans calling itself the Orzels, after the commander, had arrived in the area. At first the brigade had been friendly towards the Jewish partisans. In fact, the Jewish fighters wanted to join with the Poles; it was always better to join forces with an experienced and more numerous group of fighters. But nothing had come of these overtures. One night, when most of the Jewish fighters were out foraging for food, a dozen armed Orzels had appeared at the Jewish encampment. The Jews, assuming that the Poles were friendly, had welcomed them. But the Poles suddenly opened fire. Several Jews had fallen on the spot; the rest managed to escape. The assault had been so unexpected that the fleeing survivors had no chance to pick up the weapons of their fallen comrades.

The survivors learned from the peasants that the Orzels had been hunting for fugitive Jews and had discovered the place where Kuba and the two girls had been hiding out. The Jewish partisan group had been joined by those Jews who had been driven out of their barn *melina* by the peasant landlady. Together they roamed the woods, hunted not only by the Germans but also by the Polish partisans.

"We won't be able to survive much longer in the woods," Staszek concluded, dejectedly.

That afternoon I came upon the group of Jews who were hiding in the woods. They were living skeletons, bags of bones who could hardly stand erect. They were in tatters; some had wrapped their feet in rags or sacking. Shelter had to be found for them as quickly as possible. Once again, as so often before and after, money proved irresistible; at the sight of it not only the old peasant but also other villagers offered to harbor the Jews for a while. Shortly afterwards, I obtained a document from the Polish underground to the effect that the Jews were under the protection of the *Armja Krajowa*, the right-wing Polish underground organization. This was supposed to safeguard the Jews from any further molestations by the local Polish partisan groups.

We maintained contact with the Jews of Zelislawice until the end of the war.

43. THE LABOR CAMPS
OF CZESTOCHOWA

In a few cities in Poland the Germans left small pockets of Jews, isolated in special camps where they performed slave labor for the German war effort under conditions that defied description.

We did what we could to help these Jewish survivors and make their lot bearable. Special Jewish and Gentile couriers were sent to gather information about the Jews in the labor camps and to find ways of getting help to them.

One place where such labor camps existed was Czestochowa. I was assigned responsibility for communicating with the surviving Jews there and was entrusted with letters and funds for Motel Kushnier and Laib Brenner, two underground activists working in the German factories in Pelcery and Rakow.

My journey to Czestochowa was uneventful. When I arrived, I went directly to the only Gentile address my fellow ghetto insurgents from Czestochowa (now hiding in Koniecpol) had given me. It was a labor camp near Rakow, where an elderly Polish factory worker was to help me establish the necessary contacts.

The man was not very friendly. True, he had helped Jews some time ago, but he said he would never do it again. He was afraid. Besides, he hastened to add, he himself was cramped for space and could not receive any visitors—a clear hint for me to be on my way. I tried to sway the old man by offering to pay for his efforts, but he remained adamant; his neighbors and some of his fellow-workers, too, were watching him, and he refused to take any chances.

Instead, he advised me to go to the gate of the factory in Rakow, where Jews and Gentiles were working together and sharing the same living quarters. Perhaps one of the Gentiles there would agree to transmit a letter for me.

Leaving him, I started down the long, muddy street that led to the Rakow railroad station. The factory stood nearby, near the tracks—a huge fenced-in area with towering smokestacks. I loitered about the gate, observing that the guards inspected every person entering or leaving the compound. No Jews came out through the gates. They probably were further inside the factory.

I stopped some workers coming out of the factory, offering them bribes to take a note to fellow workers inside. Finally, an elderly Polish factory worker agreed. I jotted down a few words, addressed to Kushnier—that name sounded a little more Polish than Brenner. Just the same, I stressed that this person could be found only among the Jewish workers. The Gentile was not inquisitive; he was aware of what he was undertaking. He even urged me to be careful to word my note so that he would not get into trouble if it were intercepted. I was to return to the same spot the next day to pick up my answer.

That meant I would have to find a place to spend the night. There were no hotels for Poles in the city, and I could not be on the streets for fear of a German raid. Even the railroad station was out; the Germans might run a security check there. I would have to find a rooming house.

My fellow smugglers had told me that several poor Gentiles near the train station were renting rooms to smugglers from other cities. At one of these I found about 15 fully dressed men and women sprawled and snoring on straw mats on the floor of a dingy room. It was better than nothing. The landlady, a sickly-looking woman, informed me that she would be able to accommodate me only after curfew. At the same time she warned me that she would not be responsible for stolen articles, and that I would have to sleep fully dressed. She advised me to go sightseeing and to visit the Jasna Gora Cathedral until the curfew hour.

Having nowhere else to go until bedtime, I took her advice. Prior to the war this cathedral had attracted not only thousands of Catholics but tourists of all faiths. Myths and legends had proliferated about the treasures of the church and the miracles that had been performed within its walls.

That afternoon, the cathedral was almost empty, an island of quiet and serenity in the horror that was Poland. I had spent a sleepless night on the train and had been walking all day. Now, amid the stained glass and the candles, the statues and the altars, weariness overcame me. I stood before the madonnas and the tapestries without seeing them; I followed a guide leading a group of tourists without hearing him. The drone of his description in the huge, dark cathedral only made me drowsier. All I wanted was to rest. I gradually wandered off and found a remote nook in which to curl up. No one seemed to notice me there.

I felt I had found sanctuary. There were no German guards, no prying eyes—only a solemn serenity that lulled my anxiety. Thereafter I spent most of my free hours at Jasna Gora. The cathedral was my refuge while I looked for a contact in Czestochowa.

Nothing came of the note I gave the old man at the factory. Two days later he had still not located the people I was trying to reach. My efforts to persuade other workers to carry a message were without success. As a last resort I again pleaded with the one who had originally agreed to help, stressing the importance of his cooperation. At length—I think largely to be rid of me—he agreed to try to deliver the letter from the Coordinating Committee. But he insisted that after this mission, he would never again be party to any Jewish deals.

A full day passed. I waited at the factory gate. Finally the old man appeared, extremely agitated. He had almost gotten into trouble that day, he said, because a German guard had noticed him talking to a Jew. Fortunately, the guard had been called away at the last moment.

"Well, have you brought me an answer?" I asked impatiently.

"Yes, I have," he snapped. "But this is the last time I'll do anything like that!"

I grasped eagerly at the bit of paper he held out to me. Was it really from the Jews? Indeed, it was. The recipients wrote that they were hardly able to believe their eyes. They were overjoyed at the thought that they had not been forgotten. The offer of help from Warsaw had given them courage and hope in the midst of their misery. They would see that the instructions in the letter were carried out. The reply was signed "Jacek"—the code-name of a young Zionist in the factory who was in close touch with the Czestochowa ghetto fighters and already familiar with the clandestine assistance extended elsewhere. The address of Jan Brust, a Polish factory worker who could serve as a liaison, was also included.

A contact had finally been established! Now I had to go back to Warsaw to share the good news and await further instructions.

Several days later I was back in Czestochowa with more letters and money. This time I went directly to Jan Brust, who lived not far from the factory. He was waiting for me and welcomed me heartily, inviting me to eat and sleep in his house and to wait there for the answers to my letters. Brust was a highly skilled craftsman. On his way to work he smuggled in letters and money and, on returning, brought the replies. A regular and dependable contact was thus established. Every few weeks I visited Brust, bringing funds and instructions from Warsaw. True, he was well paid for each letter or package he smuggled in, but his humanity, kindness and reliability far outweighed every other consideration.

From the smuggled letters as well as from Brust's own estimates we learned that there were about 3,000 Jews still in Czestochowa. They worked at the factories of Pelcery and Rakow, day and night, in eight-hour shifts, at some of the most difficult and hazardous tasks.

Their most dreaded trials were the periodic "selections" conducted by the Germans during which Jewish workers were chosen, apparently at random, for transfer to other camps. Fearing, with good reason, that this meant, in effect, deportation to death, the Jews had contrived to build bunkers in the factory area to serve as hiding places.

Inadequately fed and always hungry, they sold their clothes to their Gentile co-workers for money with which to buy smuggled provisions at exorbitant prices.

German inspections were frequent and thorough. The Jews were ordered to undress completely: each garment was meticulously examined, the entire barracks and every bunk minutely combed. Should money or a smuggled loaf of bread be found, not only was it confiscated, but the Jew in whose possession it was discovered was flogged mercilessly.

Great caution and resourcefulness were needed to safeguard the money I brought to be smuggled in to be distributed among the neediest Jews. Often the recipients were unaware that the assistance came from the Coordinating Committee or even that it came from outside the camp.

Special attention was paid to the few surviving children and to the ailing workers, for whom medication and extra nourishment were provided. I also managed to smuggle in some underground Polish newspapers and Bund publications. Thus, an extensive clandestine relief activity was set in motion.

After a time, the secret Committee of Jewish Survivors in Czestochowa informed Warsaw that the Jews in the labor camp were anxious to obtain arms for use when they would be needed. "We want to fight as our brothers did in the Warsaw Ghetto!" they wrote us. "Try to get us revolvers and hand grenades."

These pleas became increasingly urgent as knowledge spread about the extermination of the Jews in the Poniatow and Trawniki labor camps. Unfortunately, our efforts to arm the Jews proved futile. We had no means of smuggling in the weapons, and had to restrict ourselves to providing money, forged documents and medicines.

The entire enterprise was put in jeopardy by the tragic death of Jan Brust, who was caught smuggling by a German guard and fatally wounded. The Jews in the factory did their utmost to save the life of this devoted friend, sparing neither expense nor effort.

Our entire relief activity continued, however. We found another trustworthy Polish worker named Mendzec, who was attached to the factory at Pelcery. He continued the task of smuggling letters to the Jews in the camp. Until the time of liberation this contact was maintained by our underground movement. Most of the Jews employed in the factories of Pelcery and Rakow survived the war.

44. JEWISH LABOR CAMPS IN RADOM

Establishing contact with the Jews in the camp at Radom posed a different problem. In Czestochowa, our aim was to set up secret relief committees inside the camp, which would cooperate with the Coordinating Committee in Warsaw. We had the names of several Jews, among them Avrom Meltzer and Kotlar who worked in a German print shop; but here, unlike the situation at Czestochowa, we knew of no Gentiles who could be relied upon as intermediaries. After conferring with Leon Feiner and Samsonowicz, I set out for Radom, to arrange for the delivery of a letter and some money to the surviving Jews.

Radom was a military center, teeming with German soldiers and guards. Few civilians were to be seen and few stores were open. What trading went on was clandestine. The city lived in mortal terror of the Germans, who enforced every regulation to the letter.

On my arrival, I went straight to the printing plant, a squat, gray building on Nowe-Miasto Street. It was closed, the windows shuttered, and the main entrance, which led to the plant offices, guarded by several Germans. On a nearby street corner, an elderly Gentile woman was selling apples. I bought two, then asked casually if she knew where I could buy some old clothes. "I've heard the Jews sell such stuff cheap," I added, "but I don't know where they are."

The old woman hesitated, looked furtively about her, then whispered, "You can't do business with Jews any more. They got rid of the better things long ago; now they're pulling the last rags off their backs—things hardly worth buying. What's more, the Germans have rounded up quite a few blackmarketeers and shot them."

"Just tell me where these people are," I interrupted her. "I'll decide for myself if they have anything worth buying."

The woman pointed to a building I had just passed. "Over there—but you can see them only at noon. Turn in at the second street, where the city baths are located. Today it's the Jews' day to bathe."

I found a vantage point and waited. About half an hour later, a group of people wearing white armbands appeared near a gray building in the compound—the city baths. These were the Jews.

Behind the bathhouse was a cluster of small wooden huts. A group of Gentile women stood nearby. I hastened toward them, hoping to get some additional information, only to be set upon angrily. They were smugglers and wanted no further competition; business, they said, was bad enough as it was. For days now they had been waiting to make their transactions. I assured them that I had come only to buy a few things for myself and pleaded with them to be patient. Grudgingly, they allowed me to remain.

All of us waited for the German guards to turn away so that we could approach the Jews. They included men and women, some adequately dressed but most in rags. They were also guarded by Jewish police. They signaled us but dared not come near until the Germans left. Then the Gentile traders rushed toward them. I followed. The Jews begged for bread, potatoes, fats.

Most of them were barely able to stand. One of them, an old Jewish woman, clutched two worn-out bedsheets. Her wrinkled face, gray hair, and sad eyes seemed to betoken trustworthiness. I engaged her in conversation and told her that I was anxious to meet some Jews in the camp, mentioning the names I had been given by the Coordinating Committee. She was a stranger in this area, she said, but would find a native of Radom who might be able to help me.

The moment she left, a voice shouted, "They're coming!" The Germans had reappeared. There was a frantic scurrying as the Jews dashed into the bathhouse and the smugglers hurried back to the huts, and I after them. It would be wise to stay with the smugglers, I decided; they were experienced at avoiding arrest.

The moment the Germans were out of sight again, the smugglers and I scurried back to the Jews. This process was repeated several times.

The old Jewish woman returned at last, accompanied by a hunch-backed, emaciated young man. Yes, he knew the people I had asked about; they had been among the first batch of deportees. He spoke slowly and seemed in complete control of himself. I decided to take him into my confidence.

He listened in sullen silence. Then his face became ashen and con-torted. With a scornful sneer, he hissed.

"Stop telling me stories about relief!" he said. "You asked me about the Jews and I gave you that information." Then he added sarcastically, "Don't think you can fool Jews just like that!" and started to walk away from me. For a moment I was stunned—that one Jew should be so much in fear of another—I let him move off a short distance before hurrying after him. With no one else around, I spoke to him in Yiddish. He stop-ped in his tracks and his jaw dropped.

"It could be that you're telling the truth," he managed to say after I had finished. "However, I will not accept any of your relief money."

"Why not?" I countered. "After all, it's for your own good."

"There have been plenty of informers and spies at our Radom camp," he replied. "Several Jews have already paid with their lives for keeping in touch with Gentiles—who later reported them."

No, he said, he would not take anything from me. It would be better if I got in touch with the Jews working in the print shop. They were more likely to help me with my project. He himself would not risk it. All my pleading was in vain. As the man left me, he was actually smiling.

I was angry both at myself and the stranger. It would be so easy to transmit the money through him and to confer with him in the future. Yet nothing had been accomplished!

On my second visit to the city baths, I succeeded in talking with a cer-tain Gruenblatt—or Gruenhaus. He agreed to help me and promised to get in touch with the Jews working at the printing plant. I entrusted him with 10,000 zlotys. I never saw him again.

Twice frustrated, I decided on a desperate stratagem. Taking advan-tage to escape the German guards, I dodged behind the huts and headed straight for the print shop.

Several Polish children were playing near the factory, and two Polish women were pacing to and fro before the gates. A Jewish policeman was on guard. Through the bars I could see the Jewish laborers hurrying about with mess kits and bowls—evidently it was lunchtime.

I asked the Jewish policeman to call a woman named Meltzer to the fence. Within a few minutes he returned with a young woman. I whispered to her that I had brought some letters and money from Warsaw. On hearing this, she hurried over and whispered something to the policeman, who then opened the gate and admitted me to the compound.

Tears sprang to her eyes as she gradually understood the purpose of my visit: we had not forgotten about them. She begged me to wait a moment, and then ran off, soon to return with her husband and brother-in-law. Together we spoke about the money I had brought for them and about the relief activities of the Coordinating Committee. Their faces beamed. The husband repeated several times with quiet fervor that he could hardly believe all this was not a dream. At the end of our conversation, the three promised to set up a clandestine relief organization in Radom. The money, they said, would save many from starvation. But their incredulity persisted; and they kept repeating, as if to convince themselves, that we had not forgotten about them.

The Jewish policeman signaled from the distance that my time was up and that I would have to leave the compound. As I turned to go, the Meltzers showered me with last-minute questions about the outside world, the war and our underground activities. I answered briefly and handed over the money and a letter of instructions for organizing a relief apparatus within the camp. They, in turn, undertook to produce within a half hour a letter stating their immediate needs, as well as a list of the *melinas* in which the children of some were hiding. They were particularly concerned about the children who had been placed with Gentiles.

I left the print shop delighted and paused near the gate. At last a contact had been established! The Polish women had left, but the children were still playing a short distance away. Everything had gone well. Now I only had to wait for their answer. Suddenly, I felt something hit my back. I turned around; three little boys stood poised to throw stones at me. I was puzzled by their hostility, but the next moment everything became clear.

"Look," one of them shouted, "she didn't buy anything from the Jews!" "She must be one of them," another cried out, and this was

followed by a chorus of, *"Zhidowa! Zhidowa!"* (Jewess!) My protests
were useless; the children only became rougher and noisier. The situation
had quickly become dangerous; I took to my heels and turned into
another street but the gang followed, still shouting, *"Zhidowa!
Zhidowa!"* Passersby were being attracted to the scene. Frightened, I
darted into one courtyard and out of another, emerging on a different
street. To my amazement, no one tried to stop me. Still somewhat confused, I hailed the first available droshka (horse and carriage) and asked
the driver to take me to the railroad station—the only building I knew in
the town. In the distance, I could still hear the children's voices,
"Zhidowa! Zhidowa!"

I spent the night at the railway station. Should I return to Warsaw, or
try to follow up my uncertain contact? In the morning, I headed for the
print shop in the hope of picking up the letter to the Coordinating Committee. The Gentile boys were not likely to be around so early. The
Jewish labor gangs, guarded by the Jewish police, were marching to work
in small groups. I joined them for a moment, asking again for Meltzer.
Somebody pointed him out to me. I took the letter from him and left.

There were at that time about 4,000 Jews in Radom. They lived in
wooden barracks behind barbed wire on the outskirts of the town. From
there, groups of Jews were sent to work at various local
industries—primarily the munitions plant and the print shop. As in all the
other camps, the prisoners worked under severe hardship and deprivation. The mortality rate was extremely high. Starvation was even worse
here than in Czestochowa.

One hundred destitute Jews benefited from the preliminary efforts of
the relief committee set up by Meltzer, Kotlar and Gruenberg, and
others. The children of Meltzer and Kotlar were supported by our
underground relief organization until the end of the war.

The next time I came to Radom I had some more money (50,000
zlotys), illegal literature and more letters from the Coordinating Committee. Once again I went straight from the station to the print shop, and
once again no one was to be seen. I waited nearby. Even during the lunch
break, no one appeared. I circled the plant, which was surrounded on all
sides by barbed wire displaying posters warning that anyone approaching
the plant did so at the risk of his life.

Turning off into a lane, I saw some Jews behind the barbed wire. The compound itself was now guarded by Germans and Ukrainians. Hiding behind a building, I deliberated on tactics for transmitting the money, letters and bulletins. I would contrive to pass them through the fence. Rolling the letters and the paper money into small rolls, I concealed them in my smuggler's sack.

How to get to the fence? There was no way to do this without being noticed. I decided to go straight out and ask the guard's permission to buy something from the Jews.

With what calm I could muster, I walked toward the barbed wire. The guard, of course, motioned me to halt and came toward me. I casually asked him to let me stay.

"I'd like to buy a pair of shoes from them," I said calmly.

The guard was brusque at first, but gradually became more friendly, evidently taking an interest in me. He was Ukrainian, and his Polish was very poor. Those few minutes of conversation seemed an eternity.

Meanwhile, the Jews were watching us from behind the barbed wire. Finally, the guard allowed me to come near the fence, but urged me to hurry so as not to arouse the suspicion of the other sentries. Hurriedly, I asked the Jews nearest me whether Meltzer and Kotlar were still in the compound and, on being assured that they were, I asked that one of them be brought to me. My friendly guard joined me, calling out aloud in German, "Does anyone have shoes to sell to this woman?"

"Yes, I'd like to buy a pair of shoes," I repeated in Polish. The Jews, regarding me as just another smuggler, offered me a skirt and a sweater.

"No, I only want shoes," I insisted.

Meltzer appeared and whispered something to another Jew who then called the guard over to the fence and engaged him in conversation. Meltzer now stood facing me through the barbed wire. The moment the Ukrainian turned away, I slipped my package to Meltzer, who hid it under his prison clothes and vanished.

The other Jews watched in silence. I felt a little more at ease now. Someone offered to sell me shoes. While trying them on, I kept talking and smiling at the guard who had returned by now. Again the guard was called away and one of my contacts slipped a letter out to me. The mission was completed! The Jews had received assistance right under the Ukrainian's nose.

I did not buy any shoes, but I promised to meet the Ukrainian later that evening. Needless to say, I never kept that appointment. As I turned to go, I could see my Jewish contacts furtively waving their hands in farewell.

Our smuggling missions were not always so successful. My friend Ala Margolis (the daughter of Dr. Anna Margolis) had a narrow escape from the Germans. Ala had succeeded in gaining admittance to a factory in Piotrkow where Jews were employed and, with the help of a Polish guard, had managed to transmit letters and 50,000 zlotys to them. Two passing Germans had taken her into custody and accused her of trespassing in a restricted area—an offense punishable by death. The Jews whom Ala had helped immediately aroused the whole camp. The inmates joined in imploring the German officers and officials to free the "innocent Aryan." In the end, she was ransomed with the money that she had brought to relieve the distress of the captive forced laborers.

45. THE WARSAW REVOLT

July, 1944: the news from the battlefields was heartening. The Germans were being defeated, retreating on all fronts. The Polish underground movement launched some daring attacks against the Germans. Prisoners were rescued from German convoys; shipments of gold and currency were confiscated; ammunition dumps were captured; Gestapo agents and high-ranking officers were assassinated.

Every day, Warsaw thrilled to another sensational exploit. The Polish populace derived grim satisfaction from the reports of these daring deeds, but not without anxiety. How might the ruthless Germans react? The answer was not long in coming; German "punishment" squads swarmed over the city like demons. German posters appeared, listing the names of Polish hostages to be executed the moment a murdered German was found. Every face reflected the same concern, the same question: Who would be next?

But the dimensions of the German rout became more apparent daily. All over Warsaw and nearby areas Germans troops headed westward. The rumbling of tanks and armored cars and the thunder of artillery filled the air. Convoys of peasant carts packed with glum and grimy German soldiers seemed endless.

"They must be on the run for sure," speculators whispered with subdued glee.

The crowds in Warsaw's streets milled about, going about their daily business or just keeping on the move, pausing now and then to listen as the noise of bombardment from the front came closer and closer. Knots gathered at gates and corners, whispering, "It won't be long now . . . perhaps tomorrow . . . Just let the signal come. . . ."

Listening, I became apprehensive. It was obvious that the Red Army was approaching Warsaw and the Polish underground was mobilizing and preparing for an uprising against the Germans.

The Jewish Coordinating Committee was making preparations of its own. Some time before, when the Soviet forces had reached the Bug River, the Committee had brought some of the partisans, including Hannele Frishdorf (who was pregnant), Franka and Yanek Bilak, from the Wyszkow woods to hiding places in Warsaw. In times of danger it was best to be united.

The Jews in hiding were provided with enough provisions for two months. To some of our "clients" we allotted dollars instead of zlotys—$35-$40 per person. We also succeeded in obtaining a limited quantity of canned meat from a Polish relief organization and were able to buy a small supply of sugar. Our couriers distributed the funds and provisions among the Jews in hiding so that they would be able to take care of themselves if we lost contact with them.

They were in better spirits now. True, during the frequent night bombardments by the Soviet forces these Jews had been forced to find other quarters because the landlords were afraid to let them enter the bunkers. Nevertheless, the atmosphere was more cheerful. The pall of fear lifted somewhat. Emotions long suppressed found expression. People embraced; some wiped away tears. Battlefield maps were scanned nervously, and guesses were made as to the date the Soviet forces would reach Warsaw. Some peeped through the curtains of their *melinas* in the hope of obtaining news from the outside. The long-nurtured dream of witnessing the enemy's defeat was at last about to materialize.

Yet, the expectation was tinged with a new anxiety, a fear of facing again the struggle for survival in a bleak and hostile world outside the now familiar *melinas*.

"After the liberation, we will feel our misfortune more keenly," someone said.

Benjamin joined me now at my quarters at Twarda 36, leaving the hiding place he had occupied with his parents. It had been his decision. "We must not be separated now," he had declared. It was good to know that he was always close, that we shared the same deep feeling for each other. This knowledge sustained me as we rushed from task to task, keeping in touch with associates, digging trenches in the streets.

The excitement in the city mounted as the German retreat gained momentum; the distant bombardment intensified, drawing ever closer. Warsaw quivered with anticipation, waiting for *something* to happen.

At five o'clock on August 1, 1944, the wail of factory sirens suddenly rent the air. this was followed almost immediately by the crack of gunfire, then cries of *"Na Szwaba! Na Szwaba!*—Attack the damned Germans!" and an urgent call for the people to come out and build barricades.

The Warsaw uprising had begun!

Benjamin and I hurried out of our hideaway, joining the thousands of Poles who streamed from every doorway. There were no Germans in sight. The red and white flag of Poland already fluttered from numerous buildings. Here and there men with red and white armbands issued terse commands. Barricades were being erected at street intersections to block the German tanks. They had to be in place by nightfall. Men, singly and in teams, dragged planks, boards and broken furniture through the streets. Others pried cobblestones from the pavement with iron crowbars. Heaps of such assorted material grew throughout the city.

How strange that these sweat-drenched young Poles laboring with such fervor and determination shoulder to shoulder with us in the common cause of liberation were the same callous and sometimes vicious Poles who had caused us so much pain and sorrow! But this was no time to think—there was work to be done. I joined a group dragging an overturned trolley to one of the barricades. In the group was a young Jew named Jagodzinski. He had been in hiding on Panska Street, but no longer wanted to stay hidden.

"I must square accounts," he grunted as he threw his full weight into the task.

All of Warsaw erupted; no one, it seemed, remained uninvolved in the fight against the hated occupiers. Together with units of the *Armja Krajowa*, which had organized and directed the uprising, the populace stormed the German fortifications and participated in the most hazardous military operations, exulting whenever the Germans were captured. At first the early bombardments of the city by the German heavy artillery were greeted with silent bitterness. After all, the people thought, this could very well be the last gasp of the Germans. We must steel ourselves, be patient. The Soviets would march in any day now.

In addition to the *Armja Krajowa* the rebellion was supported by other military organizations such as the Democratic Socialist *P.A.L.* and the Communist *Armia Ludowa*, as well as by several hundred Jews who, under assumed Polish names, had been incorporated into the combat units, not only as soldiers but as officers.

After the revolt had been underway for several days, the surviving officers of the Jewish Fighting Organization, together with the Coordinating Committee, went on the air to urge all their fellow Jews to participate in the struggle against the Germans by joining the Democratic Socialist combat groups. There was no talk now of forming exclusively Jewish units. During the first few days of the uprising, the Germans fortified certain streets to protect their retreat, dividing the city into five zones: Zoliborz, Old City, Vistula, Mokotow, and Center City. The street battles and intermittent gunfire made it impossible to maintain proper communications among the various zones, and the Coordinating Committee consequently lost contact with the Warsaw Jews it had been assisting. As we had feared, they were now left to fend for themselves.

However, a small group of couriers and ghetto fighters who lived around Leszno Street managed to stay together in the Old City and Zoliborz and to fight in the ranks of the *Armia Ludowa*. In general Jews enlisted in the *P.A.L.* and *Armia Ludowa* combat groups, not primarily because these Jews were Socialists or Communists, but because the *Armja Krajowa* was filled with anti-Semitic agitators. Even while fighting the Nazis, the Jewish insurgents in the *Armja Krajowa* units suffered persecution from their Polish comrades. The Poles assigned them to the most dangerous missions and the most difficult tasks—and on occasion shot them in the back. Jews naturally chose to enlist in those groups where they felt they would be welcome.

Despite their inadequate arms, the freedom fighters briefly gained control of the entire city of Warsaw. They also managed to free about 300 Greek and Hungarian Jews from the jail on Dzika Street. Those Jews knew no Polish at all and had difficulty communicating with the rest of the population. Nevertheless, they joined the insurgents fighting in the Old City. The Jews who participated in every phase of the struggle came from every walk of life. They served as ordinary soldiers, officers, physicians and nurses. They distinguished themselves by their courage and stubborn determination.

The street fighting became ever more intense, but there was still no sign of the Russians. Even the distant bombardment, which had been so clearly heard before the uprising, ceased.

"Could the Soviets have suddenly stopped their advance?" people asked in dismay.

Terrible days followed for Warsaw. Streets that were controlled by the rebels came under ceaseless bombardment. The Germans were determined to force the insurgents to surrender, even if it meant destroying the city. Warsaw was ablaze. The sky glowed red by night, as tongues of flame shot up now from one district, now from another. During the day, a thick cloud of smoke rose from the wrecked buildings, obscuring the sun. The heat from the fires billowed through the streets, and the air was filled with the stench of charred bodies rotting in the ruins of the buildings. The hospitals and stations of the Polish Red Cross were crowded with the wounded. Public squares, parks and any other spaces were soon filled with fresh graves of both fighters and civilians, each grave topped with a wooden cross. Under a hail of shells and bullets, ragged and confused people scurried among the rubble and debris with sacks on their backs, clutching their children and trying to escape from both the enemy and the toppling buildings. Death lurked everywhere.

As the Germans shelled the city and the buildings collapsed from the bombs and fires, some of the Jewish *melinas*, too, were reduced to rubble. Those occupants with Jewish features were forced to come out into the open. And although the Poles showed unusual courage and self-sacrifice during the uprising, imbued as they were with the spirit of liberation and freedom, some were guilty of criminal acts which discredited even their heroic struggle against an overwhelming foe—acts attesting to the hatred which most of the Polish population felt toward those Jews who had been forced to emerge from their hideouts.

Haika Belchatowska, Boruch Spiegel, Maszele Gleitman, and her husband Jakubek—all friends and former ghetto fighters—appeared unexpectedly in my quarters during the uprising. They all had been sheltered in a *melina* by Wojciechowski, a Gentile who lived at Zelazna 64. When that house caught fire and the Germans had invaded the street, the group had succeeded in escaping through the underground sewers and had made their way to my home at Twarda 36, which was in the area still controlled by the insurgents. After our joyous reunion, my first concern was about their reception by the rest of the tenants. There could be no talk of hiding them. The neighbors frequently visited each other both in the apartments and in the bunkers and were bound to discover anyone hidden anywhere. The typically Jewish faces among the group would be noticed at once. And, indeed, they were quickly discovered.

"There are Jews here!" the Gentiles remarked to each other in astonishment. They had become reconciled to the idea of having one Jew in their midst—Mrs. Topas' husband. His refuge on the fourth floor had been destroyed by fire, forcing him to come out into the open. But admitting any additional Jews was against their Polish principles.

"Where does this pestilence come from? They were supposed to have been finished long ago . . . We ought to get rid of them right now!" some of the Poles complained. But others were in favor of granting shelter to the Jews.

"The Russians will be here any moment—and they might make us pay if anything happens to the Jews," they argued.

Still others considered it beneath Polish dignity even to waste time on such a matter as a few Jews at this critical juncture. "Let them crawl around! Who gives a damn?"

But most of our neighbors did give a damn. The newcomers were barred from the bunker in the cellar. Two days after my friends had been given asylum in some bombed-out rooms on the first floor, they were interrogated by guards of the Polish insurgents. One of the tenants had reported to the authorities that the recent Jewish arrivals must be German spies, whereupon the Polish police investigated the matter—but found nothing suspicious. Such malicious harassment only served to intensify the general hostility, and one day an honest Polish woman secretly warned Topas to leave; the "boys" were likely to hurt him.

Clara Falk, her son, and an engineer named Golde, who had been living in a hideout on Sliska Street, had a similar experience. Their quarters had been demolished by a hand grenade and they had barely escaped to the underground bunker alive. But once inside, they were informed by their Polish neighbors that they were not welcome. After several days of persecution and anti-Semitic insults, the engineer was forced to leave the bunker during a heavy German bombardment. He was killed by shrapnel. The day before the outbreak of the uprising, I had delivered some money and a food package to Golde. He had thanked me; "Now I am certain that we will survive to be liberated," he had said.

A savage crime was committed in a building at the corner of Zelazna and Chmielna Streets. On the fifth day of the uprising several Jews sought refuge from the German bombardments in this huge building, which belonged to the Polish railroad employees' organization. Three of them, with distinctly Jewish features, were detained by an insurgent guard of the *Armja Krajowa*. Despite their insistence that they were Jews, the Polish guard took them into custody on the charge that they were German spies. While they were being searched in an abandoned house, several other uniformed and armed men entered and beat them, declaring that there would be no place for Jews in liberated Poland. Two of the Jews—Lutek Friedman and Adek—managed to jump out of a window under a hail of bullets. Lutek broke his leg, but both escaped and remained alive. The third, Yeshieh Solomon, was killed on the spot and, after being stripped, was buried under the Polish name of Julek Leszczynski.

Typical of the tragic situation of those with Jewish features was the experience of the Jews who took refuge in Sienna 28. The building was a ruin; all its Gentile inhabitants had fled; the cellar had been hastily turned into a graveyard. Some 20 Jews from various parts of the city clung together in this dark, debris-filled hole, because it offered them comparative security: Polish hoodlums were not likely to attack such a sizeable group. Once, following a particularly heavy bombardment, I visited there to talk with Shifra Mozelszo. It was a scene of horrible carnage. Handkerchiefs covering their noses and mouths, Jews were picking up pieces of human flesh from the ground. The stench was nearly intolerable. A German hand grenade had struck several of the graves, disinterring and disintegrating the recently buried corpses. Nevertheless, the Jews preferred to stay in this gruesome sanctuary with its suffocating atmosphere and rebury the bits of human flesh, rather than cope with the hostile Gentile hoodlums outside. Without food or water and terrorized by the intermittent bombardment, they prayed only that the uprising would continue until the Red Army entered the city. Before long, the districts of Mokotow, Old City, Czerniakow, and Zoliborz capitulated to the Germans. The downtown area, with its various government offices, still held out, but it, too, was on the verge of collapse. Exhausted by weeks of relentless bombardment, those who lived in that area stumbled about half dead. It was all too evident that the uprising had been a dismal failure. The bitter resentment of the crushed populace was now directed exclusively against the Russians. "Why didn't they come to the rescue of Warsaw?" anguished voices asked.

But it was the Jewish survivors who found themselves in the most desperate straits. What would be their fate when the Germans resumed control of the city? With the hiding places destroyed and the friendly Poles concerned for their own survival, where would these Jews find refuge? The more enterprising among them began seeking new hideouts in the ruins that now littered the city. At night, under hails of bullets and shells, they searched for food and fetched water to tide them over for a few weeks, until the Red Army would march in.

Benjamin dug through the rubble to build a bunker in some ruins near the corner of Sienna and Sosnowa Streets. Breaching a thick wall and following a circuitous passageway, he came upon a deserted cellar. Each time I had to crawl through the narrow tunnel, I felt that I was about to be buried alive.

After a bloody struggle of two months, the leaders of the insurgents announced over the radio that the city of Warsaw had capitulated to the Germans. It also became known that the Germans were set on evacuating Warsaw; the local population would have to abandon the city within three days. The Poles received the news of the capitulation almost with a sense of relief; at least the bombardments would be over and they would be able to get out of those dreary cellars. But the Jews were thrown into a panic.

Rumors circulated through the city: All the young and able-bodied were to be transported to camps in Germany. Everyone would be interrogated by a commission under German supervision at the Pruszkow camp, where the fate of each individual would be decided separately. Considerate treatment by the Germans was certainly not to be expected. The prospects for all of us seemed terrifying. We roamed through streets littered with debris and burrowed through cellars and tunnels, hunted creatures eluding their unrelenting hunter.

A group of us made our way to Zurawia 24, where we found Mikolai and Fishgrund. Having recently received a quantity of American dollars from abroad, they were doing their best to locate and aid Jews in direst need. American dollars by now were the only currency that could be exchanged on the black market for clothing, food and other necessities—including guns. A weapon was essential equipment for a Jew going into hiding.

But Mikolai and Fishgrund had no advice to offer us. For two years we had done what we could to support the Jewish survivors on the "Aryan side." Now, this underground relief network, with its central head-quarters in Warsaw, was completely disrupted. We did not even know what had become of those Jews we had assisted who had been in the districts already recaptured by the Germans—Mokotow, Old City, Vistula and Zoliborz. How were the Jews hidden there managing to survive? Who knew how many Jews had fallen in the struggle or had been buried alive under the debris of bombarded buildings?

We, the survivors among the activists to whom the others had looked for aid, were now helpless and without directions. Should we try to hide in the city or should we attempt to escape? Most of the couriers had already decided to leave the city along with the Poles. Their "good" Aryan features, they thought, would enable them to pass as Polish refugees and perhaps save them from deportation to the German death camps. Possibly—just possibly—at their next destination, they could revive the Jewish relief organization. But would Benjamin and I, and others like us, succeed in avoiding the German camps? That was another question. We were young and had little hope of eluding the Germans.

"You'll just have to risk it," Mikolai told me. "It's hard to tell how long you'll have to remain underground." He was emaciated, weak and ill, scarcely able to stand without aid—I was told he was suffering from cancer—yet he tried to give us courage and confidence. "Don't lose heart. You'll make it yet!" he assured us.

Benjamin and I deliberated for days before deciding to leave the city. The specially camouflaged bunker near Sosnowa and Sienna Streets over which he had toiled so long and hard was turned over to another group of Jews who had to remain in hiding in the city because of their Jewish appearance.

We guided them there through the devious passages of the bunker;

then shouldering our sacks we stood outside for a while where some friends had come to see us off on our hazardous journey. It was raining. People pushing carts and lugging bundles hurried past us. We did not speak much. We looked at one another mutely, finding nothing to say. "You had better hurry along," someone said quietly.

Maszele Gleitman pressed my hand. "Keep well, Vladka. Let's hope we'll see each other again."

"Here are some biscuits I happened to bake today," Shifra Mozelszo said, handing me a warm package, wrapped in paper.

"When you come back, don't forget to get us out of the bunker—dead or alive," Clara Falk observed grimly.

Choking back tears. I sought for a fitting word of farewell. It might be the last. Who knew who, if any, of us would survive? An old ghetto expression came to mind. Turning to Boruch Spiegel, who was now the leader of the group, I managed to force past the lump that seemed to be growing in my throat: "Hang on, kid, hang on."

Benjamin turned away, brushing tears from his eyes. The last handshake, the last embrace . . . we were on our way, "Let's hope, let's hope we shall meet again!" following us as we trudged off.

Benjamin and Vladka Meed in their first photograph taken together after the Liberation. Lodz, Poland, February 1945.

Picture of one of the first groups of Holocaust survivors to arrive in New York, May 24, 1946 aboard the S.S. Marine Perch. Second row, 3rd and 4th from the left are Benjamin and Vladka Meed.

The Ghetto in ruins

The famous Tlomacka Synagogue was blown up by the Germans
as a symbolic act of the suppression of the uprising

The Ghetto Monument
in Warsaw

Memorial stone at Mila 18,
site of the Ghetto Uprising
headquarters

Benjamin Meed at the ruins
of the Warsaw Ghetto, 1945

Vladka Meed and Itzhak Zuckerman at
the Ghetto Fighters House in Israel, 1967

The devastated "Gesia" Jewish cemetery, Warsaw 1978

Vladka and Marysia Sawicka at the grave site
of Vladka's late Polish "mother", Warsaw 1978

46. WE RETURN

We did see each other again. Our reunion took place five months later, days after the Red Army had entered Warsaw. Benjamin and I had succeeded in eluding the Germans. Drifting through towns and villages, we had located the remnants of the Jewish Coordinating Committee in the small town of Grodzisk; like us, they had survived the chaos and savagery before the liberation. Our friends who had remained in gutted Warsaw had been fortunate, too. Their bunker had been among the few to escape the Germans.

But our reunion was brief, and our rejoicing charged with uneasiness. An irresistible, nagging imperative drew us back to the ghetto. Though dreading what we would find there, we were obsessed by an unconquerable urge to return to the place where our ordeal had begun.

Benjamin and I made our way among the somber ruins, through gaping holes and over heaps of rubble and debris, bricks and stones and rusty gratings. We moved warily, careful not to dislodge anything, not to change anything among these ruins, all that remained of the lives of those we had loved best.

Quiet, heart! Stop racing so. There is nothing and no one to be afraid of now. Don't you see that there is no one here, that there are only desolate ruins and rubble and wreckage wherever your eyes turn? Why, then the fear and trembling? Remember, you have already witnessed horrible scenes here amidst roaring tongues of flame and billowing smoke . . .

True, then there was still some small spark of life; people still tried, still struggled . . . there was still a glimmer of hope . . .

262   ON BOTH SIDES OF THE WALL

But how different this scene! It is best not to think of all that now. Perhaps it is better only to gaze in silence upon this dead and desolate wilderness, where every stone, every grain of sand is sodden with Jewish blood and tears.

Silence . . .

The aching eyes devour the scene; every stone, every heap of rubble is a reminder of the Holocaust. Here a protruding length of pipe, there a bent iron rail, there a charred sapling—these are what is left of our devastated world. My eyes fall upon the remains of a torn, soiled prayer book, on a rusty, dented pot, and I see my home again—my father and mother. . . .

But what of my own grief? The scene is the same in a thousand other towns, a hundred other ghettos; my sorrow repeated ten thousand times. But the figures, the incredible statistics, how do they compare, how can they express what has happened?

Once again the eyes go searching. They recognize every spot. The bombed-out blocks, the mountains of rubble, cannot obliterate the memory of the streets and houses which once stood here. Over there was Dzielna Street, and further on, Pawia, Gesia and Nalewki. Once they swarmed with Jewish traders and workers; Jews in business suits and Jews in overalls; women in kerchiefs and hats; young people and children. The scene had throbbed with life and activity. Now, all of it was gone—nothing but ruin and devastation.

But I still had something left. My father's grave, in the Gesia cemetery, not far away. I remembered the spot distinctly—Row No. 105, the seventh grave from the left. We made our way to the entrance of the cemetery. It had not been spared in the bombardment. The cemetery wall stood broken in several places; there was no gate, nor was there anyone in sight. Only silence . . .

Wherever I turned, there was nothing but overturned tombstones, desecrated graves and scattered skulls, their dark sockets burning deep into me, their shattered jaws demanding, "Why? Why has this befallen us?"

These were the handiwork of the so-called "dentists"—Polish grave-robbers who ghoulishly disinterred Jewish corpses to extract the gold-capped teeth from their mouths.

Why, then, the guilt that tinged my revulsion and rage; why the shame—my shame—that persecution followed my people even into their graves? Carefully, so as not to trample the skulls or fall into an open grave, we made our way through this place of eternal rest to the spot where my father's bones had lain. Though I knew the location, I could not find his grave. The whole area had been desolated, the soil pitted and strewn with crushed skulls and broken grave markers.

Was one of these desecrated skulls that of my own father? How would I ever know?

Nothing. Nothing was left me of my past, of my life in the ghetto, not even my father's grave.

EPILOGUE
33 YEARS LATER

After thirty-three years of absence, my husband and I had the unexpected opportunity to go by ourselves to visit Poland. Our visas were only
valid for four days.

Whom should we visit? As it was, neither of us had any living family
there. And yet, we felt drawn to return once again and see those places
where we used to live, or more accurately, to see if we could find any
trace of the life that we had known there. Of the pre-war Jewish community of three and one-half million, it is estimated that only some six to
seven thousand Jews remain. And, of this number most are retired and
elderly, or else assimilated, partners in mixed marriages. The remaining
Jews clung to their few possessions but, more importantly, they clung to
their old-age pensions.

Some of these Jews are connected with the handful of Jewish institutions which exist, supported by the Polish government. Thus, it was
possible to find a few Jews in the spacious, well-heated offices of the
Yiddish weekly, *Folks-Shtimme*, or at the Social Cultural Association of
Jews in Poland. Fewer still could be found in the offices of the Jewish
Historical Institute, which still serves as the depository of valuable Jewish
documentation, as well as of the entire Ringelblum Archive.

Even there, the work was conducted mostly in Polish. In fact, the only
place in Poland where we could find young people speaking Yiddish, was
on stage, by the performers of the Jewish State Theatre, which plays
three nights a week before an almost entirely non-Jewish audience. There
are simply not enough Jews left to fill the theatre.

We also met an old Jew who had come to eat a kosher meal at the community house, a neglected and dilapidated building standing next to the Nozyk Synagogue, which was closed when we arrived. These, then, were the only places where we could find the sorry remnants of Jewish life in Warsaw.

You are left with a feeling that even this meager life exists only because the Polish government has an interest in maintaining the facade that Jewish life still goes on in Poland.

We felt ourselves drawn to the part of the city where we had once lived, to the long-gone streets of our Jewish yesterday. Of course, we knew that the streets were no longer there. Nevertheless, we had to see up close what had become of those things we had known.

Today, the old Jewish quarter is covered with broad, barren streets that radiate and intersect in a network of unfamiliar Polish names and places. Tall, alien apartments rise above them, housing thousands of strangers. Some areas are unexpectedly hilly, as if there hadn't been time to level the rubble of the old ghetto, before the new quarter had been built.

A familiar name, Nalewki! Before the war, this had been the main commercial and retail thoroughfare in Jewish Warsaw, the center of the textile trade, its streets crowded with merchants and wagons and cars from every part of Poland. Now, the name "Nalewki" is attached to a small residential court, a handful of apartment buildings. Around the corner there is another broad avenue lined with tall structures and bearing another Polish name, Nowotki Street.

We arrived at the corner of Pawia and Zamenhofa Streets. Not far from here, to the left, at Number 3, had been the house where my family had lived, and I had been born. But the building was no longer there. In its place is another apartment tower with a different number. Further down, at Number 31 Pawia Street, had stood the house of my husband, Benjamin. Now, there stands instead a small plaza with a few forlorn trees. Everything has changed.

Another familiar name, Pawiak, the once infamous jail for criminals and political prisoners: the structure had stood in the very center of the Jewish quarter and, during the Nazi occupation, it had been the setting of a particularly brutal and bloody chapter in the history of the Warsaw Ghetto. The entrance gate remains unchanged, but the prison itself no longer exists. In its place stands a small museum and monument. Inside, the visitor is shown what the prison cells used to look like, the instruments of torture, and documents and photographs relating to the long Polish struggle for freedom. A special section is devoted to documentation of Polish martyrdom under the Nazi occupation. But nowhere is there a photograph, a document, even a single word, to indicate that this was also a place of Jewish suffering and destruction; this despite the fact that within the walls of this terrible prison, thousands of Jews had been tortured and executed. Their lives and their deaths are totally erased, as if they had never been.

That evening, the Polish television had a program on the liberation of Warsaw after the German defeat. January 17th marked thirty-three years since the Soviet Army had entered the Polish capital. Polish government officials, scientists, artists, workers, and students participated in the program. They spoke for hours about life in the capital city, how they had found only total destruction after the German defeat, and how everything had been gradually rebuilt and reconstructed. Again, I didn't hear a word about Jewish participation.

The few Jews remaining in Warsaw were not easily visible or recognizable as Jews. Gone forever were the Jewish streets, Jewish stores, Jewish tradesmen and Jewish professionals; gone were the Kaftans and the sound of Yiddish in the streets. In fact, the first "Jewish" thing we could find openly and obviously in Warsaw was the monument to the Ghetto Martyrs and Heroes. It is a powerful monument—36 feet in height, with heroic figures of Ghetto Fighters carved out of granite, by the sculptor, Nathan Rapaport. Once it had stood alone in a sea of rubble but now it seemed incongruous—dwarfed by huge, faceless, apartment blocks to which it had no relation. It is as if the monument had come from another time or another world, intruding, almost by force, into the smug grey world of contemporary Polish reality.

When we found the monument for the first time, the few passersby in the vicinity seemed to ignore it completely. The place felt forlorn, frozen, its lower stones covered with hardened snow. Two miserable red flowers lay on the side. A feeling of hopelessness, abandonment, and isolation seemed to emanate from this monument, the symbol of Jewish resistance and suffering throughout the Holocaust. I looked at the chiselled figures and saw again those days, thirty-five years ago, when tongues of flame roared over the ghetto and the air was filled with the sounds of gunfire and the screams of Jews being burned alive. Above, the sky was red and empty, and, around us, not a sign of help. And now this place was built up with modern apartments towering over this lonely monument. At other times, though, the place becomes more crowded and alive, especially whenever special visitors arrive in Warsaw or when "Yahrzeits" are observed, or whenever Jewish organizations decide to undertake some action. As it happened, we too were asked to participate in a public ceremony at the monument. This was at the request of Stefan Grajek, the representative of Yad Vashem in Israel, whom we had run into during our visit to Warsaw. Grajek was there on a special mission, to help Polish officials plan the reconstruction of the Jewish pavilion at the Auschwitz museum.

On January 18, 1978, with several dozen elderly Jewish men and women, and with representatives of Jewish institutions, we assembled at the monument to mark the 35th anniversary of the first organized resistance in the Warsaw Ghetto. We stood in total silence. Several floral wreaths were placed on the monument. There were no speeches. The only sound was that of a lone photographer as he worked his camera to record the ceremony. I did not see any Polish representatives, nor did there seem to be any interest evoked among the Poles passing by. Our small group of Jews at the monument felt like an isolated band of abandoned people.

This feeling followed us everywhere. We felt it most strongly when we went to Number 18 Mila Street to look for the memorial stone marking the location of the bunker where, on May 8, 1943, the general staff of the Ghetto Resistance, including its commander, Mordechai Anilewicz, finally succumbed to the German onslaught. I remembered Mila Street vividly, for here I had gone to school. I remembered every brick and every doorway. But, again, it is not the same street, not the same doorways. The street has been completely rebuilt, widened, with new dwellings lining both sides. At Number 18, finding no such monument, we wandered about aimlessly, searching for the marker. We asked several people. Nobody knew. But the stone *had* to exist. We had seen it in many photographs; it had to be here somewhere! Finally, a woman said that she *thinks* that down at the very beginning of the street, near Number 2, there is some kind of memorial. At last! We climbed an icy mound and reached a stone half-buried in the snow. Forlorn and abandoned, too, was this Jewish gravestone.

Not far from this spot is the site of the Umschlagplatz, the railroad siding at the corner of Stawki and Dzika Streets, where the Ghetto Jews were assembled and loaded onto the cattle cars to be taken to their deaths in the gas chambers and the crematoria. Here now stand blocks of new houses. We went around the square, looking for a trace of what had once been there. On a low brick wall we found a plaque inscribed with a few sentences in Yiddish, Polish, and Hebrew. "This is the place from which the Nazis sent tens of thousands of Jews to their deaths." That was all.

An inner anxiety drove us from one former landmark to the next, wanting to take in as much as possible. We proceeded to the one place where we were sure we would find some familiar reminders of the past, to the cemetery on Gesia Street. Maybe there I would find the grave of my father, who died in the ghetto. The little shack at the entrance stood boarded up. No one was there. There was no one to ask for directions. The cemetery itself stood neglected. Only the first few rows past the entrance had their gravestones in reasonably decent order. But as we went deeper into the cemetery, we were confronted with a scene of devastation: a sea of broken gravestones, some lying upside-down or flat on the frozen ground, some hidden by broken trees and branches. It was impossible to penetrate any further into this vast resting place. In one place I noticed a stone wall, made up of bits of various gravestones from unidentified graves.

Over 360,000 people lie buried in this tragic historic wilderness of a cemetery, their remains exposed to vandalism and gradual destruction. And the world talks about human rights! A few weeks before, President Carter, who made such an issue of human rights, was received with much pomp in Warsaw, and laid a wreath at the Ghetto Fighters Memorial. They should have brought him here. He would then have seen the deprivation of the human rights of the dead in whose defense nobody raises a voice.

We never found my father's grave, but we did find several others: the great urn of I. L. Peretz, the graves of Esther Rachael Kaminska, Beinish Michalewicz, as well as those of several fighters of the ghetto uprising like Michael Klepfisz, Jurek Blones, and others.

The sight of the Gesia Street cemetery engraved itself upon our hearts, together with that of the other vast cemetery we visited: Treblinka. There, too, no one was in attendance to give directions. For more than two hours, we rode through the frozen Polish countryside, past towns and villages, and when we got near the former concentration camp, we actually got lost. There was no sign or indication of the way to one of the most horrible centers of the Nazi destruction machine. Finally, we turned onto a small side road through the forest, and then found ourselves in the midst of a vast, empty, snow-covered field filled with huge stones of many sizes and shapes, all pointing toward the sky.

We looked and looked at the big graveyard and, suddenly, I felt as if the stones had come to life, turned into Jews, men and women, the elderly, Jews with sacks, with children. Among them, I saw my own family, my mother, brother, and sister, my friends, and neighbors. They filled the vast, empty field of Treblinka, and my heart wanted to cry out, to reassure them that while they were in a hostile Poland that has remained almost devoid of Jews, they are not alone, that they are with us in our hearts and our souls, and in the memories of our people. . . .

In the center of Treblinka there stands a monument resembling a tall gate. Next to it there is another stone with a small inscription in several languages: "Never Again." Nearby, there are heavy wooden ties, symbolic of the railroad tracks that brought the hundreds of thousands to Treblinka. Here were brought most of the Jews of Warsaw, including my nearest and dearest, to this awesome factory of death. Here they were gassed and burned.

There are no longer any gas chambers to be seen in Treblinka, nor can you find any crematoria. Everything has been cleaned out. The Germans even ploughed up the ground to remove the last traces of their crime. What remains is this vast and empty field, covered with 1500 pointed stones that rise toward the heavens with a silent but piercingly eloquent accusation.

Treblinka, 1978

INDEX

A. NAMES

B. PLACES